BITTER STRENGTH

A History of the Chinese in the United States

1850–1870

GUNTHER BARTH

HARVARD UNIVERSITY PRESS

Cambridge, Massachusetts

Second Printing, 1971

Distributed in Great Britain by Oxford University Press, London

Publication of this book has been aided by a grant from the Ford Foundation

Library of Congress Catalog Card Number 64-21785
SBN 674-07600-1
Printed in the United States of America

The Center for the Study of the History of Liberty in America
is aided by a grant from the Carnegie Corporation of New York

TO OSCAR HANDLIN

FOREWORD

UNTIL the appearance of the Chinese on the Pacific Coast in the middle of the nineteenth century, the traditional American policy of open migration remained inviolate. Any free man could enter the United States and, after a short waiting period, could become a citizen fully equal to the native born; Africans, taunted by slavery, alone were excepted. The strains of adjustment occasionally produced short-lived expressions of xenophobia, but not even the Know-Nothings questioned the national utility of the pattern of unimpeded entry. The first demands for genuinely restrictive laws that would exclude some potential immigrants were generated by hostility directed against the Orientals. And, for a considerable period the Chinese remained the only people to be barred from the New World.

The enmity toward the Chinese has generally been explained as the product of a deep American antipathy to color. Although the attitude toward Orientals was initially favorable, accumulated prejudices against the Negroes and the Indians had developed an underlying suspicion of men whose skins were not white. The Chinese, the first substantial group of colored immigrants to come to the United States, inherited that hostility.

Dr. Barth's careful analysis shows that the explanation was not quite that simple. The forces that led to exclusion reflected a novel discrepancy between immigrants and Americans. The Chinese newcomers differed significantly from other arrivals in the United States both in motives and in experience. These people did not intend to form a permanent part of the American population, but were sojourners who expected before long to return to the place of their birth. They did not bring with them a commitment to settlement and the mode of their migration left them unfree and incapable of involving themselves in the life about them. Yet the California setting made Americans especially sensitive to the danger that unfree labor might impede or distort the growth of the state. Not until the strong operations of humanitarian sentiment and American ideology in time converted some of the sojourners into immigrants could they participate in the promises of American life.

This perceptive study throws light on a significant aspect of the history of liberty in the United States. By illuminating the conditions that prevented the full acceptance of a group of unfree newcomers, it indirectly reveals the terms upon which the majority of free immigrants were integrated into American society.

OSCAR HANDLIN

PREFACE

OFTEN, an American miner puzzled over the strange sight of the blue-clad men with great broad hats and swinging queues, with their bundles and packs, their picks and shovels, dangling from poles across their shoulders. The miner spotted them marching one behind the other on a nearby trail. When he learned that these men were Chinese he laconically observed that they were here and that was that, and abruptly shut off the multitude of questions besieging his mind. The following pages try to satisfy the inquiries into the newcomers' background, their arrival, and their life in the United States. The answers will also throw some light on the implications of their presence for the encounter of Chinese and Americans.

The entire book is a rather inadequate acknowledgment of my debt of gratitude to Professor Oscar Handlin, who opened avenues to a compassionate understanding of history that goes beyond the gathering of data and the mechanics of exposition. The task was carried out under fellowships offered by the History Department Committee on American Far Eastern Policy Studies at Harvard University for which I am deeply grateful. The help and encouragement I received from members of the Committee enabled me to gain such insights as these chapters may contain.

Many have contributed in various ways. I am indebted to Professor John K. Fairbank for kindly reading the manuscript. He and Professor Ernest R. May were always available for counsel. The friendship and practical advice of Professor Kwang-Ching Liu have been an inspiration and a guide. I am further obligated to him for his calligraphy in the glossary of Chinese characters. Dr. John Barr Tompkins's untiring interest and erudite perception saved me from stylistic mistakes and factual errors. Professor Walton E. Bean and other members of the History Department of the University of California at Berkeley freely contributed knowledge and good will. Mr. Michael Lau unraveled problems of the Cantonese dialects and scene. Mr. Valentin H. Rabe gave leads on materials, as did Miss Edith Colignon and Miss Vivian Walker. The Center for the Study of the History of Liberty in America at Harvard University aided greatly with the editing and typing.

Assistance from numerous sources lightened the task of research. I am beholden to the librarians of Widener, Houghton, and Baker Libraries, and the Interlibrary Loan Department of Widener which patiently borrowed books and on many occasions obtained microfilm files of newspapers. The staff of the Bancroft Library never tired of answering my inquiries and making available their resources. A Summer Faculty Fellowship from the University of California helped considerably in the final stage. The custodians of the American Antiquarian Society in Worcester, the Essex Institute and the Peabody Museum in Salem, the Boston Public Library and the archives of the American Board of Commissioners for Foreign Missions in Boston, the New York Public Library, the Newark Public Library, the Presbyterian Historical Society in Philadelphia, the Library of Congress and the National Archives, the California State Library in Sacramento, the Library of the University of California at Berkeley, the California Historical Society in San Francisco, the Stanford University Libraries, and the Huntington Library gave cordial aid. Sister Mary Clement generously placed manuscripts of her father, Inspector John J. Manion, in my hands. The Pastor of Notre Dame des Victoires in San Fran-

cisco allowed research in the marriage register which survived
the fire of 1906. Miss Fern Medley of the Carnegie Free Library at Beaver Falls, Pennsylvania, lent a paper by Mr.
Charles Reeves May.

Ellen Wood Barth has shared all the work.

G. B.

CONTENTS

INTRODUCTION

IN the 1850's and 1860's a tidal wave of Chinese surged into California in pursuit of a dream. The newcomers came with a vision; they would make money to return to China with their savings for a life of ease, surrounded and honored by the families which their toil had sustained. Their goal kept the Chinese apart from the flood of other immigrants who came to America as permanent residents. The vast majority of arrivals from the Middle Kingdom were merely sojourners and they shaped the initial encounter with Americans, molding the impact made by all Chinese newcomers. These legions of sojourners are the focal point of this history. The investigation traces their coming, delineates their world in the United States, and depicts their course until they joined the main stream of immigrants to America.

The sojourners' pursuit of their limited goal influenced the reception of the Chinese in the United States who were, as a result, excluded from the privileges and obligations of other immigrants. They became the docile subjects of bosses and headmen, still directed in California by the dictates of the Chinese world. Strife and acculturation left their daily life unchanged. Only when they modified their original narrow goal were an ever-increasing number transformed into Chinese immigrants. However the impression which the sojourners created in the United States dominated the relationships between Chinese and Americans for decades.

The conditions of Kwangtung and California shaped the nature of the first contact. The sojourners' specific goal emerged from the chaos of the Pearl River Delta which endangered their established way of life. At the middle of the nineteenth century disturbed social conditions compelled Cantonese to emigrate and to earn overseas the means of supporting the extended family. Surrounded by political and economic disorder, the villagers chose to leave parents, wives, children, relatives, and friends in their defense of this last bastion of the good life. News about the discovery of easy riches in California determined the destination of these emigrants.

The California scene contributed additional elements to the encounter between Chinese and Americans. The Westerners' faith in the American nature of California dominated their vision of the state's future. The sojourners, like the Indians, Mexicans, Europeans, and Negroes, were obstacles in the road to the realization of the Californian dream. The vision destined the young commonwealth to an elevated position among the states similar to that of the United States among the nations of the world. The Chinese represented also, like millions of newcomers to the United States before them, another object for the humanitarian elements of American culture.

The Cantonese sojourn in California took place within the framework of Chinese oversea emigration. Poverty turned the mass of sojourners into indentured emigrants resembling those who formed the backbone of the Chinese migration into the Malay Archipelago. Akin also to the coolie trade, the credit-ticket system reproduced all aspects of the nefarious traffic but one: indentured emigrants fell into their creditors' clutches at their own volition. The California setting demanded adjustments of the pattern which made possible the use of the traditional mode of Chinese emigration and continued the hold of the Chinese world on the indentured emigrants.

The adaptation of the credit-ticket system to the passage between Hong Kong and San Francisco extended the social structure of the Chinese world to California. The maintenance of this world within the United States required further modifications to sustain the method of indenture without the aid of courts or of local custom. Although Californians opposed the intrusion of the concept of debt bondage into their state, Chinese merchants adjusted the pattern successfully by utilizing district and kinship organizations as instruments of extralegal control. The sojourners' loyalty to their families in the villages of the Pearl River Delta enforced the creditors' hold over the indentured emigrants. A Chinese California emerged, isolated from, yet part of, the Golden State's development. Under merchant leadership the control system pervaded Chinese California, spreading through isolated mining camps and crowded Chinese quarters. With the aid of loyalty and benevolence, through perfidy and malice, in the interest of merchant-creditors a limited group of men controlled the mass of indentured emigrants in Chinese California.

The system of controls ensured the sojourners' work in mining companies and railroad construction crews. Regimented labor guaranteed the merchant-creditors a constant return on their investment in indentured emigrants. The sojourners' dominant concern in their new environment was survival, not liberty. "Bitter strength," the literal translation of the Chinese term *k'u-li* for these laborers, suggests the dimensions of the sojourners' experience. At the mercy of their bosses, their ability to endure generated stamina to survive the ordeal while their determination guaranteed constant efforts to reach the goal. Labor in Chinese California furnished the mass of sojourners with compensation high enough to ensure their submission to the system and to perpetuate their dreams of success, yet small enough to secure their continuing dependence. In this machinery of control and work, Chinatown provided an ingeniously supervised outlet for pent-up emotions and suppressed desires. Chinatown also furnished lonely sojourners drudging in strange environs with the illusion of home for a few fleeting hours.

The wider significance of Chinatown and work camp obscured their specific functions. These institutions not only sustained the machinery of supervision and drudgery but also brought the sojourners into contact with the alien world outside the system of control. Work camp and Chinatown provoked strife and stimulated humanitarian attempts at acculturation. From the beginning Chinese mining camps were catalysts in the strife with Americans which magnified the sojourners' bitter experience. Chinatown only slowly assumed its part in the struggle. However, long after other areas of employment attracted the mass of Chinese laborers and took over the role which mining camps had originally fulfilled in California, the quarter continued to occupy its essential function as safety valve of the control system. Chinatown remained for decades the major center of strife between Chinese and Californians.

Occupational changes increased Chinatown's problems. New industries attracted growing numbers of sojourners within the teeming blocks of the quarter. Chinatown continued to harbor hordes of indentured emigrants in dilapidated structures and to support gambling houses, opium dens, and brothels. After the failure of their reform drives Californians came to consider filth and immorality as the sojourners' second nature. They projected the original struggle over specific grievances into the framework of an irresistible and perpetual conflict. Yet even while Chinatown remained the major focal point of strife, the concentration of human misery also stimulated humanitarian attempts to alleviate the conditions by bringing the Chinese into the realm of American culture.

The process of acculturation accompanied the strife which, as the other extreme of reaction, also marked the emergence of Chinese California. On the one hand, the development turned around the American response to the humanitarian challenge presented by hordes of downtrodden newcomers. On the other hand, acculturation involved the sojourners' reaction to the strange world which they encountered. The different goals of Californians and Chinese accounted for these phases of acculturation. In response to the humanitarian challenge Californians endeavored to bring all Chinese into the encompassing realm of American culture. They extended the universal blessings of their institutions and values to the newcomers as a group.

For the vast majority of sojourners these overtures lacked significance in relation to their aim to make money quickly, to pay off their indenture, and to return to their families. They had left relatives and friends and had shouldered the burden of daily drudgery in an alien world in defense of their own system of values. They therefore clung tenaciously to their culture and rejected the new standards. Only a few sought to gain in the process of acculturation those advantages which speeded a realization of their dream.

Incidental encounters between Californians and individual Chinese provided another basis for bringing the sojourners into the realm of American culture. Personal contacts eroded the dominant image that Americans had formed of Chinese. They led to the discovery of the sojourners as individual human beings and slowly dissolved the stereotypes of anonymous hordes of docile slaves. The new concept and the sojourners' modification of their goal undermined the structure of Chinese California. Together with the movement of Chinese into the South and East, they contributed to the disintegration of the most oppressive features of the control system.

The extension of the Chinese problem to the national scene expedited the process of acculturation. The growing realization that the United States furnished means of existence outside the regimented world of work camp and Chinatown inspired individuals to break away from the control system. The new perspective on American life and the impact of Western concepts on filial piety and familism eased the acceptance of an altered goal. A mounting portion of Chinese came to consider the United States as their home. Their changed outlook initiated the laborious process that transformed sojourners into immigrants.

By that time, however, the Chinese had become a national issue manipulated by politicians who obscured the different influences that had formed Western and Eastern attitudes toward the Chinese. The expediencies of politics depicted the emergence of the Chinese question as the inevitable outcome of economic, social, and moral laws governing the destinies of nations. This policy obliterated the limited nature of the initial opposition. The reaction of the West had been formed by California's attitude toward slavery. In the context of the Pacific Coast the Orientals hardly represented an intrinsic economic threat. Only in specific settings, such as the strike-ridden factories of the East, did the sojourners endanger the economic welfare of workingmen. However, in the settled world of the East, in contrast to the unstable conditions of the California scene, the Chinese were no social problem.

The two decades between 1850 and 1870 left a lasting memory which long cast a shadow over the contact between Chinese and Americans in the United States. Stereotypes and misconceptions faded but slowly. Laws and customs, construed to restrain sojourners and to offset the particular world of indentured emigrants, continued to keep Chinese immigrants from their rights as Americans. Opponents readily absorbed the clichés into their arguments for exclusion. They adopted the rationale developed in reaction to the emergence of the Chinese question as a national problem and conveniently disguised their specific opposition to Chinese immigrants behind the general objections to the sojourners. Scheming legislators ignored the concrete grievances which accounted for the initial strife in West and East and made political capital of the sojourners' heritage.

The experiences of the 1850's and 1860's also distorted the outlook of the newly emerging Chinese immigrants. With years of regimentation and strife as inheritance, they only hesitantly entered into the process of assimilation. Acculturation offered them such unfamiliar values as political, economic, and social equality, grossly contorted by the violence of the 1870's and 1880's. Stranded in the United States, they were haunted by the memory of their former goal and they adopted a crude mixture of both cultures. Having failed in the major task of their lives some cared little for the details of a solution which remained second best since their value system recognized only one criterion of excellence. Others accepted regular visits to their homeland as an alternative to their original objective. Only the passing of decades slowly neutralized the sojourners' impact on the encounter between Chinese and Americans.

The sojourners left little written record of their experience. Illiterate or poorly educated, their struggle permitted no leisure for reflection. Newspaper accounts furnished the major source for this history of indentured emigrants. The correspondence of missionaries as well as legislative and municipal records, diaries and journals, reminiscences and travelogues written by Western observers helped to place the countless bits of information in perspective.

The Chinese are the center of the picture. The running debate among Americans about their presence in the United States received attention only in so far as it shed light on the plight of the newcomers. The records of the schemes of planters and entrepreneurs helped to trace the movement of Chinese into South and East. Filling the void characteristic of the early life of the Chinese in the United States, the bits of evidence enliven the world of silent sojourners.

In early California, with a few exceptions, individual Chinese disappeared within the legions of newcomers. A court trial or a coroner's report at times shattered the anonymity which obscured their background; however, these specific cases brought to light only variations of the theme that dominated their life. During the fleeting hours of a visit to Chinatown or to the Chinese store of a mountain camp, their suppressed nature found an outlet. In the gray morning of the working day the single-mindedness of purpose again ruled their world. Relegating their life to the pursuit of their dream, the sojourners' determination furnished the strength to endure bitter years. For many Chinese these years ended only with the abandonment of their goal. Gradually the acceptance of a life in the United States as Chinese immigrants began to hold out the promise of a future defined in terms of liberty, and not survival.

CHAPTER I

DELTA OF CONTRASTS

THE missionary came well prepared. He carried an elaborate statement, his answer to the list of twenty-seven topics upon which the Joint Special Committee of the Senate and House of Representatives to Investigate Chinese Immigration desired to be informed. Methodically, the Reverend Augustus Ward Loomis read his answer to the thirteenth question, "From what part of China do they come?" While speaking he drew from his coat pocket a chart of the empire, prepared by his associate from a Chinese gazetteer. After a brief reference to the eighteen provinces he pointed at Canton and produced a map of the province of Kwangtung, designed by missionaries to show their stations. The sketch disclosed the "names of the towns as represented in the six [Chinese] companies [of San Francisco]," he emphasized. But, he added, there were scattering Chinese from many townships not mentioned there. The rooms of the Palace Hotel in San Francisco known as A and B were the scene of the brief lesson in geography on November 9, 1876.[1]

The missionary's allusion to the Pearl River Delta hardly stirred the three senators and the one representative in their leather-upholstered chairs. They felt at ease in the masculine chambers of the "Bonanza Inn," owned by Senator William Sharon of Nevada, the ex-King of the Comstock. From the glass-roofed Grand Court around which the impressive rectangular structure of seven stories and eight hundred rooms was designed, the congressional visitors faced Montgomery

Street through an arched driveway. Arriving guests were driven inside the hotel and deposited on the marble-paved floor in the midst of a forest of potted plants and palm trees.[2] The splendor of the "world's grandest hotel" kept the dingy alleys of Chinatown at a greater distance than the few blocks intervening suggested.

There, on the edge of Chinatown, on the busy intersection of Sacramento and Stockton Streets, the missionary of the Presbyterian Board of Foreign Missions to the Chinese in California lived on the second floor of the Chinese Chapel. Augustus W. Loomis had been a missionary in China before he had come to San Francisco. Actually, Loomis had seen the Pearl River Delta only briefly, having spent the major portion of the years between 1844 and 1849 seven hundred miles to the northeast of Canton, at Ningpo, in the province of Chekiang.[3] But his experience had provided a picture of the Chinese scene at the middle of the nineteenth century, when the discovery of gold in California directed the migration from the Pearl River Delta to the Bay of San Francisco.

Other Americans, before and after him, missionaries, traders, and travelers, viewed the delta in detail. John Ledyard, corporal of marines in the *Resolution* in Captain James Cook's last exploring expedition, was one of the first Americans to gaze at the landscape from the anchorage at Macao when his eyes followed the boat that took Captain James King in his quest for stores to Canton as guest of the British East India Company.[4] Major Samuel Shaw established the initial commercial contact with the Middle Kingdom and served as first American consul in Canton.[5] In the years to come, in company with other "outside barbarians," Americans wore down some of the barriers created by geography, custom, and law. Every glimpse which the eager eyes of newcomers cast upon the landscape, sharpened the contours of the picture. Recorded in sketches and ship logs, letters and reports, learned articles and chatty journals, the views added color to the outline which the Reverend Loomis drafted for the Committee. Like the stones of a mosaic these pieces of information arranged themselves into a panorama of contrasts.[6]

The topographical diversities of the Pearl River Delta paralleled the social and cultural divisions among its inhabitants. The geography of the Delta, the character of its people, and the function of emigration in their way of life at the middle of the nineteenth century transmitted the influence of these diversities to the migration to California.

Vast numbers of fishing boats guarded the shadowy outline of the coastal hills that flanked the Pearl River estuary. Scattered in almost every direction, the craft sailed in twos before the wind, with a net extended between each pair. Strikingly rigged, the square sails set upon two or three masts formed a vivid contrast to the bluff, barren peaks of the Ladrones.[7] These rugged islands studded the mouth of the river and bordered a bay which absorbed half of the total length of the waterway. Deep channels abruptly intersected the granite formations opening up into the bay which was dominated by a solitary peak. The view from Lintin Island embraced the vast body of sickly-green water, dotted with boats, extended mud flats, and the bleak islands on the coast, their broken hills worn into deep furrows. Vegetables grew on a few terraces, but the higher hills often terminated in sharp peaks and the lower ones were frequently enveloped in sand. No trees grew from the water's edge to the summits.[8]

In the southeast the island of Hong Kong hid behind the neighboring highlands of Lantao. The Queen's Road, which marked the extent of Victoria, skirted and twisted along the foot of hills washed by the waters of the bay. After the town began to leave Queen's Road it climbed up the mountainside which stood out with sharp angular features. Serpentines were fringed with shrubbery and gardens. The yellow-washed castle of the British governor, with the Union Jack in front, the residence of the Bishop of Victoria, the cathedral, military quarters, and the pretentious palaces of successful merchants caught the breezes of the hilltop. Victoria's Peak looked down from an elevation of eighteen hundred feet, over city and bay, sampan, lorcha, and junk, and the men-of-war and the merchantmen of many nations.[9]

To the southeast of Lintin, isles and distant hills formed familiar volcanic scenery up to the bay of Macao which introduced a strikingly different panorama. A long line of white European buildings which burst into view at once wound with a gentle sweep around the crescent shore of the bay. Macao stood upon a peninsula of the island of Hiangshan, with the romantic bay in front and a sheet of water in the rear, the pillared gateway of the Portuguese governor's residence occupying the center of the half-moon. The spacious promenade in front, on an embankment faced with stone, was interrupted, occasionally, by jetties and steps. Military and ecclesiastical structures crowned the summit of the hills; however, the Chinese dwellings, one story in height, were concealed by Portuguese and English houses that surrounded them. The irregular surface of the town changed from every viewpoint. Covered with hills and valleys, scattered hamlets and cultivated fields, inlets and bays, the peninsula narrowed down to the breadth of a hundred yards within a mile, and here the Barrier, a wall built by the Chinese, barred entry into the empire.[10]

The shores of the bay above Lintin Island slowly forced the reddish-yellow water of the Pearl River into a narrow channel. The muddy waves rolled and flowed around rocky islets clothed in green and the shore began to exhibit the peculiar delta scenery. Lofty hills bordered the banks, with intervening valleys and villages. Every plain or cove showed its populous town or hamlet. Wherever the soil, washed from the hillsides, accumulated in masses large enough to support a community, settlements planted themselves on the fertile ground. Graves, which formed a horseshoe-shaped enclosure of masonry, one within another, were sprinkled over the green mountain ranges, their wide semicircles resembling an old-fashioned, large, oval-backed sleigh, high behind and low in front. High hills commanded the river, about thirty miles above the pyramidic peak of Lintin. Fanciful names enlivened the bizarre rock formations, masses of red and yellow sandstone that confined the stream to a narrow passage. The "Dragon's Eye" watched the entrance to the gateway and scanned Lintin Bay which no longer appeared as a river but as a large lake, lending weight to the Chinese notion that the sea began at the Tiger's Mouth, the Bocca Tigris or the Bogue.[11] Tiger Island lay higher up in the current of the passage and furnished the Chinese name for the gateway, Hu-men, Tiger's Gate. The walls and bastions of several forts, flanking the streams, provided a martial facade, their embrasures painted with figures of tigers and demons. A fleet of war junks anchored below the strongholds while small cruisers patrolled the channel behind the islands.[12]

As the Tiger's Mouth widened into the Sea of Lions, the grotesque hills receded and rice fields covered the flats on the eastern shore. Many streams, arms of the river, divided the extensive plain into countless islands. On the west bank the land rose abruptly. A large pagoda of nine stories, standing on a bluff of red sandstone, crowned the summit of the hill. From the precipitous river bank, a narrow path led up to the top. Plats of vegetables and fields of rice, raised on numerous terraces, covered the larger portion of the hill. The lofty view from the eighth story permitted a glance backward at Lintin Island and forward over the city of Canton. The wide expanse of the Pearl River lay to the east; the barren hills of the Bogue shut out most of the prospect to the south; and in the west and southwest a plain dotted with fields and villages embosomed in groves, stretched further than the eye could reach. Canals and creeks, connecting countless settlements, ran in every direction, the masts and sails of boats peeping out of the rice fields revealing their course. Hills framed the landscape to the north.[13]

During the winter months the great width of the Pearl River attracted innumerable wild fowl which were caught in nets and with decoys. Ducks were plentiful and wild geese not uncommon, while coots and other water birds fed in the weeds during the cold weather. Every spring, the tide overflowed the multitude of flat islands, unprotected by embankments. These places were chiefly given over to the cultivation of rice. The soil was prepared with a plow drawn by a buffalo, and afterward hoed by hand. The plow consisted of three pieces of timber, roughly joined together. The hoe was made of hard wood, the edge shod with iron and the handle lengthened to increase the force of the blow. Men, women, and children worked on the fields, planting, setting out the young rice, and bringing in the harvest.

Mulberry plantations were elevated artificially above the reach of the tide and the moisture was drained off by deep trenches and numerous fish ponds. The young shoots sprouted with the beginning of spring, and when the first crop was ready, usually in April, boys, women, and girls stripped them off and packed them into baskets. Men, in little boats propelled by paddles, darted back and forth on the canals and rushed the baskets to the market places where they were purchased by the owners of silkworms. The cocoons, when ready to be unwound, were plunged into hot water and dried. Women, sitting by their doors, wound the gossamer threads from the cocoons. The refuse fed the fish in the ponds. On clear, warm days boats glided up and down the canals while men and women rolled up the silk which hung on frames along the top of the boats and dried in the wind.[14]

A great pagoda, visible for many miles, revealed the location of Whampoa Island. Brushwork covered the shell of the monument, and trees grew in crevices of the eaves which divided the stories. The remains of a conical roof, nearly as high as a regular story, crowned the summit. The town of Whampoa, hardly perceptible from the river, was concealed behind the shady trees planted around its wall. Plantations of sugar cane, rice, bamboo, and vegetables stretched from the edge of the river to the wall and were irrigated with tortuous canals, sluices regulating the flow of water from the stream. Banana, litchi, and peach trees grew on the embankment. The anchorage attracted the huts of the poor which were often taken for the town itself.

The Chinese town on shore faced a foreign settlement in ships on the water, the anchorage of the foreign merchantmen that were not allowed to proceed the remaining thirteen miles to Canton and in most cases could not have done so because of their size. During the trading season from October to March, the vessels discharged their cargoes into barges and waited several months in the reaches between Dane Island and Whampoa to take aboard the teas which came down the river. The gothic windows of a church, a doctor's office with Venetian blinds, a grocery, and a ship chandlery lent color to the floating city.[15]

Above the city of Whampoa fisherboats searched the stream for shellfish. They drifted slowly with the current while two men pressed the dredges over the river bottom. Boys washed out the mud and threw the mussels into a heap on the floor of the boat. Stakes cut off branches of the river and supported long nets, arranged in parallel rows, which at ebb and flow caught the fish as they were borne by the current in either direction. Just when the tide began to slacken, the fishermen lifted the nets and collected their catch in baskets. Others, on the embankment, tanned nets in large cedar vats to preserve them and to make them less noticeable to the fish. Portions of the flats were fenced in with coarse bamboo mats to trap fish during ebb tide. At low water, when the shoals were dry, women and children waded knee-deep through the mud in search of shrimps.

Further up the river another pagoda of nine stories stood on a small mound at a narrow canal cut for boats through one of the islands. Several trees flourished on its mouldering cornices. Farm houses and sugar mills surrounded the tower while a large assembly of boats moored in long, regular streets formed a floating city. "The river itself is teeming with human life." [16] Craft of every description drifted by the luxuriant vegetation on the banks. Salt junks discharged their cargoes into canal boats. Vessels from the interior and immense rafts of bamboo and timber drifted down with the tide. The floaters dwelt in huts built upon the rafts or lived in small boats attached to them. Brightly colored revenue cruisers policed the river, their moveable roofs thatched to protect the sailors from sun and wind, the large triangular flags with vermilion characters at the stern, and the cannons with red sashes tied around their muzzles distinguishing them from lesser craft. Minute ferry boats dotted the water. Gigantic junks, gorgeously embellished with dragons, viewed the pandemonium with huge eyes painted on their bows. At dusk the tremendous din of gongs, the shouts, the music from flower boats, and the glare of flaming paper set on fire by the boatmen and thrown into the stream as evening sacrifice, increased the excitement.[17]

The tiled roofs of Canton barely rose over the phantasmagoria of the floating city. At first sight the entire town was one solid mass of low houses, the narrow streets being scarcely perceptible. The far-stretching dull level of gray

A shirt, drawers, a long gown, or a pelisse buttoned in front over them, stockings, and shoes formed the principle articles of dress, the climate determining the number and quality of these garments. The humidity accounted for cold winters and hot summers although the mercury hardly rose or fell to extremes. The long summer began in April and ended in October. In July and August the thermometer registered a hundred degrees in the shade. Vicious typhoons marked the passing of the summer. Autumn began in October and lasted till January which brought cold, northerly winds. Heavy rains fell in the spring, in February and March, and during the summer, in July and August.[21] On a hot day the thinnest grass-cloth robe over a light shirt, thin silk drawers, stockings, and shoes constituted the attire of most respectable persons in the streets. In the winter fur jackets or thickly wadded cloth served as outer garments. The poor wore durable blue nankeen or quilted cotton of dark color. During the warm months boatmen, laborers, and porters donned nothing but a pair of wide drawers, fastened around the waste with a silk string. A large bamboo or straw hat protected them against the scorching sun. When the heavy rain poured down, they covered their shoulders with a cloak of dried rush leaves which farmers also used as protection against the fierce sun during the hottest hours of the day.[22]

The labyrinth of streets within the walls of Canton knew neither beginning nor end. It resembled the intricate waterways of the delta which the provincial capital dominated. A long street, transecting several separate neighborhoods of the city, changed its name as frequently as the Pearl River. Even though the name Pearl River designated the course between Shimun, about fourteen miles west of Canton, and the Bogue, common people hardly recognized the term more than a few miles. The fork at the head of an island, or the entrance of a brooklet, supplied sailors and boatwomen with new names for each branch, reach, channel, or passage. Three rivers united to form the waterway. The West River and the North River mingled at Sanshwui, roughly fifty miles west of Canton. The East River joined them near Whampoa, a few miles east of First Bar. The West River, rising in the eastern part of Yunnan and receiving tributaries throughout Kwangsi, was by far the largest of the three streams. Its main course reached the China Sea west of Macao, and the Pearl River often appeared as its northern mouth. The North River and the East River, both draining the northern part of Kwangtung, joined the Pearl River after an independent course of several hundred miles.[23]

The delta formed a rough triangle, each side about hundred miles long. Merchantmen passed through the Bogue, about thirty miles up to Whampoa. Only sampans, lorchas, and junks could pass the thirteen miles due west to reach Canton. Rivers, creeks, and canals intersected the area in every direction. Boats linked the towns, villages, and hamlets. Away from the crowded metropolitan center business was conducted in market places. The surrounding villages harbored the people. At night, when the quick pulse of the delta slowed down and silence covered water and land, a barking dog could be heard in twenty villages, none of which contained less than a thousand people.

The eastern and central parts of the delta cultivated rice; the west grew mulberry shrubs and reared silkworms. Between the two rice crops the land produced fruits and vegetables. The mountain regions raised large quantities of pears, oranges, plums, mangoes, peaches, and litchis; entire hills were covered with pineapples. Fruit trees lined the fields and separated the windswept barren plateaus from the level plains, partially covered with yellow flood water at high tide. The rich green of the growing rice enlivened the gray monotony of the bizarre sandstone formations. The grain rose and fell with the wind like billows in a sea of verdure. Misty valleys led up to bold hills crowned with white clouds towering over dusky mud flats and brown, marshy lowlands, and blurred mountain ranges that framed a delta of contrasts.[24]

The administrative divisions increased the complexities. Nine districts of the Kwangchau prefecture divided the delta as arbitrarily and rigorously as creeks and hills, rivers and mountain ranges. The district of Nanhai and the district of Pwanyü bisected the city of Canton, the former administering the western, the latter the eastern portion. The Pearl River originated in the district of Sanshwui, passed in westerly direction through the districts of Nanhai and Pwanyü and, after turning south on its way to the China Sea, was flanked in the east by the districts of Tungkwan and Sinan [Sanon, Sunoan], and in the west by Hiangshan [Chung Shan]. The West River was bordered on its southern course by the districts of Shunte, Sinhwui, and Sinning [Toi Shan]. The districts of Anping, Haiping, and Hohshan, of the Shauking prefecture, completed the administrative structure; they guarded the southwestern boundary of the Kwangchau prefecture in the shape of a dagger that pointed at the populous city Kowkong on the West River in the district of Nanhai.[25]

The boundaries of the twelve districts failed to disguise the diversity of the delta. Language barriers and cultural divisions disregarded the administrative units. The sophistication of the metropolitan center contrasted with the rustic simplicity of sleepy hamlets tucked away in the delta. The courtly luster of the splendid entourage of the Viceroy of Liang-Kuang, ruling Kwangtung and Kwangsi, and of the illustrious favorites of the Hoppo, the Superintendent of Maritime Customs, pervaded the provincial capital. The attendants of the Governor of Canton, the hangers-on of numerous provincial officials, and the clerks in the hongs of merchant princes disseminated the tone and the air of the great world outside of yamens and palaces.

Foreigners were confined to the area between the western suburbs and the Pearl River. For decades this had been the only foothold of the "outside barbarians" in the empire; at the middle of the nineteenth century, it was one of the five treaty ports. The presence of foreigners turned the citizens' feigned self-consciousness into haughty pride. The residents of the Thirteen Factories were catalysts in the process which charged any urban mob with enthusiastic loyalty to the provincial capital. At regular intervals the metropolis also attracted the scholars of the province who competed in official examinations for degrees which opened the coveted road to officialdom. At the same time, the floating city on the river, under the wall, welcomed at any hour the failures and outcasts of society.[26]

The luxury and riches as well as the misery and vices of the inhabitants of Canton elevated to a superior position the people of the Sam Yap, a collective name for the three districts of Nanhai, Pwanyü, and Shunte, which encompassed and surrounded the provincial capital. Their purer Cantonese was hardly understood in Sinhwui and Sinning, the two districts of the Kwangchau prefecture farther from Canton, whose coarser dialect was readily accepted in the adjacent districts of Anping and Haiping in the Shauking prefecture. This bond between the dialects linked the two districts of the Kwangchau prefecture to the districts of the Shauking prefecture, to form the Sze Yap, the Four Districts. Sometimes the people of the Hohshan district in Shauking prefecture were lumped together with the Sze Yap to make the Ng Yap, the Five Districts. Even the stolid peasants of the district of Hiangshan, in the heart of the Pearl River Delta, looked at a hardy mountaineer from the Sze Yap with contempt.[27]

Yet tensions permeated the day of a rice farmer in an isolated village or of a charcoal worker in a lonely mountain valley as thoroughly as they filled the precarious existence of a courtier in the viceroy's yamen. Field and creek, hilltop and valley, pond and fountain were peopled with demons controlling air and earth and water. The welfare of a man, of a family, or of an entire village depended upon the good will of the gods whose reign was more effective than the limited power of the faraway mandarin. In the face of these forces, pirates, robbers, and other formidable enemies who posed a constant threat to life and property appeared less dangerous, as did the long, sanguinary internecine wars which often arose among villages and clans from trivial causes. During the fighting women and children were corralled in fortified places, the *wai,* garrisoned by boys and old men which also protected the villagers against bands or robbers and crews of pirates scourging the hamlets of the delta.

The mandarins faced the chaos in their districts helplessly. People paid taxes, but they did not allow the officials to tamper with local affairs. The walls surrounding yamens and district capitals symbolized the lack of communication which handicapped the officials who in most cases did not speak the local dialect. The gentry attempted to settle disputes, but if there was no agreement, communications were broken off and the rival factions started a predatory war without any declaration of hostility. Bloody battles marked the struggle, hundreds of men perished, and entire villages were destroyed. The combatants generally tolerated neutral villages, but it frequently happened, when a league of powerful clans struggled with their enemies that they plundered any man who fell into their hands unless he belonged to a clan whose strength they feared.

Brotherhoods stood ready, for a compensation, to furnish the mandarin with bribes, ransom many, false witnesses, and guilty persons in case the riots gained the attention of higher officials who were able, with the aid of the soldiery, to establish momentarily a modicum of order. The people of Kwangtung easily became bandits, Governor Hwang Ngantung [Huang En-t'ung] lamented in an exhortation of his subordinates. They were unwilling "duly to appreciate life" and stole and kidnapped in order "to obtain ransom-money, thus appreciating gain and lightly esteeming life." [28] The endless feuds and conquests turned the bucolic landscape into a quarrelsome world, metamorphosing simple villagers into scheming rapparees who engaged in any enterprise which promised plunder.

Secret societies recruited farmers and fought pitched battles for control of the countryside. At times desperate peasants joined these leagues to counteract the intrigues of corrupt mandarins and avaricious gentry. In the middle of the nineteenth century the Triad Society, variously known as T'ien-ti Hui, San-tien Hui, San-ho Hui, or Hung-men Hui, raised the standard of revolt in Liang-Kuang. The rebels infested Canton and controlled the Pearl River Delta for several years. After their withdrawal the Manchu bannermen pacified the villages which surrounded the provincial capital and, in retaliation, drove thousands of peasants in chains to Canton for execution.[29]

Three distinct groups divided the population of the delta, the loyalty that each commanded producing further decomposition. The majority of the inhabitants of the twelve districts called themselves Punti, natives, the Cantonese pronunciation of the two Chinese characters *pen-ti*, in distinction to the Hakka, *k'e-chia*, the guest families or strangers, who migrated to South China from northeastern provinces in the thirteenth century. The Hakka had drifted into the mountain regions of the Pearl River Delta during the turn of the seventeenth century and occupied a broad belt of land, a short distance north of Canton and running southeast and southwest. They first served as hired laborers, but through industry and thrift acquired most of the land of their masters. These people diligently guarded their independence and lived in separate villages, willing to endure new adventures rather than to submit to suppression. A talent for organization and a strong group spirit marked their action. Simple and naïve, they withstood all privations. The women did not bind their feet and were able to work as hard as men. Taller and stronger, if a little darker, than the Cantonese, the Hakka spoke their own language, different from the local dialects but closer to the Mandarin of the officials.

The struggle between Punti and Hakka reached a climax in 1854 when, in the turbulent years following the withdrawal of the Taiping Movement to the lower Yangtze River, members of secret societies and rioters known as Hung-chin-tsei captured towns and villages in the vicinity of Canton. In the face of these Red Caps most Hakka clans remained loyal to the Manchu officials while the Punti joined the bandits until brutally suppressed by Yeh Ming-ch'en, Governor-general of Liang-Kuang. After the extermination of the rebels the Punti attacked Hakka villages in retaliation for their support of the Manchu government. The struggle turned into open warfare in which the officials were powerless to interfere. The Hakkas, greatly outnumbered, were driven from their settlements and roamed the mountains in bands that ranged from a few hundred to many thousands. In the southwest of Canton, in the districts of Hohshan and Sinning, the Punti also fell upon the Hakka to settle old scores.[30]

The third group, the Tanka, *tan-chia* or boat people, disturbed the tranquillity of the life on the river. For centuries they were treated as outcasts. Born and raised on boats, these men and women earned their living as ferry men and by transporting or smuggling goods to and from Canton. They were not allowed to intermarry with the Cantonese or to compete in the official examinations; their women did not practice footbinding. A successful piratical venture was a Tanka's sole hope for a better life.

The chaotic state of the districts in the Pearl River Delta stemmed from disturbances which shook the structure of the entire empire. The upheavals originated partly in the unique world of the Pearl River Delta. For decades Canton was the only port where foreign merchants were allowed to trade in season with the Co-hong, a limited number of licensed Chinese under the supervision of the Hoppo, the Superintendent of the Maritime Customs. With the legitimate produce of foreign trade two items of contraband, long known in China, found their way into the empire in steadily increasing quantities: opium and Christianity. Well-armed opium ships anchored in the Bay of Lintin in the open roadstead and transferred the chests of opium to receiving ships and floating warehouses. Centipedes and scrambling dragons, two-masted fifty-oared craft manned with Chinese smugglers, took over directly part of the opium, evaded the custom's patrol, and ran it ashore at small creek villages, whence agents distributed it over the countryside. Sometimes Western firms delivered a consignment at a port further up the coast. With the connivance of provincial officials, smuggling, on the eve of the Opium War, was three times as lucrative as all other forms of trade.[31]

The success of the Protestant missionaries was negligible if viewed with the eyes of the traders. Restricted to Macao and the Thirteen Factories at Canton, they pursued their calling before the Treaty Days under the protection of the foreign merchant community, recognized by the Chinese officials as physicians and interpreters. Yet their mere presence stimulated the first intellectual revolution in China. In the 1830's Hung Hsiu-ch'üan, a candidate for examination and the future leader of the Taiping Rebellion who in 1814 was born in a Hakka village thirty miles north of Canton, heard a foreign Christian evangelist preach in the provincial capital. He picked up a set of nine Christian tracts written by Liang A-fa, apparently the first ordained Chinese Protestant minister, who was born in the district of Kauming, north of Hohshan, about fifty miles west of Canton. In later years Hung Hsiu-ch'üan professed to have found in the tracts the key to his vision of being a son of God, second only to Jesus in his new trinity. In 1847 he received religious instruction at Canton for two months from Issachar J. Roberts, an American Southern Baptist missionary. In the ensuing three years his religious movement combined with an intense antidynastic sentiment and the desire for agrarian reform to initiate the Taiping Rebellion.[32]

The First Anglo-Chinese War (1839–1842) destroyed the military reputation of the Manchu dynasty; the Taiping Rebellion (1851–1864) almost destroyed the dynasty itself. The incompetent successors of the Ch'ien-lung Emperor (1736–1796) failed to solve the ordinary tasks of any Chinese dynasty and lacked the vision to counteract the extraordinary efforts of Westerners to gain improved conditions of trade and diplomatic relations of a Western type. Dynastic decline, political corruption, inadequate administration, Chinese resentment against the alien Manchu overlords, secret societies, agrarian distress, population pressure, rebellions, and foreign penetration created a dilemma in which defeats in any one area of conflict increased the difficulties in all the others.

The hardships which the peasant suffered scarred his personality. He was no longer the naïve and frugal farmer. Cunning and deceiving undertones dampened his forthright spirit. The ready jokes which still delighted him, lost their rough innocence and became brutal.[33] But the more the countryman deviated from his old image the more tightly he clung to the established guides of his conduct, the family and the clan. In the turmoil the recognized rural values maintained their validity. These bastions of the rustic way of life remained unshaken, while a handful of "outside barbarians" and rebels humiliated the boastful soldiers and the mighty minions of the Manchus in view of the people of the Pearl River Delta. The vainglorious soldiers were dead, their officers disgraced, yet the peasants lived and venerated their elders for engineering the survival of family and clan.

The family, *chia*, and the clan, *tsu*, safeguarded the value system of the villages against disintegration under the erosive process of official oppression, "natural" calamities, and foreign intrusions. These institutions molded the life of the individual and, in a chaotic world, shaped social relations into an orderly and stable pattern. In the tightly knit life of the rural world the family whose members had close contact with one another was the basic instrument of social control. The clan consolidated the numerous component families which traced their patrilineal descent from a common ancestor who first had settled in the locality. Kinsmen were not so much relatives of an individual but of the family.[34] The authority to manage the common property rested with the head of the family, usually the father. The family controlled not only the income of members and their joint consumption but also their social conduct.

The clan was deeply rooted in the rural world of the delta. It played no role in the city which was not the abode of one's family but a place away from home. Clan members working in the city sent money to their homes in the country. A clan maintained graveyards and the ancestral hall where rites of filial piety were performed and group activities sponsored. Wealthy clans supported schools to prepare promising members for the civil service examinations. The individual prestige of the degree-holder enhanced the reputation of the clan which accumulated social honors and public distinctions in a common pool. The group also sought to punish members whose social disgrace damaged its reputation and it assumed collective legal responsibility in relations with the government. The clan sent recalcitrant guilty members to the mandarins for punishment while the officials recognized its judicial power. The family shared many of the characteristics of the clan and both guaranteed the same basic values: stability, continuity, and perpetuity.[35]

The intensified loyalty to family and clan demanded ever-growing sacrifices. The turmoil made it increasingly difficult to keep the units intact for a poor peasant could no longer sustain wife, children, and dependent parents on his small plot. When he found it economically impossible to maintain a large family, the rustic continued to pay tribute to the ideal. Deprived of his resources by the existing disorder, he aimed to support wife, children, and dependent parents by emigrating into the Chinese oversea communities. There he intended to labor and live with his kin who in earlier decades had followed the lure of the Nan Yang (Southern Ocean) and acquired wealth and reputation as successful merchants.[36]

Devotion to family motivated the peasant to abandon land and family, home and friends, in exchange for the uncertain fortunes and the certain privations that awaited him in Burma, Siam, Indochina, Malaya, on Sumatra, Java, Borneo, and the Philippines.[37] There he planned to work until he was fifty or sixty when he would return to his native village, a wealthy and respected man, to enjoy the rest of his life venerated by the large family which he had kept intact with his earnings and savings during the long years overseas. Visions of personal wealth and glory, dreams of choice rice fields, shady gardens, and the palatial estate of a merchant prince mingled with illusions of grandeur that placed him, clad in the insignia of office, into the seemingly unperturbed world of the inner courtyard in a mandarin's yamen.[38]

During the long absence from the scene of his dreams, he hoped to visit the Pearl River Delta several times, to marry the girl chosen by his family and to beget children. His wife would remain in the native village and bring up his offspring with his family. Overseas he would maintain a very low living standard and save the larger part of his income for his family which depended on his remittances. The long years in the strange world would not break the emigrant's emotional ties with his family. The tablets of his ancestors in the clan hall and his children in the family home, the veneration of his parents, and the desire to live leisurely in China would sustain his loyalty during his adventurous years ahead until the sun of the Pearl River Delta and the joy of his family again warmed his homesick heart.[39]

The Pearl River Delta shared the social function of emigration with the villages in South China which for decades sent an unending stream of their men into the Nan Yang. In these emigrant communities the majority of the inhabitants depended for their living, in part, on remittances from members of the family who were abroad.[40] One or more sons of less prosperous families, or the sons of every family in a certain clan, ordinarily went overseas in each generation. The adventurers usually selected the same city in which their kin worked. Whole districts preferred specific settlements for their emigrants.[41] The visions of easy fortunes and the opportunity for travel offered by proximity to the sea and to trading vessels influenced the individual decision. Sometimes the dream came true. The returning emigrant entertained his village with a great banquet, firecrackers, and a three days' theatrical performance at the temple. A beautiful concubine warmed his declining years, a new house was built and land bought — and from the land the newly dispossessed were driven overseas to seek their fortunes. The cycle was complete, the stream of emigrants flowed, but only a few drops returned.[42]

Within the empire itself working arrangements paralleled the pattern of oversea emigration. Large groups of people from the hinterland considered the city only a place to work and to earn money. For months these workers filled the contractors' demands for hired laborers while their wives and children lived in the old home to which the earnings were forwarded.[43]

The social conditions of the Pearl River Delta at the middle of the nineteenth century compelled the Cantonese to test the value of the emigration system as defense of their way of life. Engulfed by political and economic disorder the villagers chose to emigrate to protect the foundation of their world. The rumor of easy riches in California determined their route. The story of the Golden Hills in America reached Hong Kong in the spring of 1848. Trading vessels began to link the Bogue to the Golden Gate and to overcome the lack of favorable monsoon winds.[44] Slowly and thoroughly the news penetrated the Pearl River Delta and set the dreams of sojourners into motion.

CHAPTER II

AMERICAN CALIFORNIA

A SMOOTH sheet of water stretched far beyond the reach of the eye. The gigantic mirror appeared "altogether different from mountains, rocks, snows, and the toilsome plains we had traversed," Zenas Leonard observed on November 20, 1833. In sight of the Pacific, about forty miles south of Yerba Buena Cove, the fur trader brought his diary up to date. Auspicious omens had accompanied Joseph Reddeford Walker's party in the last stages of their trip through Mexican territory. The distant thunder of the ocean's pounding surf had kept the first Americans to cross the Sierra Nevada awake at night. The thought of being "within hearing of the *end* of the *Far West*" inspired each "with a patriotic feeling of his country's honor." The falling of the stars, a meteoric shower recorded on November 12, 1833, throughout the United States, spurred them on to the Pacific.

A ship seen dimly riding on the water caught the company's attention. Two white blankets, hoisted on a pole, brought the vessel closer to the shore. To their "joy and surprise" the trappers spotted the American flag "waving majestically . . . at the masthead." Captain John Bradshaw's *Lagoda*, owned by Bryant and Sturgis of Boston, had reached the West Coast a few months earlier. This ship was one of numerous American northwest traders that visited California after Captain Ebenezer Dorr, Jr., had on October 31, 1796, sailed the *Otter* into the harbor of Monterey, the first American vessel to touch at a California port. When the sailors met the trappers, Zenas Leonard noticed, "their astonishment was as great as ours" to find out "that we were children of the same nation." [1]

In the following decade the United States, almost in a single leap, spanned the territory from the Mississippi to the Pacific. A stream of trappers, settlers, explorers, soldiers, and miners cast their eyes for the first time on their Bucolia or El Dorado. Many newcomers discerned familiar American elements in the strange scenery. In 1841, John Bidwell, one of the promoters of the first emigration of American settlers across the plains into the Mexican province, stumbled with his motley group down the western slopes of the Sierra Nevada in search of California. The emigrants chanced to run into an Indian. "Marsh" was one of the few words he used that the men understood. "Of course we supposed," John Bidwell rationalized, it was the name of "the Dr. [John] Marsh . . . who had written the letter [inspiring the promoters] to a friend in Jackson County, Missouri, and so it proved." [2] Three years later, Captain John C. Frémont and his companions, following a river through the foothills of the mountains, strayed into a large Indian village. Here the explorers learned that they "were upon the Rio de los Americanos." Never "did a name sound more sweetly," Captain Frémont rejoiced. "We felt ourselves among our countrymen; for the name of American, in these distant parts, is applied to the citizens of the United States." [3]

When the trickle of settlers to California turned into a stream, the manifestations pointing to an American California grew clearer. On August 30, 1846, Edwin Bryant saw the first issue of the first newspaper published in California, after his overland party had reached the ranch of the New England sailor William Johnson on Bear Creek, near the edge of the Sacramento Valley. The editorial of the Monterey *Californian* called on the people of California to organize a territorial government in preparation for annexation to the United

States. "We have been travelling in as straight a line as we could," the future alcalde of San Francisco pondered, "crossing rivers, mountains, and deserts, nearly four months beyond the bounds of civilization, and for the greater distance beyond the boundaries of . . . our government; but here, on the remotest confines of the world . . . we find ourselves under American authority, . . . to be 'annexed' to the American Union." [4]

A multitude of events revealed to Californians the American character of their new world. These signs foreshadowed the natural growth of the United States destined to culminate on the shore of the Pacific. California formed the pinnacle in the structure which reached from ocean to ocean and harbored the best form of human society. Among all social organizations, past and present, the United States seemed to occupy the highest rank. By adding the crowning touch to the edifice California was chosen for a similar position among the states of the Union.

Californians derived an exalted sense of obligation from a contemplation of the process. They considered themselves selected to realize a vision and cherished the elevated role of *the* American state which California aspired to fill. "Our State is a marvel to ourselves," Justice Nathaniel Bennett readily confessed in his oration heralding California's admission into the Union, "and a miracle to the rest of the world." [5] The struggle over slavery which they had witnessed "back in the states" filled Californians with moral fervor for their task. They hoped to realize their goal without re-enacting the dilemma of the Union on the Pacific Coast. Californians strove to limit the impact of slaveholders, abolitionists, and slaves on the development of their young commonwealth. However, the free society which they envisioned faced equally corroding influences that obstructed the pursuit of their ideal.

A series of obstacles blocked the road to the true American

state. The Indians and Mexicans on the scene were the earliest impediments. Their way of life thwarted the Californian dream. The infiltration of Europeans and Negroes increased the difficulties. The resulting strife frustrated the high hopes of Californians for the spectacular development of their commonwealth and reduced their beliefs to ever-diminishing fragments of a general outlook. These surviving tenets barely eased the insecurity of the young society. The growing tensions made the concepts of Californians increasingly rigid and inadaptable to new problems. Each encounter with new obstacles produced new realities which demanded new compromises that shattered old hopes.

The vision of the state's future rested on the faith in an American California. Various influences sustained the creed. The institutional growth, the physical isolation of the young state, and the gold rush strengthened the American nature of the new commonwealth. At the same time these influences introduced elements which obstructed the realization of the vision, heightened the insecurity of the young settlements, increased the particular difficulties of the Indian problem, and sharpened the encounter with the slavery issue.

When ever-growing numbers of Chinese arrived on the California scene, their reception had two aspects. On the one hand the process was another act in the struggle for the realization of the Californian vision. On the other hand the meeting with the newcomers demanded that the American tradition of providing a refuge for suffering humanity be extended to the Chinese. The constant struggle of Californians to realize their exalted dream produced one segment of the background for the Chinese contact with Americans. The concepts of American culture which permeated the new state formed the other. The first encounter between Chinese and Americans thus included both strife and acculturation. The emergence of American California, the frustration of the Californian vision, and the movement of American culture to the Pacific Coast set the stage for the coming of the Chinese to California.

In the nation's capital, a general, a statesman, and a politician expressed various facets of the belief in an American California. On March 5, 1849, on the day of his inauguration, General Zachary Taylor, riding with the outgoing president in a carriage to the Capitol, expressed the view that the settlements in California and Oregon were too distant to become parts of the Union; it would be better for them "to be an Independant Government." After reflecting in his *Diary* that these were alarming opinions to be entertained by the President of the United States, James K. Polk reiterated his fears that the "fine territory" might be "lost to the Union by the establishment of an Independant Government." [6]

William M. Gwin, who was to play a major role in California's first constitutional convention, witnessed the inauguration parade. On the previous day the former commissioner of the New Customhouse at New Orleans had arrived in the capital to settle his account with the Treasury Department. While the procession passed the spectators on Pennsylvania Avenue, Gwin remarked to Stephen A. Douglas that he intended to leave the next morning for California. He counselled the Senator that the failure of Congress to institute territorial government in California would force the people to form a state government independently. Gwin stated that he intended to advocate that policy, and announced himself, in front of Willard's Hotel in Washington, a candidate for United States senator from California. Within a year, Gwin predicted, he would ask Douglas to present his credentials to the Senate. Eleven months later he handed his papers to the Senator from Illinois.[7]

William M. Gwin's accurate prediction placed the development of the new commonwealth confidently within the established concepts of American growth. Familiar elements dominated the development of pioneer California. The old story of adventure, optimism, and western opportunity, of economic concentration, and of striving for cultural achievement took shape again on the Pacific Coast. The process in California occurred on a larger scale and faster than before, but fundamentally, it was the same. California was an intensified, not a different American experience. While Daniel Webster depicted it in his Seventh of March Oration as "Asiatic in . . . formation and scenery" as late as 1850, the new commonwealth paralleled the familiar political experience of other areas in the expanding American West.[8]

When California failed to gain territorial status as a result of the division in Congress, self-government was the substitute. The military, ruling the conquered land, permitted limited self-government with striking readiness. The wide degree of autonomy in local affairs actually fostered the development of American communities more readily than the three departments of a territorial government would have. The gold rush, which made California abnormal, also made her more a part of normal American growth: it broke down the appointed alcaldes' authority in the older towns, attracted a new majority of men from the Eastern states, and submerged the early pioneers and the old Spanish-speaking element.[9]

The Mexican War and the gold rush crowded California with federal office holders. Their activities compensated for the lack of regular territorial officials. They served, in the absence of a more formal system, as a channel of political acculturation through which the new communities moved into the currents of national politics.[10] The contest over patronage directed attention to the national capital. Professional politicians flocked to California, attracted by the prospect of statehood and the wealth of litigation over mining claims which supported large numbers of lawyers. The formation of parties coincided with the organization of the state government, but preceded formal statehood by nearly one year. "It was curious," Bayard Taylor noted in San Francisco toward the end of 1848, "how soon the passion for party politics . . . emulated the excitement of an election in the older states." [11]

Physical separation from other states and the gold rush safeguarded California's specific American character. Geographic isolation linked California not to another section but directly to the Union. The aureole which surrounded, in the eyes of Californians, this most perfect political creation mankind had devised, naturally drew into orbit the rising commonwealth based upon "principles as high and holy as the laws of eternal justice." [12] The affinity between the young state and the Union compounded Northerners and Southerners into Californians: Eastern men, with some additional experience, became Western men. Yet the attributes of heart and mind which their actions revealed, showed the diverse trends of American thought at their time. At the middle of the nineteenth century the youngest American experiment effectively bridged, within its limited world, the diverging sectional loyalties of the other states which the Compromise of 1850 aimed to alleviate.

The gold rush accentuated the American character of California. The stampede of polyglot adventurers to the diggings directed attention to the future of the newly discovered El Dorado while luckless miners, settling for less than the pot of gold, awakened the country to the other potentials of California. General Persifer F. Smith did not regard "the mere loss of . . . gold carried off . . . so great a misfortune as the introduction of the worst kind of population, and the probability of their combining together to resist . . . the regular administration of laws and government." [13] The "wonderful gold discovery . . . threatens California with an emigration overwhelming in number and dangerous in character," Thomas J. Green warned the first session of the legislature.[14] The "prosperity of our State . . . and the happiness of society generally," the San Francisco *Daily Alta California* lamented, "are in a great measure affected by those who come from foreign climes to seek their fortune in this country." [15]

The miners' reaction to foreigners reduced these lofty sentiments to the reality of the camps. But the scenes in the mining districts did not place California outside the realm of American experience. Elsewhere in the country similar tendencies marked other phases of life in the United States. California revealed only its extreme aspects. Confronted with the insecurity and mobility of their society, Americans were not satisfied to rely only on the efforts of their government to secure communal ends. Settlements outran government in many places and rapid changes invalidated established forms. Riots and spontaneous violence occurred in every part of the country as well as in California.[16]

The cosmopolitan character of California's urban centers eliminated the political impact of foreigners as effectively as the rough rivalry of camps and settlements. Educated foreigners, like Californians, tried to follow politics in the homeland. Transplanted Easterners found it easy to form new allegiances with branches of the Democratic or Whig parties. Rootless Europeans, however, continued to peruse, in their newspapers, the wavering fortune of the Second Empire in France, the rise of Prussia, and the *Risorgimento* in Italy. Between 1850 and 1860 alone the French, German, Jewish, Spanish, Italian, and Chinese groups launched thirty-six newspapers in San Francisco.[17] They chose to remain immigrants rather than become Californians.

Mexicans and Spaniards had been placed earlier under a benevolent tutelage. They became a part of American California. The spearheads of the American infiltration of California provided the guiding rationale for the process which reclaimed native Californians for the realm of free men.

Seafaring Massachusetts traders and roving Kentucky trappers had reached the same conclusion: California was in bad hands. Captains and supercargoes compared the ranchos of the scantily developed littoral with thriving New England farms. They marveled at the rich soil, and wondered why the land was not in the hands of the men who would use it properly. The mountaineers despised the oppressive restrictions of the Mexican feudal system. They were accustomed to roaming vast territories, subject to no order but their will.

Each group expressed one of the expansive tenets of Manifest Destiny. The sailors argued that the land be used by men who carried out the design of Providence which called for the cultivation of wheat fields and orchards where wild cattle grazed. The trappers advocated the continuous extension of the area of freedom, based on the rule of free men.[18] Their unbounded confidence in the superiority of American life and institutions made it their duty to propagate these concepts in the world, and to liberate and educate their fellowmen suffering in unnatural bondage. Native Californians became citizens of the United States by the treaty of Guadalupe Hidalgo, unless they individually declined the opportunity.

The gold rush and the growing legend of Old California obscured the new status which native Californians gained. The low position of Mexican and Spanish-speaking miners reflected a change in the American attitude toward segments of the group. The areas of acceptance began to vary as conditions in California altered and the value of Mexicans to American society fluctuated.[19] In the legendry that was created about Old California, the Mexican ranchero was conceived as a noble grandee, and the mission father as a gentle patriarch. The Indians whom both had exploited were happy and well protected innocents. Helen Hunt Jackson's *Ramona*, intended to be the *Uncle Tom's Cabin* of Indian life, at the height of the sympathetic nostalgia for Old California, idealized kind padres and fine old Spanish families, which diverted interest from the author's thesis.[20]

The insecurity accompanying the growth of the new American society impressed upon Californians the reality of the struggle. The citizens of the young state were also alerted to the obstacles that blocked their exalted vision of the future role of the state. While the foundations of an American California were being secured on the West Coast, Californians showed an increasing awareness that their American heritage included such liabilities as the Indian and the Negro questions. The peculiarities of the California scene added new difficulties to these old problems. The resulting struggle to solve the dilemma absorbed the idealism of Californians, obstructed the realization of their dream, and relegated the exuberant young commonwealth to the level of an ordinary state, pressed hard to find solutions to the common problems troubling the Union.

Indirectly, the American acquisition of California helped to break down the established Indian frontier. The Indians, numbering at least one hundred thousand in 1846, roamed through the entire state. They were everywhere, as one Californian complained, "not only . . . on our frontiers, but all among us, around us, with us — hardly a farmhouse . . . without them." [21] Conditions in California were a striking contrast to the "permanent" Indian frontier of the trans-Mississippi West, where white settlers lived in organized settlements and Indians in the unorganized Indian Country. The neophyte Christians added to the confusion. After the secularization of the missions many baptized Indians had rejoined their wild kinsmen and their mission background concealed the convenient division between Christians and pagans which followed the color lines.

The constant search for new mining claims uprooted the few Indian tribes with independent social and economic systems. The California frontier did not settle down as others

did; its development was more repetitive than progressive.
The miners were always on the move. Bands of Indians,
roving the countryside, added to the insecurity which permeated the new diggings and spread resentment among
miners and farmers. The Federal government failed to understand the problem and its early efforts to cope with it
closely resembled the Black Codes of the South. The development of the reservation system ended the long contest by
concentrating the surviving bands on valueless tracts of land
where they received some measure of protection.[22]

The struggle with the Indians roaming among them made
Californians particularly sensitive to the related issues of the
slave and the free Negro. Their memories prejudiced Californians in favor of an exclusively white population. The
"Indians amongst us," the San Francisco *Californian* emphasized, "are . . . a nuisance." We "left the slave States,"
the editor stated explaining his opposition to Negroes in
California, "because we did not like to bring up a family in
a miserable . . . condition, which . . . would be inevitable,
. . . surrounded by slavery. . . . We desire only a white
population in California." [23]

Californians joined readily to exclude slavery from their
new commonwealth. Their strong attachment to the Union
as the embodiment of an absolute set of principles produced
a conservative attitude. The legislation and the judicial decisions of the state reflected neither the extreme attitude of
Southern slaveholders nor the radical views of Northern
abolitionists. The general tendency favored the owners of
slaves in the disputes involving property rights, and white
men in criminal cases where testimony of non-Caucasians was
submitted as evidence.[24] The California Fugitive Slave Law
of 1852 copied the provisions of the federal law, passed as one
of the measures which admitted the state into the Union.[25]
But the continuing debate about slavery showed the underlying emotions. Newspaper editorials and letters to the editors

kept the dispute in the open. They indicated a determination to act as "Western men with constitutional principles" and to gain a neutral position between abolitionists and slaveholders.[26] We "are of neither class," the *Alta* emphasized, "and it is our pleasure to aid in frustrating the one as we have always opposed the other." [27]

Random awareness of the issue turned into a passionate preoccupation with the problem when it threatened to interfere with the development of the state. The California boundary controversy, the movement for state division, and the contest between the warring factions of the Democratic party became linked emotionally to the slavery question, although each emerged from a setting unrelated to the problem. From the constitutional convention in 1849 to California's ratification of the Thirteenth Amendment in 1865, the slavery question agitated the citizens. The "barbarities inflicted upon" Indians by their "inhuman masters," the San Francisco *California Police Gazette* moralized in an exposé of Indian slavery in California after the Civil War, "would put to blush the most unfeeling wretch that ever lorded over a gang on a Southern plantation." [28]

The rich soil of California attracted speculators in search of land grants, to develop slave colonies for the cultivation of rice, cotton, and sugar. Even after California had been admitted into the Union as a free state, the mirage lost nothing of its attractiveness. We will reach California overland "with both Negroes & animals," James Gadsden in Charleston informed his confidant Thomas J. Green in San Francisco on December 7, 1851, "if you only make the grants." Senator Green, a member of the first California legislature, in 1849 had moved from Texas to the West Coast, with his slaves, and engaged in mining.[29] Another member of the legislature, a native of Virginia, suggested to an Eastern correspondent that the gold mines could be worked more profitably by slaves than in any other way; the legislature would probably pass a measure admitting them.[30] In February 1852, twelve hundred and eighteen citizens of South Carolina and Florida petitioned the California Legislature for permission to "colonize a rural district with a population of not less than two thousand slaves." [31]

The influx of "servants" whose masters aimed to retain their control stimulated a more open advocacy of concessions to slavery. Newspapers chronicled the constant arrival of Negroes. These reports increased the irritation of Californians who intended to uphold the legal restrictions against slavery. In the spring of 1852 the San Francisco *Herald* quoted a report from the Charleston *Courier* that one steamer, on her last two trips to California, had carried seventy-four slaves belonging to passengers bound for the mines.[32] The phantom of the Slave Power, conspiring to debase California to the level of a slave state, came to haunt Californians. Even the missionaries of the Methodist Episcopal Church, South, appeared to threaten the free state. In April 1852, an attempt was made to place a spy in the secret councils of the Pacific Annual Conference of the Church to gain information about the alleged Southern conspiracy.[33] Arrests and trials of fugitive slaves lent poignancy to the continuing debate over slavery. In the *cause célèbre* of 1858 which occupied the state for several months, the United States Commissioner in San Francisco finally terminated the last fugitive slave case in California when he gave Archy Lee his freedom.[34]

In *Ex parte* Archy the California Supreme Court had invalidated a convincing legal argument through a diametrically opposed decision.[35] The Court, it appeared to some editors, gave the "law to the North and the nigger to the South." The decision was a "disgrace to the judges," which "would bring odium upon the State," and "render the Supreme Bench of California a laughing stock in the eyes of the world." [36] The legal farce symbolized the vanishing California dream. Repeated encounters with obstacles had shattered the vision and had relegated California to the troubled ranks of ordinary states. Rapidly growing communities provided a mounting degree of security; but settled conditions also brought a share in the disputes of the Union. In the campaign of 1859 David C. Broderick and William M. Gwin climaxed their bitter personal feud with debates about the larger questions which agitated the electorate of the United States.[37]

The growing participation in the affairs of the Union long antedated the completion of the Transcontinental Railroad in 1869 which represented California's true admission into the sisterhood of states. But the flow of Eastern culture to the West had already completed a portion of the process. While Californians looked ahead to the bright future of their commonwealth, they looked back to the East as source of law, learning, literature, manners, and morality. From these roots emerged the concepts of Manifest Destiny which inspired and sustained the faith in an American California. On the Pacific Coast, the spectacular growth of art and literature in the form of theaters and newspapers sustained some hopes about the future role of California. In diametrically opposed endeavors, in fashionable as well as religious pursuits, Californians strove to excel the other states. American culture provided a vehicle for the realization of the Californians' dream, but its commonly accepted tenets undermined their exclusive vision.

Adventurers and soldiers facilitated the flow of American culture to California. On September 5, 1846, the chaplain of Governor's Island, in the harbor of New York, made his appearance in the midst of Colonel Jonathan D. Stevenson's California Volunteers. The regiment was drawn up in a hollow formation while a chain of sentinels kept spectators at a respectful distance. Sergeant Felix Wierzbicki's name was called. When the Polish exile who had found his way to

America twelve years earlier stepped up, the chaplain presented him with a Bible. "In behalf of the American Bible Society," he instructed the author of the first, original book written in English to be published in California, "go to California not only with a sword, but with the olive branch of peace." [38]

The candle and salt boxes of pioneers soon replaced the knapsack of the volunteers. Mrs. Louise Clappe described the little library which she and her physician-husband kept at Indian Bar in 1851. The collection contained a Bible and a Prayer Book, Shakespeare, Spenser, Coleridge, Shelley, Keats, Lowell's *Fable for Critics*, Walton's *Complete Angler*, and some Spanish books. "Spiritual instead of material lights," Dame Shirley emphasized.[39] A great number of educated men gave up professions in the East and came West to the California frontier. Sea lane and land routes brought a heterogeneous population which provided a better setting for the development of culture than existed on the agricultural frontier. Lawyers and doctors, teachers and preachers, professors and business men, attracted by the irresistible metal, flocked into the diggings and worked the mines. The wisest among them discovered soon that it was easier to turn to vocations more in line with their talent and training.

Easterners, as soon as they became Westerners, joined in building not only the new Tyre but also the new Athens of the Pacific. The exalted concepts of Californians demanded that they have their theater and their Shakespeare. During the first decade Californians had an opportunity to see twenty-two of Shakespeare's plays, an accomplishment which challenged the hegemony of Boston, Philadelphia, and New York.[40] The acquisition of wealth and the achievement of law and order absorbed the ambition of these men who consumed three times as much tea, and almost as much sugar and coffee, as people in the East. For every bottle of champagne drunk by Bostonians, they emptied seven.[41] Leading citizens boasted that New York dressed better than Paris, and San Francisco better than New York. Mrs. Eliza Farnham carried her fight for more sensible female fashion to California where the stylish garb and all it symbolized were incongruous with the spirit of the time and the locale. The lady, however, adapted herself to the California frontier by donning the Bloomers that were just achieving notoriety.[42]

Protestant preachers answered readily the challenge which California represented. They came in amazing numbers. Even before the gold rush, Methodists from the Oregon mission had looked upon California as a promising field. The prejudices of the American newcomers thwarted the influence of the Catholic missions. The earliest systematic attack against sin waged by the Protestants of San Francisco came as a communal enterprise. Methodists, Baptists, Congregationalists, Presbyterians, Episcopalians, and Mormons joined in the campaign at the end of 1849.

In the field of religion Californians took early a broad view of their responsibilities. On New Year's Eve, 1849, the San Francisco group held a prayer meeting for the conversion of the world. By the beginning of the 1850's, the Methodists, Baptists, Presbyterians, Episcopalians, and Congregationalists all had organized churches. Many of the missionary preachers combined teaching with their spiritual vocation. Since the state was slow to provide adequately for schools, higher education came to be regarded as a special field for the work of religious groups.[43]

The rapid influx of people, the extraordinary number of educated persons among the newcomers, and the wealth released by the gold mines accelerated the development of American culture on the California frontier. By the time the *Alta*, one of the first thriving newspapers in the West, celebrated its fifth birthday, San Francisco counted twelve other dailies and several times that number of weeklies. Nearly every small town in the state also had a local journal. The papers varied widely in quality, but they provided reading matter and enlightenment for thousands. During political campaigns, editors and readers filled the columns with their opinions. The diverging views showed the aspects of American culture thoroughly entrenched on the California scene.

These developments brought not only esteem in the eyes of the world but also new obligations toward it. One of these responsibilities, expressed in the concept of America as asylum for suffering humanity, found its way to the Pacific Coast. The welcome which Americans extended to all newcomers was an element in the growth of American culture in California, but it also placed a heavy burden on those who realized that adherence to the humanitarian principle continuously narrowed the depth of their dream.

The roots of the concept went back far into America's past. The colonists permitted every type of future settlers to build homes in the New World, regardless of heredity or origin. Men were free to come to the United States without any distinctions as to national characteristics or place of birth. The benefits of the immigrants to the country, the general assumption about the nature of nationality, and the course of history supported this attitude. Regardless of their origins, Americans were a people because they lived under free institutions. Any person who came to settle under the influence of these free institutions would be Americanized. Willingness and capacity to live as citizens of the Republic were the desirable qualities of immigrants.[44]

In February 1848, the American brig *Eagle* from Hong Kong landed two Chinese men and one woman in San Francisco. These newcomers were another threat to the realization of the California vision like the Indians, Mexicans, Europeans, and Negroes. They were also another group of downtrodden humanity destined to find succor on American soil. The chaos of the Pearl River Delta and the sojourners' attempt through emigration to maintain the extended fam-

sans, and laborers filled Chinese settlements in the South Seas.

The types of emigrants — indentured, contract laborers, and coolies — varied with locale and period. Indentured emigrants relied on the credit-ticket system under which they obtained their passage from Chinese merchants who were reimbursed by relatives of the travelers or by their future employers. In return, the newcomers worked for whoever extended the credit until the debt was paid. In other cases the merchant-creditors utilized the working power of the migrants in any way that guaranteed a profitable return for their investment. The system camouflaged a debt bondage that turned indentured emigrants into slaves of their countrymen who ruled through influences unfamiliar to outside observers.

Foreign importers and Chinese middlemen played the principal role in the contract system hiring laborers to fill the specific demand for workers in Malaysia and in America. The service contract differentiated the arrangement from the debt bondage of the credit-ticket.

The coolie traffic to the West Indies, Latin America, and the Indian Archipelago produced the extreme form of the contract system at the middle of the nineteenth century.[2] Force alone sustained this trade. Kidnaped or decoyed into barracoons, the coolies were sold into service. The term coolie which originally designated any hired laborer, porter, or carrier came to describe one pressed into service by coercion. Indentured emigrants and contract laborers faced similar hardships but they fell into their creditors' or contractors' clutches at their own volition. They were but one step removed from the despotism of the coolie trade. The nefarious traffic stimulated compassion for its victims and an increasing urge for control by Western powers. The oppressive nature of the contract labor system and the subtle tyranny of the credit-ticket system escaped observers whose awareness was already blunted by the coolie trade's cruelty. The variations among the three types were less important than the basic enslaved nature of the indentured emigrants, contract laborers, and coolies alike.

Indentured emigrants and contract laborers were the backbone of the movement into the Malay Archipelago. Chinese merchants in the ports of Southeast Asia transported shiploads of their poorer countrymen to the plantations, mines, and godowns of Malaya, Java, Borneo, and the Philippines where the emigrants bound themselves into servitude until they had repaid their passage money and the accrued interest. Then they were free to accumulate the modest fortune, the vision of which had lured them across the sea. Only the completion of this task assured the successful workers a return to their native villages as respected men. The steady demand for laborers in Southeast Asia perpetuated the system, which English, Dutch, and Spanish officials tolerated for its immediate value to colonial development.

This mode of emigration did not receive detailed attention. Confucian scholars "would have scorned to chronicle the adventures of . . . coolies or fisher-folk amongst the . . . barbarians of the West." [3] The mandarins were indifferent to unfilial emigrants who themselves were illiterate or poorly educated and left few records.[4] In the 1780's when poverty drove a scholar of literary refinement into their ranks for a dozen years, he felt called upon to comment on almost everything but his fellows in his account of the Malay Archipelago.[5] Yet contemporary travelogues, histories, and magazine articles furnish glimpses of Foochow, Amoy, Penang, Malacca, Singapore, and Sambas in the early decades of the nineteenth century and show the system in operation.[6]

On his second voyage along the coast of China, in March 1832, Charles Gutzlaff noticed the junks which regularly carried indentured emigrants into the Nan Yang. The vessels reminded him of African slavers. Emigrants crowded the decks, at the mercy of the elements, for cargo filled the junk below and there was no place of shelter for them. Subsisting on dried rice and an allowance of water, many starved during long passages.[7] Regular trading junks carried the bulk of emigrants, but now and then special transports also made their appearance.[8] A single vessel was known to convey twelve hundred passengers to Bangkok in the first decades of the nineteenth century when seven thousand Chinese arrived annually at the Siamese port.[9]

Chinese traders on the scene handled the migration to the Malay Peninsula. In April or May, merchants at Penang and Malacca chartered vessels and traveled with them as supercargoes to Macao or Amoy. Into the countryside, they sent agents who cajoled peasants and artisans into accepting a bounty by promises of an easy fortune and a speedy return. The unwary victims were huddled aboard while the agents received one Spanish dollar per head. The emigrants arrived at the Straits in January, February, or March.

There, resident Chinese bought the newcomers who, after the Amoy dialect pronunciation of *hsin-k'e* (new guest), were called Singhés, Singkehs, Sinkehs, or Sinkays. A master workman, a tailor, goldsmith, or carpenter, brought ten or fifteen Spanish dollars for the charterer, a laborer six to ten, and a sickly man three or fewer Spanish dollars. The cost of transportation which the employer had to pay differed with the number of passengers and the number of Singhés for which a planter, trader, or mine owner contracted. The Singhés served for a fixed period, receiving food, clothing, and a few dollars as compensation. Two to three thousand landed every year at Penang and spread into Wellesley and the Siamese and Malay territories; three thousand arrived annually at Malacca.[10]

Siah U Chin, a Chinese merchant who had come to Singapore from Swatow in 1825, observed the laborers who arrived at the port from South China after a voyage of thirty or forty days. They intended to return to their homeland after three or four years. Only one of ten, however, managed to go back to their native villages with a small fortune. Some did so after five or six years, others after eight or ten. A great number worked at Singapore up to twenty years, only to die in the Straits.

In the 1840's, Siah U Chin estimated, ten thousand laborers arrived annually at the port. A compilation by the editor of the Singapore *Free Press* for the first months of 1848 listed 10,475 men who came from South China in one hundred and eight junks and eleven square rigged vessels.[11] G. F. Davidson, who viewed the scene in the 1820's and 1830's, recorded that junks transported annually from six to eight thousand emigrants, "ninety-nine hundredths of whom land without a sixpence . . . beyond the clothes they stand in," the majority having embarked without funds to pay their way.[12] These "defaulters remain in the vessel," George Windsor Earl noted, "until they are redeemed by their friends . . . or by strangers engaging their services for a stipulated period, and paying their passage money as an advance of wages." [13]

On Borneo thirty thousand Chinese operated the gold mines of the Sambas district, at the beginning of the nineteenth century. Each work camp employed at least three hundred and fifty laborers. The proprietors rented the mines from native rajas and paid a capitation tax of three dollars on every miner. About three hundred Chinese returned annually to their homeland on trading junks which called at Pontianak.[14] Eleven junks sailed every year from China and transported new emigrants to the island.[15] J. H. Moor, who at various times edited the Malacca *Observer*, the Singapore *Chronicle*, and the *Free Press*, noted that each year about three thousand Chinese emigrants arrived at the west coast of Borneo, between the Sambas and the Pontianak rivers, in the first three decades of the nineteenth century.[16]

Missionaries of the American Board of Commissioners for Foreign Missions depicted the junk traffic and the social organization that linked the Chinese settlements. A "democratic anarchy" controlled the "great mass" of "rude adventurers." As their head they recognized the "great Chief of Montrado," the so-called Chinese Governor of Montrado. American missionaries were not permitted to locate in Chinese villages, on territory nominally under Dutch rule, without the formal sanction of the Chinese headmen.[17] If the Chinese had not been constantly returning to their homeland, Malaysia would very soon have become a second Chinese empire, one chronicler of the Malay Archipelago concluded from his survey of the settlements on Borneo.[18]

The movement of indentured emigrants to Southeast Asia was the model for that to the Golden Gate. The adaptation of the system to California, however, required some modifications. The changes resulted in part from the dictates of geography, in part from American conditions, in part from the objections of Californians to any form of bondage or slavery. In March 1852, the *Alta* described the movement of Chinese indentured emigrants into the Malay Archipelago as the prototype for the traffic of Cantonese to California. The newcomers at San Francisco, the paper explained, "had either contracted with wealthy Chinese at home to labor at the mines . . . , or had agreed on certain rates per month with the foreigners who brought them." But the ease with which "all contracts could be set aside, the temptation of the mines, and the impossibility of coercion, caused . . . these contracts to be broken with severe loss to the holders." [19]

The bulk of the Chinese migration to California depended on the credit-ticket system. Chinese brokers, merchants at San Francisco or at Hong Kong, paid the expenses of the travelers who remained under their control until the debts were paid. To facilitate the repayment the Chinese merchants in California employed the laborers in their own enterprises or sold the lien on the emigrants' services to other employers. For transport, Western sailing vessels took the place of junks, while the kinship system supplied an extra-legal control in a country where courts and customs failed to support any form of contract labor. During their sojourn the majority of the emigrants never left the narrow confines of the Chinese world which demanded their allegiance from the moment they turned their back on their native villages.

In 1877, a congressional committee's report furnished evidence about the operations of the system in the 1860's and 1870's. The testimony and the report may have been partisan in interpretation. But neither the defenders nor the foes of indentured emigrants questioned the existence of the pattern. Several witnesses, favorable to it, emphasized that the credit-ticket system was not based on service-contracts but on debt bondage. They never discerned the oppressive features hidden behind this technicality which assured the toleration of this form of servitude in the United States. Even Frederick A. Bee, the attorney of the Chinese companies at San Francisco, stated that the repayment of the debt was the obligation under which the Chinese in California labored. Other witnesses dwelt on the very limited number of women among the indentured emigrants. Only a few noticed in passing possible parallels between the Chinese pattern and the indentured servants of America's colonial past.[20]

The preoccupation of committee members and witnesses with the coolie question obscured those portions of the testimony which threw light on the nature of debt bondage. Statements about indentured emigrants were unwittingly mingled with tirades against coolie labor and indignation over the latter blocked an evaluation of the machinations of the credit-ticket system and an understanding of the indentured emigrants' plight. Since the Chinese newcomers to California were no chain-carrying coolies but technically free, most observers failed to perceive the invisible web of controls that oppressed them. The distinctions between indentured emigrants, contract laborers, and coolies sustained humanitarians in their spirited defense of the Chinese against the frequent charge of being coolies, much to the detriment of an understanding of the oppressive nature of the credit-ticket system which was the dominant mode of transporting emigrants between Hong Kong and San Francisco.[21]

The pattern suggested itself readily as model for the emigration from the Pearl River Delta to the Golden Mountain, Chin Shan or California, and was again utilized in the rushes to the New Golden Mountain, Hsin Chin Shan or Australia. On November 4, 1848, a correspondent of the *Californian* argued the advantages of Chinese indentured emigrants for the development of California. Eighteen months after the first Chinese had reached San Francisco, auction and commission merchants advertised the sérvices of two Chinese blacksmiths, "engaged for the term of three years." The "contracting party, not requiring their services at present," offered to transfer the agreement with the Chinese who were "bound to make themselves generally useful." [22] Toward the end of 1848 and in the spring and summer of 1849 William Redmond Ryan observed "numerous Chinese, . . . consigned, with houses and merchandise, to certain Americans in San Francisco, to whom they were bound by contract as laborers." [23] The price of a Chinese frame house, including the labor of Cantonese carpenters, in 1850, amounted to fifteen hundred dollars.[24] In March 1851, six Chinese workers, "who were under contract, in consideration of a free passage," ran away to the mines. The contractor failed to obtain a warrant for their arrest. Since the "offence was not cognizable by a criminal tribunal," the Court recommended he "obtain his remedy in a civil suit." [25]

A large portion of the Chinese in California, an editorial writer of the *Alta* observed in 1855, were contract laborers. Wealthy merchants pay for their transportation and take them "into the mines and derive the entire profit of their labor." These workers are "in fact little better than slaves, and their own countrymen are their masters." They "have laws of their own," and their masters customarily "enforce their contracts not only without, but in defiance of our State laws." On May 14, 1859, a reporter of the Stockton *Argus* described the arrival of the *J. Bragdon* at Stockton with Chinese miners for the Mariposa country. The laborers, "bundled on board the boat like so many cattle," were "under contract." Their countrymen, engaged in mining operations, had traveled in the cabin and "brought them from China for the purpose of speculating in their labor." One year later the Stockton *Republican* lamented that Chinese agents there forwarded "load after load" of indentured emigrants "in the [same] manner as other freight." [26]

Western sailing vessels linked California with Kwangtung after the discovery of gold attracted the shipping fleets of the world to the Golden Gate. San Francisco was outside the trade winds which facilitated the regular movements of junks in the Malay Archipelago and few Chinese craft ever reached the West Coast.[27] One of them once visited the Atlantic Coast, although it took a British sea captain to bring it there. In 1847 Captain Kellett sailed the *Ke Ying* (Ch'i-ying) from Canton, by way of the Cape of Good Hope, in two hundred and twelve days to New York. That fall and winter the "great wonder" attracted curious crowds at New York, Newport, Providence, and Boston. In February, 1848, the junk left Boston and reached London at the end of March 1848, to be shown to Queen Victoria.[28]

The American brig *Eagle* completed the first direct run between the Pearl River Delta and the Golden Gate on February 2, 1848. Captain Lovett sailed the vessel in forty-six days from Canton via Macao and Hong Kong to San Francisco. Damage in a storm off Japan made the swift passage more remarkable in a decade when voyages of fifty-five to sixty-five days were good for the course.[29] In the following year Captain Fisher A. Newell accomplished the round trip with the *Honolulu* in four months and sixteen days. In April 1850, the American schooner *Anonyma* bettered the *Eagle's* record by one day. Two years later, the voyages of American clippers set new standards. The *Game Cock* covered the distance between San Francisco and Hong Kong in thirty-four days; the *Flying Cloud* and the *Witchcraft* took a few days longer. The *Witchcraft* managed the return trip in forty-four days.[30] The crown for the quickest voyage the *Alta* awarded to the *Challenge*. The paper erroneously recorded thirty-three days for the run, but the clipper left Hong Kong on March 19, 1852, stood off the coast of Japan on April 5, and arrived at San Francisco on April 22.[31] The reporter's mistake had no import for the record since one year later the clipper bark *Mermaid* reduced the time to thirty days.[32]

For more than a decade the marks of the *Game Cock* and the *Mermaid* remained unchallenged. The clipper race added regularity to the route between Hong Kong and San Francisco, while the monsoon winds governed the junk traffic in the South China Sea. In 1855 forty-five days were regarded a normal voyage for a clipper-built vessel, but the average passage amounted to sixty-two days.[33] Fifty-four days formed the average for 1859.[34] In January, 1867, at the inauguration of the direct steam communication between America and China, the first steamer, the P.M.S.S. *Colorado*, covered the distance between San Francisco and Hong Kong in thirty-one days.[35]

The transportation of Chinese emigrants relieved the depression in one sector of an overexpanded trading community when the California boom of the early 1850's vanished. The traffic afforded employment for shipping at moments of great demand for freight. The transportation of Cantonese passengers solved the cargo problems of many masters and furnished new opportunities for British shipping, which had felt the influx of American clippers into the tea trade. The circulars of the house of King & Co. at Canton and the firm of Rawle, Drinker & Co. at Hong Kong readily documented the possibilities of the traffic with detailed lists of the ships carrying Chinese passengers.[36] Chinese merchants, furnishing emigrants and cargo, contributed to the eventual employment of four hundred thousand tons of American shipping in the China trade.[37]

Chinese merchants, recently established in San Francisco and without lines of communication to Hong Kong equal to those of the traditional junk routes in Southeast Asia, came to rely on Western sailing vessels to transport their countrymen. The clippers, after being hastily unloaded at San Francisco, were dispatched to China, where they "either competed successfully with English ships for return cargoes to the Atlantic, or were profitably employed" in carrying Chinese emigrants to California.[38] As charterers or owners of an illassorted fleet, Chinese traders, with the aid of such San Francisco commission merchants as Cornelius Koopmanschap, controlled the flow of emigrants to California as effectively as to Malaysia.[39] In the first six months of 1852 the "new field of enterprise" gave "profitable employment to 82 vessels with . . . 42,724 tons." [40] Although there existed no relationship between the amount of tonnage employed and the number of emigrants carried to California, the great emigration of 1852 attracted an unusually large fleet. During the twelve months of 1857, only twenty-two ships with a total of 23,593 tons reached California from China.[41]

Here and there, the names of Chinese shipowners or charterers appeared in the columns of the San Francisco newspapers. When the *Hamilton* arrived at San Francisco from Hong Kong on June 1, 1853, the marine reporter of the *Alta* thought that the ship was the "first vessel owned by a Chinaman which has ever entered this port under their flag." Ton Key was the owner, Captain Keller the master of the craft.

The "embarking of the Chinese in their shipping trade between their country and ours is certainly an interesting and curious event," the editor reflected, "and in time will lead to important results." In October 1853, A Choo chartered the clipper ship *Gazelle* for eight thousand dollars; Captain Dolland and his American crew returned three hundred and fifty Chinese to Hong Kong on the merchant's account.[42]

About one month earlier, in September 1853, Mou Kee acquired the *Potomac*, a ship of 450 tons, for about five thousand dollars. The new owner spent ten thousand dollars on repairs and alterations and transferred "an old hulk into a good ship." At Hong Kong the *Potomac* was subsequently sold for fifteen thousand dollars. In the meantime an extra deck had been added to the vessel. On a single voyage the Chinese owners transported more than five hundred emigrants to San Francisco who represented the equivalent of thirty-seven thousand dollars in passage fees. From 1853 on, besides the *Potomac* and the *Hamilton*, several large vessels carried emigrants for Chinese owners. In October 1855, one of the Chinese companies at San Francisco chartered the French ship *St. Germain* to convey a considerable number of laborers back to Hong Kong.[43]

High freight rates between Hong Kong and San Francisco made the passenger traffic lucrative.[44] Frequently ships would not wait for additional cargo, but took passengers aboard and sailed in ballast. Contemporary observers at times speculated about the financial gain of shipowners or charterers. But only Western shipowners profited immediately from the transportation of emigrants through the money which Chinese charterers paid for the vessels. To Chinese merchants, as shipowners or charterers, the passage represented a considerable investment since they speculated not on the shipping venture but on the labor potential of their countrymen in California.[45]

The fare, at the lowest estimate, amounted to forty dollars for transportation to San Francisco and twenty dollars for the return trip. The "present rate . . . for a Chinese is fifty dollars," Peter Parker informed Secretary of State Daniel Webster in March 1852. "One vessel, which recently cleared for San Francisco, received $18,000, . . . another . . . $19,000 for passage money," the acting United States Commissioner in China reported.[46] Two California newspapers considered fifty dollars the average.[47] On August 1, 1852, the editorial writer of the *Herald* argued that the passage fee of twenty-eight thousand Chinese travelers amounted to $1,120,000 within the first six months of the year. At the beginning of 1856 William Speer, the missionary of the Presbyterian Board of Foreign Missions to the Chinese in California, calculated that all Chinese in California had paid a total of $2,329,580 for the trip.[48] During the year 1852 alone, thirty thousand Chinese who embarked at Hong Kong for San Francisco paid $1,500,000 for the voyage, Ernest John Eitel estimated.[49]

The easy profits attracted a multitude of vessels; however, the size, type, and nationality of these ships varied. Slowly, American craft overcame the numerical superiority which British bottoms enjoyed in the early years.[50] The fleet included extreme clipper ships, such as the *Bald Eagle*, 1703 tons, built by Donald McKay at East Boston in 1852, and such nondescript barks, as the *John Mayo*, of 297 tons.[51] Its mixed composition reflected the rapid changes in the shipping business which the period brought about. In the 1840's a sailing ship of five hundred tons burden was still a respectable craft. A decade later, nearly half the vessels at Hong Kong registered over a thousand tons,[52] their owners representing most nations trading with China. The New York firm of Olyphant and Sons, and other great names in the China trade, contributed to it as did outsiders from Hanseatic towns who, on a trading venture around the world, no longer waited for cargoes in the Orient but carried Chinese emigrants on the return trip to America.[53]

Tradition selected the second of February 1848, as the date for the coming of the first Chinese to San Francisco. On that Wednesday Charles V. Gillespie reached San Francisco from Hong Kong in the American brig, *Eagle*. He brought with him three Chinese — two men and one woman. These, he stated in his manuscript memoir, were the first Chinese in California — with the exception of some drifters who had strayed earlier to the West Coast as servants, stewards, or cooks of vessels and had left no trace.[54] Russell H. Conwell's suggestion that the earliest Chinese in California were fugitives from Peruvian masters who found employment as sailors on two ships that put in at Callao for repairs, *"en route* from New York to San Francisco in 1848 or 1849," could not have been true; the first Chinese laborers did not reach Peru before October 1849.[55]

The traditional date lacks the support of convincing evidence. The arbitrary choice, however, illustrates the uncertainty which surrounds the coming of the early Chinese. The two San Francisco papers registered the *Eagle* in their marine journals, but differed on the arrival date. They excerpted the brig's log, listed Charles V. Gillespie, his wife, and Edward Cunningham as passengers, but failed to mention the Chinese newcomers. At the time there were no Chinese at San Francisco; they were still a curiosity. Rice, sold at the beginning of the year, was imported from the Carolinas and the Philippines. While about one hundred Indians, Kanakas, and Negroes among the six hundred inhabitants of the town received the editors' attention, the three Chinese evidently did not arouse their interest. Three months after the event the excitement engendered by the discovery of gold finally upset the tranquillity of the scene.[56]

In the meantime the *Star,* in an editorial about the "Prospects of California," commented once more on the "recent arrival from Canton" which showed the "practicability of voyages" between California and China "in forty-five days," without mentioning any Chinese passengers.[57] A private letter describing the bay and town of San Francisco, published in the *Star* on April 1, 1848, referred to the passage of "only 46 days" from Canton, but ignored the Chinese passengers. In the same issue, however, the editor mentioned a reliable source that suggested a large emigration from China to America, and registered for the first time the presence of "two or three 'Celestials' " in San Francisco, "who have found ready employment." This statement strengthened the *Eagle*'s case. No other vessel reached San Francisco directly from China between February and April 1848.

A steady trickle of Chinese merchants prepared the way for the arrival of larger groups of laborers. In the first three months of 1849 vessels from China never carried more than ten passengers. From April until the end of June the total number of Chinese increased to thirty-four men and two women. In July the harbor master counted nine Chinese newcomers. In the following month this figure grew almost seven times; sixty-two Chinese landed at San Francisco in August. The first vessel to carry more than one hundred passengers arrived on October 15, when the British ship *Amazon* disembarked one hundred and one Chinese. One month later, on November 19, three hundred men gathered at the Canton Restaurant for the first public meeting of Chinese residents.[58]

By the end of 1850 the reports of Chinese who returned to their homeland, had "created quite an excitement" at Hong Kong. One hundred and fifty Chinese, having "caught the gold fever," crowded the Swedish bark *Antelope*. The circular of the firm of King & Co. at Canton alluded to the development and described the excitement in the capital of Kwangtung province, and the unexpected employment for shipping "at a moment of great depression in freight." At the beginning of 1852 the handsome clipper ship *Wild Pigeon*, for the first time, carried a greater number of Chinese back to the Pearl River Delta. Some thirty or forty, in the *Flying Cloud*, had started the return movement in December 1851. Sixty-five men and one woman left in the first three months of 1852. Most of "these singular men" had come to San Francisco "a year or two ago, with a few packages of tea or rice, and by their industry, frugality, and strict attention to business, have all made money, and some of them amassed fortunes." On their arrival "in the Celestial Empire," the editor predicted, "they will doubtless give a very favorable account of the golden land, and many more of their countrymen will come here to try their fortunes." On March 26, 1852, on a single day, six hundred and four Chinese landed at San Francisco; the British ship *Land O'Lakes* disembarked 289 passengers, the British bark *Henbury* 236, and the Prussian bark *Fred Boehm* 179 newcomers. Four months later a single vessel, the *Baron Renfrew*, transported the same number of Chinese travelers to California.[59]

Isolated news items, merchant circulars, and Chinese notes furnish a composite picture of the passage.[60] With some exceptions, Hong Kong served as point of departure. Twenty-two out of twenty-nine ships which carried Chinese to San Francisco between February 19 and June 6, 1852 sailed from there. Two came from Whampoa, two from Macao, two from Shanghai, and one from Mazatlan. During the year 1856 only one of the thirty-two vessels which reached San Francisco came directly from Shanghai; all others departed from Hong Kong. In 1859 twenty-eight of the twenty-nine ships which called at San Francisco left from Hong Kong; one sailed from Macao.[61] The chaotic state of the Pearl River Delta, foreign wars, internal unrest and rebellion, drove Western shipping into the British colony. Hong Kong also freed sea captains and Chinese emigrants from the clutches of avaricious officials at Whampoa or the barracoons of coolie traders at Macao. Proclaimed a free port in 1841, Hong Kong required no duties, not even bills of health since, according to the bon mot of United States Consul James Keenan, no new diseases could be imported.[62]

The laws of the Ch'ing Dynasty explicitly prohibited emigration from China.[63] All nations beyond the confines of the Middle Kingdom were barbarian. The experience of the Manchu with Koxinga (Cheng Ch'eng-kung) had strengthened the feeling at Peking that emigrants from the disaffected South would almost certainly be anti-Ch'ing and plotting the overthrow of the dynasty. The law, although impossible to enforce, discouraged emigration and provided officials with an opportunity to exact payments from departing and returning emigrants and their families in China.

In theory the Manchu law held until 1860, but it was not actually repealed until 1894.[64] In the Conventions of Peking, in 1860, the Chinese government recognized the people's right to emigrate. About a decade later, the Burlingame Treaty first incorporated the principle in international law. Long before the official acknowledgment, the results of the Arrow War had turned the dynastic law into a dead letter. After the capture of Imperial Commissioner Yeh Ming-ch'en, Governor-General of Liang-Kuang, an allied commission administered the city of Canton for almost four years, from January 1858, to October 1861.[65] In 1859, with the aid of Harry Parkes, British Consul at Canton, the colonial government of British Guiana, anxious to encourage the migration of laborers from China, obtained the official recognition of the Chinese authorities in Kwangtung to the right of the people of that province to emigrate.[66]

The emigrants to California traveled in junks, lorchas, or sampans over the waterways of the Pearl River Delta from their native villages to Hong Kong.[67] Letters from Chinese in California circulating through the hamlets of the Delta, reports of returned emigrants reminiscing on their success in the Gold Hills, broadsides and open letters for and against emigration, and the rumors about the distant riches emanating from the shipping centers of South China filled the imagination of the travelers.[68] In company with other emigrants they cast off before daybreak to ensure the probability of a safe voyage. In this way they avoided an encounter with other villagers and the possibility of hearing unlucky words which might endanger their enterprise. A roll of bedding and a bamboo basket with netting on the top, containing shoes, hat, and provisions, were their worldly possessions. At Hong Kong passage brokers provided a bunk in a dormitory, or friends and relatives furnished a domicile until the day of departure.[69]

While the credit-ticket system was the dominant mode of traveling from Hong Kong to San Francisco, the passage was made at times under arrangements similar to the thinly veiled slave trade of the coolie system. The credit-ticket system, by which the passage money was advanced to laborers in Chinese ports and repaid out of their earnings in California, became partly a disguised slave trade, managed chiefly by Chinese crimps and compradores who lured artisans, peasants, and laborers into barracoons and sold them to ticket agents. At the Chinese ports and at San Francisco they were kept in confinement, watched, and terrorized by the agents of Chinese societies who acted in the creditors' interest. On a single day in 1854, within twenty-four hours, eight hundred and forty laborers, consigned to the Chinese companies of San Francisco, arrived at the Golden Gate.[70]

The travelers, waiting for the day of departure, were induced to gamble and lost money. Additional costs were added to the passage money. Skippers frequently charged the emigrants for fitting up bunks or water tanks in the steerage. Harry Parkes, the Chinese interpreter of the Superintendent of British Trade in China, noted that the merchant-creditors paid fifty dollars for the passage and twenty dollars as additional expenses of the emigrants, on "the condition of receiving" in return "the sum of two hundred dollars." Most of the travelers accepted any arrangement that promised their transportation to the Golden Hill without realizing the extent of their future financial obligations. The prospect of returning to China with two or three hundred dollars was inducement enough for men whose total annual income at home rarely amounted to one tenth that sum; no venture for such princely gain was deemed too arduous.[71]

The agents forced the emigrants to accept employment at low wages as the creditors dictated. Ostensibly free in California, the newcomers were virtually the slaves of their countrymen operating through influences of which Americans knew little. These emigrants, a reporter of the *Alta* observed in 1860, "come to one or another Chinese house [company], the heads of which make every arrangement to send them into the country, where agents are ready to set them to work." The exact relationship "between peons and masters" was not generally understood, "but it seemed plain that the arrivals were little better than serfs." [72]

The emigrants' limited contact with the strange environment of a Western sailing vessel served as an indicator of their relationship with the barbarian world for their entire sojourn. The travelers lined up on deck for inspection. After a mate had counted noses and tickets, to see that the charterers kept within the confines of the bargain, the emigrants climbed to their quarters below. With the exception of the cooks, few came up on deck during the voyage. Several bills of lading suggest that there might not have been room for travelers on the upper deck. During the gold rush the British ship *Kelso* transported fifteen houses and four thousand planks on deck, in addition to her regular cargo below.[73] Even when ships sailed with a clear deck, the steerage was the easiest way to control large numbers of emigrants. It was one of the surest ways to avoid fights between the Chinese and the crew which from time to time marred the passage.

Length and course of the voyage varied with the season. On the average the trip lasted about two months. The *Oud Nederland* and the *Senator* made two of the longest voyages on record. In the summer of 1854 the Dutch ship transported four hundred and twenty Chinese in one hundred and eleven days from Hong Kong to San Francisco; the American ship required one hundred and fifteen days in 1856.[74] In general the vessels ran up the China coast through the Formosa Strait to the northern end of the island, to avoid the trade winds, stood east of Japan, to take advantage of westerlies in the higher latitude, and traversed the Pacific between thirty-five and forty-five degrees latitude.[75] Others did not beat up against the northeast monsoon and the heavy current to Point Breaker, the usual course out of the China Sea recommended by Matthew F. Maury, the American navigator.[76] In the spring of 1858, Captain R. Simonson, after leaving Hong Kong, kept at once southward of the Pratas Islands, and got under the coast of Luzon. The land breezes from the Philippines sent the *Daring* along with a free wind up past Cape Bojeador and the Bashi Islands. Having the northeast monsoon on the larboard beam, the clipper stood out past the southern end of Formosa and rode the Kuroshio, the Japan Current, to the north and east. The experiment carried the *Daring* in forty-five days to San Francisco.[77] "The best route of crossing the North Pacific," the Pacific Mail Steamship Company admitted in 1867, "has yet to be thoroughly determined." [78]

Between 1848 and 1867 a vast number of Chinese emigrants lived for an average of two months at the mercy of the ocean, their bosses and comrades, and the ships' crews. Before the introduction of the regular steamboat service be-

tween San Francisco and Hong Kong, a number of spectacular marine disasters tainted the run, epitomized by the
fate of the *Bald Eagle*. On October 5, 1861, the clipper left
Hong Kong for San Francisco with a cargo of rice, sugar,
and tea, cabin passengers, and Chinese emigrants. The *Bald
Eagle* was never heard from again, no traces of wreckage
were found, and it was assumed that the clipper foundered
in a typhoon in the China Sea.[79]

Calm days presented particular problems. While the ship
drifted idly on the smooth sea, and the sailors amused themselves by fishing, the emigrants gambled in their quarters or
lay in their bunks, vainly listening for the yells, creaks, and
gongs of their native junks.[80] Such tension-filled days brought
fights between sailors and travelers and quarrels among the
Chinese. In addition the quality of the provisions and the
neglect of the living quarters caused friction between the
emigrants and their countrymen who represented contractors
or charterers.

During the course of the voyages, the dark, dank depths of
the sailing vessels grew increasingly oppressive to men who
were present under compulsion and afflicted by superstition,
apprehension, and dreams of their destination. When barrel
after barrel of rotten pork had to be thrown overboard, when
rough seas prevented the travelers from using the badly constructed cooking places, arranged with an eye to maximum
economy on the crowded lower decks, when cheaply built
bunks continued to break down to the risk of heads and
limbs, the strain-charged air could explode at any moment.
While the Chinese insisted on settling these disturbances in
their own way, the sailors put down the unrest by force. In
the event of a clash with the crew, the Chinese swarmed up
from the lower decks, hurling pieces of lumber and brick-
bats from the cooking places. Forced to retreat, the emigrants usually smeared blood over the faces of their wounded
comrades and left them on the upper deck as if dead. Such

moments tested the ability of captains and officers to prevent an open battle.[81]

The average captain handled the difficult task capably. His name disappeared behind the stories of the few who bungled their job or earned the praise of their Chinese passengers. Captain Leslie Bryson's zeal for sanitation led to disaster on the American ship *Robert Bowne*. In March 1852, the New Haven master left Amoy for San Francisco with four hundred and fifty Chinese passengers. They had received advances at the rate of six dollars each and were contracted by Captain Bryson to serve for a period of five years, at three dollars per month. After eight days, having rounded the northern end of Formosa, the captain ordered the emigrants to be scrubbed with brooms and their queues to be cut off, on the plea that the passengers did not keep themselves sufficiently clean. The Chinese rebelled against the disgrace, killed captain and officers, and captured some sailors, while a part of the crew escaped in boats. The emigrants took command and ran the ship ashore on the southernmost of the Liu-ch'iu Islands east of Formosa. When most of the Orientals had disembarked, the remnants of the crew slipped the ship's cable and floated the craft back to Amoy. There were few disturbances on Chinese emigrant ships, Dr. John Bowring, Superintendent of British Trade in China, commented on the case of the *Robert Bowne*, "in which the commanders have not been blameworthy in a very high degree." [82]

The regulations of Western powers hardly affected Chinese emigration before the 1880's. The British Passenger Act of 1855 provided for the inspection of the traffic from Hong Kong in ships of any flags, but scarcely touched the movement to California. Charterers, shipowners, and captains devised ways to evade the penalties. Chinese cooks, recruited from the load of emigrants, were listed as crew members in the ships' articles, the number ranging from five to twenty-five per cent above the figure of emigrants given in the regular passenger return. Some vessels took on additional Chinese passengers at other points of the coast after they had passed inspection at Hong Kong.[83]

American legislation proved equally ineffective. The laws of 1847, 1849, and 1855 dealt with conditions on passenger vessels, but were rarely enforced in regard to the transportation of Chinese. In the summer and fall of 1854 the "fearful mortality" which had occurred on the *Libertad* and the *Exchange* momentarily directed San Francisco's attention to the traffic that threw "the most indefatigable slaver which ever sailed on the African coast completely in the shade." On board the *Libertad* one hundred out of five hundred Chinese emigrants and the captain died during the passage of eighty days from Hong Kong to San Francisco. Eighty-five of the six hundred and thirteen passengers of the *Exchange* lost their lives after the vessel cleared Macao. About an equal number of the passengers succumbed to the effects of the crowded voyage after their arrival.

A series of court trials involved these and several other vessels, as they all had reached the Golden Gate at the height of the fear about the threat which these newcomers formed to the health of San Francisco. Prolonged legal arguments concerning the meaning of a specific section of the Passenger Act of 1847 characterized the trials. The defense construed the passage to imply that besides the lower and orlop decks, the upper deck of a vessel, though not expressly allowed as such by terms of the law, might be used and counted as a passenger deck. Long before the courts reached verdicts in accordance with this view, San Francisco papers emphasized that there was little "hope of putting a stop to the pestilence-breeding crowding of the ships," since most of the craft carrying Chinese were "worthless old hulks." The owners counted upon their confiscation as a matter of course and calculated their possible loss into the expenses of the venture. On complaint of the California Commissioner of Immigration, the Police Judge of San Francisco fined one of the masters two hundred dollars for a violation of the State Law of 1853 which required the captain to report the number of passengers within twenty-four hours.

In September 1854, the United States District Court dismissed libels for forfeiture for transporting an excess of passengers from China against the *Libertad, Exchange, John Gray, Potomac, John N. Gossler, Louisa Johanna,* and *Nova Zembla.* By that time, however, the arrivals of hundreds of sick Chinese stirred San Francisco no longer. Instead the departure of one man excited the city: on October 7, 1854, Henry Meiggs escaped in the bark *America* after the discovery of his extensive forgeries.[84] Eight years later, in similar cases, instructions from Washington set aside the judgment of the San Francisco District Court for $2,800 in favor of the United States against the ship *Daphne* for bringing an excess of Chinese passengers. The suit was dismissed under a provision of the law which authorized the Secretary of the Interior to remit the penalty. The judgments against the ships *Phantom, Washington,* and *Victor* were similarly treated.[85]

Ineffective legislation went hand in hand with the lack of adequate information about the nature of the traffic. In the face of the merchant community's credo of the destiny of American commerce in China and the clamor for the undisturbed development of the trade, the San Francisco public came to view the traffic's seamier sides as symptomatic of Chinese emigration.[86] Skippers frustrated the attempts of the American consulate at Hong Kong to regulate the transportation with methods perfected in evading the British Passenger Act.[87] The confusion between the coolie traffic and the shipment of indentured emigrants to California increased the difficulties of dealing with the abuses. In 1859 an opinion of the Attorney General in Washington contended that even the coolie trade was outside the range of congressional acts against the slave trade.[88] The passage of "An Act to prohibit the 'Coolie Trade' by American citizens in American vessels" in 1862 produced little change in the movement of indentured emigrants from Kwangtung to California.[89]

As long as the characteristics of the traffic remained unaltered, it completely isolated the travelers from the world of Western shipping. Only in a few instances did the emigrants break through the invisible barriers of the Chinese world which confined them to appear more as a group of human beings than as mere figures in the registers of harbor masters or the logs of sea captains. At the end of their voyage from Whampoa to San Francisco, in June 1852, the *Balmoral*'s Chinese passengers honored Captain Robertson with a "splendid ring, made of California gold," while the masthead of the vessel flew a "magnificent silk flag" with the inscription in Chinese characters. "Presented to J. B. Robertson," it read in translation, "by 464 of his Chinese passengers who have experienced much kindness and attention from him during the voyage from Kwangtung to the Golden Hill." [90]

The Chinese aboard the American ship *Persia* also expressed their gratitude with a flag. "Gratification to our race — Presented to Captain M. M. Cook, by Leong, Assing, and others," the Chinese characters proclaimed. "Every one of us," the Cantonese travelers of the British ship *Australia* assured Captain G. Chape with the inscription on their pennant, "found a friend in you." At Hong Kong, in 1856, Captain E. Scudder of the clipper *Ellen Foster* received a "handsome Canton crepe flag" from his Chinese passengers "as a token of their appreciation of his kindness towards them." The Chinese merchants of San Francisco complimented Captain Slate who transported seven hundred Chinese emigrants without a single case of sickness or death to San Francisco in the summer of 1857. When the British ship *Achilles* anchored in the harbor, in May 1860, a large white banner of silk, about 28 by 75 feet, was flying at the mizzen. "To Henry T.

Hart," the characters translated, "from 174 Chinese, saved in September, 1859." Captain Hart had taken these passengers from the burning *Mastiff* and had carried them to Hong Kong on his outward voyage to China.[91]

When the emigrants' eager eyes finally caught the first sight of land, they strained every sense to catch the golden hues with which their imagination had painted the gateway to California. However, nothing but rocky headlands crowned with fog met their gaze. The stream of Western travelers who approached San Francisco by sea in the 1840's and 1850's sensed the "raw, cold, and disagreeable" scene.[92] To the Chinese travelers, however, the barren shore line, as far as it was visible through the mist, also resembled the bleak islands of the Pearl River's estuary and recalled an equally familiar world of unrewarding work.

Noise and confusion accompanied the disembarkation on the wharves of San Francisco. Baskets, matting, hats, and bamboo poles covered a pier crowded with boatmen, agents of Chinese merchants, draymen, custom officials, and spectators. Suddenly, as a traveler remembered, "out of the general babble some one called out in our local dialect, and, like sheep recognizing the voice only, we blindly followed and soon were piling into one of the waiting wagons." Everything appeared so "strange and exciting," he confessed, that his memory of the landing was "just a big blur." Other newcomers, with packs on their backs, walked behind the drays which carried their belongings. The Chinese quarter was the destination of groups of travelers who marched in single file through the streets, carrying their luggage suspended from the ends of bamboo poles slung across their shoulders. The first night in the strange country the newcomers slept in the dormitories of the Chinese companies under whose management they had made the long sea voyage, safely confined within the narrow limits of a world that had harbored them ever since they departed from their villages.[93]

With the credit-ticket system the social framework of the Pearl River Delta came to the United States. The basic sentiments of Californians ran counter to an extension of the Chinese concept of debt bondage to their state. However, Chinese merchants secured its continuation and the indentured emigrants' loyalty to the family reinforced the creditors' hold. A Chinese world emerged in California which was isolated from, and yet part of, the state's development.

CHAPTER IV

CHINESE CALIFORNIA

$\mathbb{S}$INCE the traditional Chinese system of indentured emigration lacked the support of American courts and customs, its adaptation to California depended upon the development of extralegal controls as substitutes. Social organizations furnished the framework which guaranteed the operation of Chinese debt bondage on American soil. Through a set of associations the merchant-creditors maintained their hold over the indentured emigrants. The Chinese quarters of American cities were symbols of that control. This visible Chinese world, however, provided only the shell for a hidden structure, kept together by the durable ties of social groups. District companies and kinship associations, transplanted to the West Coast, guaranteed the functioning of the indentured emigrant system in the United States.

District companies formed the warp of an intricate web covering Chinese California. Family associations, guilds, and secret societies strengthened the woof and sustained the invisible world. These institutions in California reflected the traditional social life of villages and towns in the Pearl River Delta. In the Middle Kingdom, the groups depended for stability upon the co-operation of their members, and not upon the Manchu government. Based on the loyalty to a native district, a family, a number of friends, a political or religious creed, they fulfilled functions which were intimately associated with the Chinese view of personal relations. Men from the same district, at work in trading centers of another province, banded together for protection and aid. Members of a clan, separated temporarily from their ancestral hall, found comfort and solace in their club house. Friends in distress joined forces to battle hardships and privations. In California, however, in addition to the traditional objectives of mutual aid and protection, these institutions contributed in various degrees to the maintenance of an invisible Chinese world which controlled the indentured emigrants.

In Malaysia merchants had used traditional Chinese institutions for similar ends. In the late eighteenth century and the early nineteenth, Chinese emigrants in Southeast Asia formed companies, or *kongsi*, under merchant leadership, along the lines of native districts or clans. The members, recruited on account of their allegiance to specific villages or prefectures in South China, assisted the needy, carried out rites, and settled disputes. In China the term *kongsi* described only an ordinary public company, as defined by the usage of the trading community. In Southeast Asia, however, the application of the term suggested a conceptual affinity to the powerful rule of the East India Company, frequently transliterated as Kong Pan Yee. With its territorial, legal, and military control, and its monopoly in trade, coinage, and diplomacy, the Honorable Company provided a striking model for Chinese merchants in their bid for control.[1]

The *kongsi* resembled guilds more than capitalistic companies, and depended for their wealth primarily on the labor of indentured emigrants, the coolie trade, opium taxes, and pawnbroking. In Malaysia they ruled their own territories with force and levied contributions. At the height of their influence, the powerful *kongsi* resembled principalities. Until the 1880's the Langfang Kongsi governed Pontianak in West Borneo.[2] In Malaya rival *kongsi* battled for more than a decade over the control of mines in the Perak district. The leader of the Yap Si Kongsi taxed tin and opium in his domain of Selangor. In addition to the *kongsi*, or as part of these companies, secret societies tightened their grip on the emigrants. These *hui* traced their origin to secret leagues in the homeland.[3]

In the mid-nineteenth century, the *kongsi* and *hui* controlled the sojourners' world in Southeast Asia. They arose out of social institutions in the Middle Kingdom, but many assumed new functions which went beyond the traditional objectives. The dividing line between outright oppression and hidden exploitation under the guise of self-help or benevolence, always remained thin. Pure benevolent associations, based on loyalties to districts or clans, differed from secret societies at times only through the restrictions on the recruitment of followers. An equal degree of secrecy frequently surrounded activities of both types of associations, although even some so-called secret societies existed overtly. Arbitrary distinctions determined the application of the terms *kongsi* and *hui*. Legitimate benevolent associations repeatedly appeared as *hui* while undisguised secret societies passed frequently as *kongsi*.

Like the numerous enclaves in Southeast Asia, a set of associations dominated Chinese California. A number of factors obscured the existence and operation of these organizations in America. They centered around the hazy American notions about Chinese society and the newcomers' deeply rooted loyalty to families and other symbols of a superior culture. Only a few American observers of the sojourners' world in California, through intimate contact with the Chinese or on account of their work in Asia, acquired clearer concepts about these organizations. They failed, however, to present a balanced picture of the associations' functions. Some onlookers extolled the benevolent aspects of these associations without mentioning the obvious oppression and exploitation, while others ignored all charitable functions and dwelt merely on abuses and tyranny. Only a composite of these divergent views makes possible a historical evaluation of the role of associations in Chinese California.[4] The indiscriminate use of terms labeling the various types of societies makes the absence of concrete information even more confusing. This account refers to associations based on allegiance to specific districts as companies, organizations requiring membership in families as clan associations, groups uniting members of a particular profession as guilds, and leagues of men drawn from various districts, families, and professions as tongs.

Behind a façade of benevolent precepts, the companies and tongs of Chinese California in the 1850's supervised or oppressed their countrymen. With the aid of district companies and clan associations, the merchant-creditors controlled the mass of indentured emigrants. Under manifold compulsions, forced into submission by their basic allegiances of district loyalty and filial piety, most sojourners readily accepted the confines and dictates of Chinese California.

Feuds accompanied the creation and the maintenance of the Chinese world in the United States. First they took the form of contests among individuals, then of struggles between individuals and companies. Later they culminated in a series of pitched battles, fought by district companies for hegemony in their spheres of influence. With their areas of control clearly established, the district companies joined in sustaining a roof organization. They co-ordinated and perfected their control over their countrymen by substituting subtle pressure for open force. The final structure of Chinese California rested on the precarious balance between the interests of merchant cliques and the goals of indentured emigrants.

Few outside forces challenged the feigned harmony of interests between oppressors and oppressed which the leading men of Chinese California strove to maintain. The concept of noninterference with the private affairs of all newcomers kept Americans away from the Chinese structure. The schemes to upset the equilibrium originated among the Chinese themselves. Men who lacked the basic allegiances forfeited their loyalty to family or native village, banded together in tongs, and feuded with the entrenched factions until they had carved out of the Chinese world their own sphere of power. Deprived of the helpful ties of social obligations which sanctioned the established rule of the district companies, the tongs controlled their domain by brute force. During these stages of the struggle, district companies and tongs emerged as instruments of social control, exploitation, and oppression.

The creation of a Chinese world in California took place without the gentry and scholar-officials who lent stability to the traditional Chinese scene. Their status within the legitimate realm of Chinese culture kept both groups out of the stream of emigration. As a result, merchants rose to leadership among the Chinese newcomers in California. The generic title of merchant embraced the occupations of traders, manufacturers, agents, contractors, proprietors, managers, and bankers. For the mass of their poorly educated countrymen, their firms functioned as clearing houses for contacts with the Chinese homeland and the American world. Unlike the China of the Manchu dynasty, where officials never served in their native districts and clan elders chafed under the rule of an alien magistrate, the Chinese merchants in California combined the prestige of mandarins, the wealth of gentry, the authority of family heads, the status of scholars, and the power of creditors in their unique position. "These self-constituted mandarins," Frank Marryat observed in 1851, exercised "so much influence over the Chinese population of the country as to subject them to fines and bastinado." The clique of the "most powerful of the Chinese merchants," he noted, "supply the Chinese emigrants, looking for their labor . . . for profit." [5]

The merchants' undisputed eminence in Chinese California formed a striking contrast to their low position in the Confucian value system. Their rise coincided with the economic development of the United States, when men with daring, keen foresight, and limited resources started and succeeded in business. Some of the early Chinese merchants sensed these liberating influences and capitalized on American notions to strengthen their newly gained position. "I am a naturalized citizen of Charleston, South Carolina," Norman Assing asserted candidly in an open letter to the Governor of California in 1852, "and a Christian too." One year earlier Norman Assing, in league with John Lipscom, had used the San Francisco Vigilance Committee to tighten his control over his countrymen. Only the interference of Selim E. Woodworth, the "Agent of the China Boys" since November 1849, saved two men and two women from being placed officially in Assing's custody. In his letter to the vigilantes' executive committee, which Woodworth signed as "Mandarin of the Celestial Empire and China Consul," the San Francisco businessman exposed Assing and Lipscom as members of a conspiracy "to deprive" their countrymen "of their liberty." [6]

Norman Assing had come to San Francisco prior to 1850. The *City Directory* of that year listed the merchant as proprietor of the Macao and Woosung Restaurant on the corner of Kearny and Commercial Streets.[7] At the first public appearance of the "China Boys," on October 28, 1850, he led one group of Chinese residents from his store on Kearny Street to Portsmouth Square. During the subsequent distribution of missionary tracts, which had been printed in Chinese on the Canton press of the American Board of Commissioners for Foreign Missions and shipped to San Francisco, Norman Assing might have been the "old celestial . . . with . . . a singularly colored fur mantle . . . and a long sort of robe," whom a reporter assumed to be "a mandarin at least." James O'Meara, who lived in San Francisco during the 1850's, remembered in 1884 "the recognized chief of the Chinese" as "a sallow, dried, cadaverous, but active and keen old fellow." He described Assing's dress as "a singular mixture" of Chinese and American garments, topped with "queue and stovepipe hat at the same time." [8]

In many public appearances at the beginning of the 1850's, Norman Assing ranked as the leader of the Chinese newcomers. Together with Ahe, Assing thanked Mayor John W. Geary on August 30, 1850, for inviting the Chinese to the ceremonies commemorating the funeral of President Zachary Taylor. "Their chief, Norman Assing, . . . commanded . . . the China Boys" on October 29, 1850, in festivities on the occasion of California's admission into the Union. During the first reported Chinese New Year celebration in the United States, on February 1, 1851, Assing "gave a grand feast at his private home in San Francisco, with a number of policemen" and "many ladies" among his guests. In the Fourth of July parade of 1852, "Norman Assing, Esq., together with Sam Wo and several other of our prominent Chinese citizens," led a "large number of mandarin [merchants] in carriages and on horseback." [9]

Reports from the Recorder's Court, notes on daily occurrences, and advertisements in newspapers attested to the shrewdness, belligerency, and ruthlessness with which Norman Assing asserted his control over early California. Only when he meted out his version of justice in the form of bastinado and imprisonment to an American offender of his autocratic code of Chinese law in January, 1853, did he learn of limits to his power. The *City Directory* of 1854, for the only time before 1879 when the first regular official's name appeared in its pages, listed among the "Foreign Consuls in San Francisco" as Chinese representative, "Norman Assing, Sacramento street, between Kearny and Dupont." The "days of Norman Assing are past," William Speer finally assured Californians in his third article on the Chinese companies in the *Oriental* in 1855, when the companies "took the law into their own hands" and inflicted "corporal punishment upon offenders in their houses." However, only Norman Assing had faded into obscurity; the system of oppression remained.[10]

Apart from merchants only one group among the Chinese newcomers perceived the liberating forces of the California scene. Its members ranked in the traditional Chinese value system even below the merchants. However, they enjoyed temporarily the favor of the San Francisco gold rush society and defied briefly the Chinese traders' timocracy. "Everybody has seen the charming Miss Atoy," a reporter of the *Alta* described the toast of the town in 1851, "who each day parades our streets dressed in the most flashing European or American style." Through the use of American courts, Atoy successfully fought off all attempts by Norman Assing and his thugs, Leidik and Chidock, to control her world. "Blooming with youth, beauty and rouge" in the Police Court, she prosecuted him and other extortionists who disturbed the order of her disorderly house through attempts to tax the Chinese women.[11]

Atoy's style of life and her wealth earned her the title of a "Chinese Aspasia." As legal counsel for other Chinese girls, she secured the immunity of her clients against the charges of Chinese merchants by exposing in court the plaintiffs' reluctance to "pay debts of honor." In August 1852, Atoy escaped the extortion rackets of A-thai, "a self-styled dictator" and "sort of High Priest" of Chinese California, who tried to tax the Chinese women on Dupont Street. "But Miss Atoy knows a thing or two," a reporter of the *Alta* assured his readers, "having lived under the folds of the Starspangled Banner for three years, and breathed their air of Republicanism, and she cannot be easily humbugged into any such measures. Besides," the journalist candidly admitted, "she lives near the Police Office and knows where to seek protection, having been before the Recorder as a defendant at least fifty times herself." The "strangely alluring" Atoy "with her slender body and laughing eyes," scored her greatest triumph when she defeated Assing's intricate schemes, avoided repatriation to China at his expense, and had the merchant bound over in the sum of two thousand dollars to keep the peace. The readiness, however, with which fifteen Chinese put their names to the bond in the court room, suggested the ultimate victory of the merchant clique over further attempts to escape from the ties of the Chinese world.[12]

The struggle for the hegemony of Chinese California lent importance to Norman Assing's and Atoy's antics. Those who viewed the panorama of early San Francisco, delighted with glimpses of an exotic scene, failed to understand their significance.[13] Norman Assing and Atoy were only two of the protagonists in the contest. The columns of San Francisco newspapers which so extensively recorded their exploits, preserved also a significant number of other Chinese names connected with merchant enterprises and wealth. The struggle created new centers of authority in the power vacuum caused by the absence of traditional Chinese sources of control and by the California notion which considered all newcomers free to shape their own destiny. The contestants for supremacy soon substituted subtler methods of coercion for the open use of the American legal system and social concepts. With the aid of Chinese interpreters and through an increasing familiarity with the newcomers, the courts had grown rapidly aware of how some Chinese manipulated American institutions for their own ends. The changing temper of California society and San Francisco's growing preoccupation with vice designated the courts' docks as the only place which Chinese prostitutes occupied during future trials.

The majority of Chinese did not participate in the struggle as protagonists. Their ready submission to the dictates of their overlords was the essence of Chinese California. The "Chinese themselves are used to this . . . despotic rule," Frank Marryat noted in May 1851.[14] "When some man came . . . and said he was a high man," and was ready to back up his threats with force, Atoy revealed, "all the Chinamen" submitted to his despotism "because they were fools, and didn't know nothing."[15] Social organizations enabled the merchant-creditors to control the newcomers without the aid or the interference of American institutions. While the undisguised struggle for the leadership of these organizations still raged, the mass of Chinese had accepted the extension of the invisible bonds of regional loyalty and familism to California. Practically, whatever limited alternatives the newcomers may have had, they sealed their fate at the beginning of their sojourn when they decided to leave their native villages only temporarily and to accumulate in California that modest fortune which guaranteed a continuation of the extended family on the Chinese scene. With parents, wives, and children as hostages within the reach of their creditors, laboring constantly under the moral compulsion to work for their return to the Pearl River Delta, the emigrants readily submitted to tradition and coercion.

The merchant-creditors controlled their investments in indentured emigrants through their powerful position in the district companies or the clan associations. In addition, their guilds linked them to other influential traders who dominated San Francisco's commerce with China. Apart from their own interest in gaining and maintaining control, the members of the merchant class represented, in the absence of mandarins and gentry, the logical choice for leadership in the district associations. Their training, contacts, and wealth elevated them to positions of dominance within their clan. All members of a clan, hailing from the same district, belonged to the same company and strengthened their elders' position in the larger organization. For the achievement of the merchant-creditors' end it was inconsequential which type of social organization came first into existence, the district company or the clan association.[16] Since the district companies developed into the most powerful social control units, the history of their growth delineates the invisible world of Chinese California.

Five district companies dominated the Chinese world in California in the mid-1850's. They emerged in San Francisco over a period of three years as a result of the feuding factions' struggle for hegemony. The contest for power disrupted the earliest Chinese organization, the Chew Yick Kung Shaw, which had embraced all newcomers regardless of the divisions separating the people of the Pearl River Delta. On November 19, 1849, a meeting of the Chinese residents of San Francisco first directed attention to the original association. At the Canton Restaurant on Jackson Street, three hundred representatives selected a committee of four, Ahe, You-Ling, Atung, and Attoon, who waited on Selim E. Woodworth and asked the businessman to act as their "arbitrator and adviser." The "Agent of the China Boys" estimated a couple of years later that at the time of the meeting seven hundred and eighty-nine Chinese men and two women lived in California.[17]

Contemporary evidence fails to reveal the name of the first Chinese organization in the United States. When Liang Ch'i-ch'ao gathered notes about his countrymen in California during his brief visit to San Francisco more than fifty years after the disintegration of the first association, he called it Chew Yick Kung Shaw, *chao-i kung-so*, Luminous Unity (Public) Office.[18] In a thesis on the basic social organization of the Chinese in America, Meng Tai Chuang reiterated in 1932 most of Liang Ch'i-ch'ao's notions and rendered the name as "signifying one or unity." [19] Ten years later, William Hoy, the official historian of the Chinese Consolidated Benevolent Association and research editor of the California Chinese Historical Society, failed to take these views into account in his summary. He labeled the first organization "Kong Chow association," a term referring to "the entire geographical region" from which the newcomers hailed.[20]

However, it is arbitrary to extend the practice of applying regional names to social units into the earliest period of Chinese life in America without contemporary evidence. Regional terms gained meaning only after the increasing arrival of sojourners disrupted the basic organization. The names of the new divisions, which followed primarily district lines, then helped to identify the factions among the Chinese in California through a reference to the district subdivisions of the prefecture. The discussion of the use of a eulogistic term or a regional name is interesting in itself, yet the application of *kung-so*, or *kung-ssu*, for the type of organization has wider significance. Possibly the first Chinese association in the United States may also have been called *kongsi*, like similar institutions among Chinese emigrants in Southeast Asia. After the formation of district companies the term Wui Kun, *hui-kuan*, the usual designation of a guild hall, prevailed. The Chew Yick Kung Shaw disappeared quickly; the first association disintegrated with the rise of the district companies.[21]

Emigrants from the districts of Nanhai, Pwanyü, and Shunte organized in 1851 the first district company, the Sam Yap Wui Kun. The name designated collectively the Three Districts which encompassed Canton. At the end of the year the formation of the Sze Yap Wui Kun forecast the tendency to extend to Chinese California the traditional divisions of the Pearl River Delta as the newcomers increased in numbers. This Four Districts Company reflected the bonds of dialect and custom which united emigrants from two different prefectures. It linked the inhabitants of the districts of Sinhwui and Sinning with the population of the adjacent districts of Anping and Haiping in the Shauking prefecture, and indicated the gulf which separated them from other districts of the Kwangchau prefecture and metropolitan Canton. The organization of the new company robbed the Chew Yick Kung Shaw of its significance.

In 1852, emigrants from the district of Hiangshan [Heungsan, Chung Shan] formed the third district company, the Yeong Wo Wui Kun. This eulogistic name, Masculine Concord, reflected the aspirations of the founders. It referred only indirectly to their native district which occupied a central position in the Pearl River Delta, along the eastern shore of the Chu Kiang estuary, with Macao on the tip of one of its southernmost peninsulas.

The same year brought into existence the first district company which was not based on regional loyalty. The new organization followed the cleavage that separated Punti and Hakka in the Pearl River Delta. The Yan Wo Wui Kun (Human Harmony), also known as the Hip Kat Company, united Hakka from their scattered settlements at Chew Mui [Ch'ao-mei], Tung Gwoon [Tung-kuan], Chak Kai [Ch'ih-ch'i], and Bow On [Pao-an] in several districts of the Pearl River Delta.

The emergence of the fifth district company in 1854, but probably organized in the previous year, signified the disintegration of the original association which had united all Chinese in California. The emigrants from the Sinning [Toi Shan] district withdrew from the Sze Yap Company, formed the Ning Yeong Wui Kun, the Association of Masculine Tranquility, and left the Four Districts Company in control of the emigrants from Anping, Haiping, and Sinhwui. The establishment of these district companies signaled the destruction of the Chew Yick Kung Shaw and marked the end of one phase in the power struggle for the hegemony of Chinese California. With the demise of the original company

Norman Assing and other early leaders of the Chinese in California disappeared from the scene. The new men ruled less through brute force and more with the hidden persuasion that went with regional loyalty and filial piety. The realization that Chinese California had grown too large for domination by one group or control by one company characterized the emergence of district companies.

The five district companies of 1854 controlled Chinese California for roughly a decade. William Speer described their strength and organization in a series of articles in the *Oriental, or Tung-Ngai San-Luk* for February and March of 1855. His compilations, the figures given by the Four Houses in 1853, and Tong K. Achick's estimate for 1854 revealed the growth of the district companies.

Name of Company	Arrivals	Speer's Returns	Figures Died	Members	Figures of Four Houses	Tong's Figures
Sam Yap	8,400	1,300	300	6,800	4,000	6,000
Sze Yap	13,200	3,700	300	9,200	9,500	11,000
Yeong Wo	16,900	2,500	400	14,000	7,500	11,000
Yan Wo	2,100	160	160	1,780	1,000	1,000
Ning Yeong	8,349	1,269	173	6,907	. . .	6,000
Totals	48,949	8,929	1,333	38,687	22,000	35,000

Allowing for about a thousand unorganized drifters, the total number of members, as compiled by Speer, approximated the total number of Chinese men in California. Roughly two thousand Chinese women were not recognized by any district company.[22]

The Five Companies concentrated their activities in their San Francisco quarters. Their respective agents and collectors, operating out of Sacramento and Stockton, the gateways to the Northern and Southern mining districts, controlled the indentured emigrants in the Mother Lode. Now and then, the address of one of the brick structures which served as headquarters appeared in the San Francisco *City Directory*.[23] "Large, substantial and commodious," the offices, dormitories, and hospitals compared "favorably with any public institution in our midst," a reporter of the *Alta* commented on the Sze Yap asylum built in 1853.[24] Buddhist temples connected with the company houses incorporated religion and superstition into their set of controls. Ceremonies and festivals centered around the joss houses of San Francisco as well as of distant mining towns. The district companies originally arranged for the shipment of the bones of deceased sojourners to their homeland, but later this service, so important for the morale of the Chinese, was taken over by small organizations dedicated exclusively to this task.[25]

The companies expressed their concern for the well being of their members in eloquent regulations. The rules exhorted benevolence in general and specifically contained provisions for invalids and stipulations concerning coffins for the poor. The companies controlled the Chinese relations with the American world, arbitrated disputes among their members, and dealt in concert with problems involving overlapping jurisdiction or quarrels which originated on shipboard during the passage. They offered rewards for apprehension and conviction of the murderers of their members. The Yeong Wo Company advertised an offer of hundred dollars for information about the death of twenty-year-old "Ching A-wai, a native of the village of Li-kai Chung, in the district of Heungshan." [26] A particular set of rules enforced the operation of Chinese debt bondage. These regulations required all newcomers to register with their district companies and pay a fee, or interest on the sum in case of delayed payment. Members planning to return to China had to inform the agents of their companies who examined their accounts and prevented them from sailing in case of any outstanding debts.[27]

William Speer's accounts of the structure and purpose of the five companies suffered from the forced analogies with American institutions which he superimposed upon his material. Speer did not, however, wholly obscure the important functions of the Wui Kun. "Great facilities are afforded through the companies for the collection of debts," he admiringly recorded. "Disputes between miners [indentured emigrants] and others [merchant-creditors] can be settled without the expense, delay, and trouble of a resort to our courts of law." Nevertheless, Speer recognized "some weighty objections" to the companies and felt that the "Americanization of the Chinese" could only be promoted by the dissolution of their Wui Kun.[28] The Report of the Grand Jury for San Francisco County on May 30, 1853, emphasized: "So great is the dread entertained" by the Chinese for their companies "that the sufferers are unwilling to complain or certify before the proper authorities." [29]

The Grand Jury report was based in part on a number of trials in the San Francisco Police Court. The evidence brought out in these investigations shed light on the machinations of the district companies and exposed the internal struggle in Chinese California which accompanied the establishment of the Four Great Houses, as San Francisco newspapers called the district companies before the organization of the Ning Yeong Wui Kun. The trials frequently involved Sam Wo, Ah Ti, the two Ah Chings, or other headmen of various companies. While the Grand Jury deliberated on its report of May 30, 1853, the Recorder sentenced Ah Ti, the "Chinese petty despot," to five days' imprisonment in the city prison. Ah Ti was convicted of having "inflicted severe corporeal punishment upon many of his more humble countrymen . . . , cutting off their ears, flogging them and keeping them chained." The court felt that the defendant had avoided earlier conviction "by his superior adroitness, influence and cunning." [30]

Ah Ti's trial illustrated the plight of the indentured emigrants. "Being generally unaware of their rights," the police reporter of the *Herald* explained, the newcomers "have long suffered themselves to be oppressed by the wealthier and more influential of their nation." The "proceeds of the industry of the lower classes," he observed, "too often serve to fill the coffers of the rich." The witnesses' ignorance of the type of evidence required for conviction in American courts, their growing timidity and constant trepidation, and the confusion of the various dialects "rendered it almost impossible to ascertain facts with any degree of certainty." The courts dismissed many cases on account of the conflicting evidence which the defendants' powerful position among their countrymen readily produced as defense. San Francisco's lawyers quickly discovered a set of legal technicalities to bypass all adverse verdicts against their wealthy clients. Nevertheless, on November 17, 1853, a trial of four Chinese thugs ended with their conviction by the police judge. The major witness had been found in a company house, bound with a heavy chain. Having embarked on the *Lord Warrington* to return to China without paying his debts of three hundred dollars, he had been abducted to the building where he was chained, starved, and frequently beaten with a rattan whip exhibited in court.[31] With the tightening of company rule, the possibilities for open protests against suppression vanished and the complaints disappeared from the dockets of the courts.

Having bullied the vast majority of sojourners into submission, each district company turned to secure its sphere of influence in California. The contests ranged over the control of mining claims and trading posts as well as of gambling houses and brothels. The Chinese wars, as newspapers called the encounters between hostile district companies in the 1850's, mixed the brutality of a cunning power struggle with the comical elements of an *opéra bouffe*. The running feuds of villages and clans which upset the equilibrium of the Pearl River Delta found new expressions in the fights among the district companies. Punti and Hakka, as well as Sam Yap, Sze Yap, Ning Yeong, and Yeong Wo, continued their old hostilities in California. The vivid imagination of some observers regarded the clashes as an extension of the campaigns between Taiping rebels and Imperial armies.[32]

The preparations for the pitched battles between the Sam Yap Wui Kun, Sze Yap Wui Kun, and Ning Yeong Wui Kun on the one side, and the Yeong Wo Wui Kun on the other, the Canton and Hong Kong companies of contemporary American accounts, occupied the California countryside for several weeks before the encounters. A blacksmith in Trinity County left a colorful account of the first war at Weaverville in the summer of 1854. For three weeks he "ran the shop day and night, making China instruments of war" for the rival companies, as did "nearly every blacksmith shop in the county." In other engagements, rifles, knives, and revolvers substituted for swords, spears, pike poles, brush scythes, and bamboo shields. Public drills and parades struck terror into the hearts of the enemies while dragon banners, proudly floating in the breeze, testified to the unconquerable spirit of the demonstrators, who restrained their warring temper on the days before the encounters by marching and counter-marching through the streets of mining towns.[33]

Public challenges of one company by another were, in translation, very concise. "There are a great many now existing in the world who ought to be exterminated," the Sam Yap Company at Rock River Branch in Tuolumne County threatened the Yan Wo Company at Chinese Camp in October 1856, in the Columbia *Gazette*. Consequently, twenty-five hundred fighters clashed on a chosen field near Kentucky Ranch. James Hanley, interpreter among the Hakka at Chinese Camp, described the battle in a detailed letter to the Sonora *Union Democrat*.

Well prepared for the fight, the Sam Yap had purchased a hundred and fifty muskets and bayonets at San Francisco. Fifteen white men, at ten dollars per day, meals and free whisky, served as instructors and drill masters. Before the fight, these vagabonds "painted themselves yellow, put on the Chinese costume, and, with a yard of horse-hair tail hanging down their backs," battled in the Punti ranks against the Hakka. The vast majority of the Chinese fought in the traditional fashion, with long pikes, butcher's choppers, and tridents. After a hundred shots had been fired, the Yan Wo who had only twelve muskets at their disposal beat a hasty retreat, discouraged by two casualties and frightened by the appearance of the fifteen scamps. The Sam Yap Company spent forty thousand dollars engineering the victory; the Yan Wo Company expended twenty thousand dollars.[34]

The number of fighters varied with the locality. In the mining districts generally about two hundred men composed the armies, but the preparations for the battle at Jackson in Calaveras County, on May 27, 1854, attracted two thousand Chinese. The sheriff prevented bloodshed by arresting the ringleaders and jailing them on defaulting a fine of three hundred dollars. The skirmishes in the streets of Nevada City in Nevada County, in Sacramento, and San Francisco seldom engaged more than a hundred participants on both sides. In September 1854, the great melee on Sacramento's I Street which involved six hundred warriors formed an exception. Regardless of the number of fighters, however, the losses remained low. No record listed more than twenty-one killed for any of the Chinese wars. In the third battle at Weaverville, on April 4, 1858, one Chinese died of his wounds; in the second, on April 12, 1857, eight casualties occurred; in the first, on July 15, 1854, twenty-one lost their lives according to the report in the *Herald* on August 1, 1854. The Weaverville Correspondence of the Shasta *Courier*, on July 23, 1854, perhaps more accurately than the San Francisco newspaper, listed ten dead and twelve severely wounded as a consequence of the first encounter. The nature of the battles and the frequent interference of Californians who stopped the fighting kept the casualty figures low.[35]

At times the engagements in the vicinity of Greenwood, Coloma, and Placerville, in El Dorado County, at Jackson and San Andreas in Calaveras County, at Swett Bar, Tuolumne County, Bear Valley, Mariposa County, Loafers' Ravine and Rancheria Diggings, Butte County, Marysville, Yuba County, Auburn, Placer County, and in Sierra County served fighters and spectators as a welcome distraction from the daily drudgeries of mining. Now and then a court trial interrupted the warfare. After San Francisco police and firemen on Sacramento Street had broken up a battle between the Sze Yap Wui Kun and the Yeong Wo Wui Kun, on October 17, 1857, the Recorder fined some of the arrested fighters for rioting. In most cases, however, the minor affairs in the countryside received no attention in California courts.[36]

With the beginning of the 1860's the rule of the five district companies over Chinese California entered a new phase. Pitched battles faded into the background.[37] Increased cooperation between the companies in matters of common concern marked the dawn of the Six Companies' era. When the emigrants from the districts of Anping, Haiping, and Sinhwui separated from the Sze Yap Wui Kun, in 1862, the division revived old and created new tensions, but it also opened prospects for a better balance between the various interest groups. Under the leadership of the Yee clan from Sinning they formed the Hop Wo Wui Kun, the Company of United Harmony. "The members of the Ho Wo Company," a reporter of the *Alta* noted in September 1862, "have literally 'taken up the Hatchet' against the See Yup Company." "Chopping affairs," street fights of the Ning Yeong Company and rows with the Sze Yap Company in San Francisco's Chinese Theater, accompanied the split.[38] A California court rejected the new company's request for incorporation on the ground that the board of trustees was not composed of a majority of United States citizens.[39] The remnants of the

Sze Yap Company later assumed the name Kong Chow Wui Kun.

The spirit of co-operation brought the Chung Wah Kung Saw (Chinese Public Association) into prominence. This was a co-ordinating council which dealt with the general affairs of the district companies. Administered by the headmen of each company, the roof organization became known to Americans as the Chinese Six Companies.[40] The constant application of this unofficial name in later years obscured the fact that only for the two decades between 1862 and 1882 did six district companies form the Chinese Consolidated Benevolent Association, the official name of the Chung Wah Kung Saw. In the 1850's Chinese and Americans used as collective term for the district companies first "Four Houses" and afterwards "Five Companies." [41] In later decades eight district companies formed the association and after 1909, seven. After 1862, Chung Wah Kung Saw, the original name, was changed to Chung Wah Wui Kun.[42] The substitution paralleled the indiscriminate use of *kongsi* and *hui-kuan*, noted among Chinese emigrants in Malaya.

With their leadership of the Chung Wah Wui Kun, the prominent merchants expanded the control which they exercised in their clan associations and district companies.[43] The headmen of the companies formed the board of directors which rotated its members as chairman of the Six Companies. Only the Yan Wo Wui Kun was excluded from the office, a result of the traditional hostility between Punti and Hakka. The available evidence proves that merchants were the leaders of Chinese California, in the district companies as well as in the Six Companies, in a manner similar to that in the Chinese settlements in Southeast Asia. "The companies," Augustus W. Loomis summed up his observations of a decade in 1868, "have been organized by merchants . . . whose business and residence keeps them in the city." [44]

The euphemistic names of the powerful commercial houses disguised the personalities of these merchant princes. Only on special occasions, such as a legislative hearing, the reception of favors in China, a voyage to Paris, an official banquet, or a funeral, did the public get a glimpse of what lay behind the headmen's splendid anonymity. As early as 1853, the heads of the Four Houses, Gee Atai and Lee Chuen (Sze Yap), Tong K. Achick and Lum Teen-kwei (Yeong Wo), Tam Sam and Chung Aching (Sam Yap), and Wong Sing and Lee Yuk-nam (Yan Wo), pleaded their cases before a committee of the California State Legislature.[45] At the end of 1860, the San Francisco *Le Mineur* surprised its readers with the intelligence that the merchant Ah Shang, who recently returned to his homeland with a fortune, had received an official rank from the Manchu Emperor and had served as barbarian expert in the negotiations which ended the Second Anglo-Chinese war.[46]

For other returned merchants the confines of the traditional Chinese world held little regard. Chow See used the Great Industrial Exhibition of 1867 at Paris to surround himself with the degree of recognition which he thought due him. This noted *bon vivant* and former head of the Ning Yeong Company drank "nothing but Veuve Cliquot from morning to night," according to a letter from China. His friend, Ah Ting, at one time the first president of the Hop Wo Company, took the Industrial Exhibition as pretext to inform his old counsel, the Sacramento lawyer James Coffroth, of his own departure for Paris in the company of "quite a number of traveled Chinamen." [47] Chow See's and Ah Ting's former colleagues at San Francisco entertained during these years an array of American politicians, diplomats, and statesmen. At the Grand Complementary Dinner to Schuyler Colfax on August 17, 1865, the presidents of the six district companies, Chui Sing Tong (Sam Yap), Khing Fong (Yeong Wo), Ting Sang (Sze Yap), Wae Nga (Ning

Yeong), Chee Shum (Hop Wo), and Mum Kuae (Yan Wo), functioned as hosts.[48]

The funeral of Chu Pak on January 6, 1866, threw some light on the life of a merchant whom the Chinese in San Francisco honored with the title "Venerable Old Man." [49] He had come to California in 1850, at the age of fifty-three. One of the leading men from the Four Districts, Chu Pak had served for many years as one of the headmen of the Sze Yap Wui Kun. For six years he presided as "Chief Director, Master and Trustee" over the affairs of the district company. In the summer of 1862, when Chu Pak was involved in a murder trial, "the heads of the five great companies . . . , Chan Yeen Lan, Head Director See Yup Company, Wong Yuk Tong, Head Director Ning Yeong Company, Chan Lae Wo, Head Director Canton Company, Lam Hew Cho, Head Director Yeong Wo Company, and Mak Mum Kwae, Head Director Yan Wo Company," came to his aid with an "address to the public" which helped to clear Chu Pak in the American court.[50] Under the management of merchants ruling through the Six Companies, the structure of Chinese California represented an advance over the traditional Chinese scene where scholar-officials governed according to the Confucian value system in a world which restricted merchants to a lowly position in society.

The district companies gained more effective control over Chinese California through the expansion of their oppressive system. The Six Companies derived its immediate power from an extension of the district companies' authority. The sailing permit which the headquarters of the Six Companies issued for a fee demonstrated the association's sway over the sojourners. Every Chinese planning to return to his homeland needed it for the purchase of a ticket. Only those who had paid their debts before the planned departure could apply. Steamship companies and independent ship masters, cognizant of the Chinese merchants' control over freight or passage contracts, acquiesced in the system and made the permit an effective instrument of debtor control.[51]

During the encounter between Chinese and Americans the Six Companies acted as spokesman for all sojourners. The association performed tasks which earlier had been handled by individual merchants or district companies in the absence of Chinese consular or diplomatic officials in the United States. Until the 1870's the Six Companies hardly favored the presence of official Chinese representatives in the United States. Semiofficial functions tightened the strict social control over the Chinese world. However, the rule not only sustained a realm of oppression in California but also re-created a familiar setting which provided a measure of relief for the bewildered newcomers in an alien world.

The system of control, disguised behind the loyalty to native districts and families and sanctioned by traditional concepts of the Chinese scene, radiated a degree of security and comfort. With a large temple on the highest point of the western ridge of San Francisco's Lone Mountain Cemetery and other joss houses in towns and mining camps, the Six Companies alleviated the spiritual anguish of the sojourners. The tight regimentation protected the emigrants not only from scheming villains among their countrymen but also from the wide range of reactions to Chinese newcomers of which Californians were capable. All in all, Chinese California provided not only oppression but also home for men who worked solely for the moment of their return to their families in the Pearl River Delta.

Custom sanctioned the rule of the companies over Chinese California. The sojourners' emotional ties to their native districts guaranteed the function of the control system and Americans, respecting the private affairs of all newcomers, tolerated its oppressive character. The major challenge to the rule of the district companies came from rebellious factions. Untouched by any loyalty to family or district, these brotherhoods, anxious to manipulate and to coerce their countrymen for their own ends, disputed the authority of the district companies. Secret societies led the onslaught against the pre-eminence of the companies and wrested segments of Chinese California away from them. These brotherhoods traced their origin to the Triad Society which found its way from China to the United States like other institutions and customs.

Men of different clans and districts, from all walks of life, for centuries had banded together in China for social, political, or religious reasons, to alleviate shortcomings in the structure of society and to further their own ends. During the Ch'ing Dynasty, the Triad Society, with tenets based upon the bonds existing between Heaven, Earth, and Man, rose to eminence south of the Yangtze River under a multitude of different names. The brotherhood's own records dated its origin in the year 1674. The Triads fought the Manchus and supported rebellions in Formosa, Kiangsi, and Kwangtung. During the Taiping Rebellion its bands held Shanghai for eighteen months in 1853–1855. Following the movements of emigrants from South China to Malaysia, branches of the secret society sprung up in the settlements of Southeast Asia.

As result of its secret nature practically nothing was known of the Triad Society by foreigners, until a set of studies provided some understanding of the brotherhood's history and activity among the overseas Chinese.[52] The emergence of Triad branches in Chinese California followed in the wake of the society's spread among overseas Chinese. Their early intrigues in San Francisco, however, attracted no witness of the caliber of Munshi Abdullah bin Abdul Kadir who, in his autobiography, described the ritual and riots of the Society in Singapore.[53]

With the establishment of clearly defined spheres of influence in Chinese California, secret societies openly challenged the district companies' control of certain fields, mostly those connected with activities on the borderline of social respectability. Gambling and prostitution fell into the domain of these brotherhoods which traced their origin to splinter groups of the original Triad branch in San Francisco. Internal rivalries, as well as open warfare between these secret societies, accompanied constant shifts in alliances which led to the sudden decline of powerful groups and the rapid success of rival factions. California newspapers briefly recorded part of the intrigues, including the feud between the Hung Shun Tong, ruling San Francisco, and the I Hing Tong, controlling the mining districts.[54] During the struggle, the expressed goals of these secret societies underwent frequent modifications, while their real objectives never changed.

The detailed history of the shifting scene is difficult to reconstruct. Information on Chinese secret societies in the United States, available at the turn of the century, found its way into one of the reports of the Industrial Commission.[55] However, the compilation throws light on the 1850's and 1860's only indirectly and recent accounts mix fantasy and sensationalism. Yet there was an intimate connection among tongs, traditional Chinese secret societies, and the oppressive forces controlling Chinese California. The manuscript material of John J. Manion (1877–1959), head of the San Francisco police's Chinatown detail between 1921 and 1946, provided some insight.[56]

In the United States a Chinese secret society came to be designated as a tong, the Cantonese pronunciation of the Chinese character t'ang. Its literal translation as hall or office has been used generally to explain its function in the brotherhoods. This usage obscured the term's specific meaning in the Chinese scene where it described a Triad lodge. It strengthened the notion that tongs were a phenomenon peculiar to the Chinese world in the United States. The extension of the term highbinder, which originally characterized Irish toughs in New York City, to a Chinese hatchet man, the professional killer of a tong, increased the distinct American air surrounding these societies. The popular label of Chinese Freemasons attached to one of the tongs facilitated the assimilation.[57] The use of the word tong, however, provided an additional link between the early brotherhoods in San Francisco and the tongs, or Triad lodges, in China and Southeast Asia. It placed the early tongs within the confines of the Chinese world which was extended to California.

The generally accepted version of the history of the Triad Society recorded that five Buddhist monks headed the Five Provincial Grand Lodges of the Triad Society, in the eighteenth century, after Manchu troops had dispersed the army of the brotherhood. The society instructed the monks to scatter throughout the Empire and to work secretly against the Ch'ing Dynasty until the opportune moment for the restoration of the Ming had arrived. One of them, Fang Tahung, went into Kwangtung province. There he organized the second lodge of the Triads in South China which received the name Hung Shun Tong, Hall of Obedience to Hung.[58] The original branch of the Triad Society in California, an offshoot of the Kwangtung lodge, set the pattern for the continued use of the traditional designation tong in the United States.[59]

In 1887, Stewart Culin, a perceptive observer, described the operation of the I Hing Tong which "embraces nearly two-thirds of all the Chinese in the country." He traced the tong's name, I Hing, or "Patriotic Rising," to the watchword of one of the first chiefs of the Triad Society.[60] The headquarters of the secret society's branch on Philadelphia's Race Street displayed a gilded sign with the inscription Hung Shun T'ong, the name of the provincial grand lodge of the Triad Society in Kwangtung. A charter from a Pennsylvania court incorporated the lodge as Roslyn Beneficial Association. The sister lodges in Baltimore, New York, and Boston also followed the traditional ceremonies of the Triad Society.[61]

The Triad Society came to sudden public attention in California when a police raid on the night of January 3, 1854 netted one hundred and forty-one of its members. The San Francisco police, alerted by victims of the brotherhood, surprised four hundred Chinese during an initiation ceremony in the upper story of a house on Jackson Street. Among the arrested was A Ching, head of a large merchant house and leading man in one of the district companies. The police officers described the fancifully decorated hall and produced the captured Triad symbols, flags, and pennants in court. Interpreted by Tong K. Achick, prominent merchant and agent of the Yeong Wo Company, the description of the ceremony clearly paralleled recorded Triad rites.

From writings confiscated in the raid, the police witness translated the oaths and regulations of the brotherhoods after the judge overruled a defense objection that the Court had no right to inquire into the secrets unless a criminal offense was committed. The articles of the "Thirty-six Oaths," partly rendered into English in court, corresponded with the "Thirty-Six Articles of the Oath" which Gustave Schlegel recorded in his study of the Triad Society.[62] Tong K. Achick labeled the association "Wide Gate Society," a literal rendition of Hung-men Hui, or Hung League, one of the many names of the Triad Society in China. Among the numerous confiscated flags, which lent power and prestige to the head of the league, the witness identified correctly "the arms of the Chinese General," which matched the "Army-standard" of Schlegel's investigation, the "warrant of the commander of the army." [63]

The raid and the trial established beyond doubt the existence in California of branches of China's powerful secret society. At the time of the raid on the San Francisco lodge

Triad factions in China controlled the walled city of Shanghai by force of arms, from September 7, 1853, to February 17, 1855. But the incident on Jackson Street produced no further results. The Triad members remained secure within the confines of their transplanted community. In March, the members of the brotherhood, "an extensive secret political organization of the Chinese in this city," the reporter of the *Alta* observed, paraded to the Yerba Buena Cemetery in a spectacular procession, "a large red banner fancyfully decorated with the insignia of the society" stirring in the noon breeze. The color identified the flag as the great pennant of the Triad lodge in the province of Kwangtung. Within the realm of the Triads, black was reserved for Fukien, crimson for Yunnan, white for Honan, and green for Chekiang. Fifty Triads on horseback, two hundred marchers in festive robes, and a long procession of carriages composed the impressive spectacle.[64]

A series of trials in San Francisco courts in the mid-1850's revealed the true nature of the California branches of the Society. The evidence conformed to the general picture of their activities among overseas Chinese. Indicted for extortion, larceny, or false imprisonment, the Triads saw shattered the trappings of a benevolent society behind which defense lawyers and witnesses tried to disguise their tyrannical rule. In the opening days of the trials, trembling plaintiffs and intimidated witnesses still mustered sufficient courage to levy charges against their oppressors. Their testimony dwelt on the highhanded methods of the society's tax collectors, gathering forced contributions or extorting tribute. Other witnesses accused thugs who meted out punishment against recalcitrant subjects of Triad rule.

With the court's recess the trials entered their perjury stage. On their return to the stand, the witnesses for the prosecution showed the effects of the persuasive influences to which they had been exposed in the meantime. With the aid of writs of habeas corpus, naïvely issued by superior courts, the Triad henchmen almost regularly gained hold of those witnesses whom the police judge kept in protective custody to secure the continued validity of their testimony. The witnesses now failed to remember vital details of their previous testimony or lost all recollections of their initial charges. In the final stage of the trials, the "quirks and squibbles of lawyers," to whom the Triads paid "fat fees," and the silenced or perjuring witnesses in most instances forced the police judge to dismiss the cases or the district attorney to drop the charges.

Toward the end of the futile attempts by San Francisco police judges to break the hold of the Triad branches on segments of Chinese California, the Chinese interpreter of the court appeared as the only witness against the Hung Shun Tong. Charles T. Carvalho, a native of Batavia, educated in the British consulate at Canton and in St. Paul's College at Hong Kong, read Chinese and spoke Mandarin and the various Cantonese dialects with "facility and accuracy." However, his intimate knowledge of the machinations of the brotherhoods, with which his background provided him, failed to produce results within the rigid procedural framework of an American court. The interpreter frequently stated that "he was unable to produce in Court any evidence against . . . accused" Triads, "owing to the fear and dread in which they held . . . their victims." He repeatedly urged the court to accept confiscated records of the brotherhoods, sufficient to ensure their members' decapitation in China, in evidence against the hatchet men. On one occasion, in February 1855, Carvalho averred that the Hung Shun Tong relied on eight hundred members in San Francisco and counted four thousand followers in the entire state. The annual income of the tong from forced contributions in his estimate amounted to "upwards of $150,000." [65]

Closely related to the Hung Shun Tong, the Kwan Ducks,

the Kwang Tek Tong (Broad Virtue Tong), appeared in San Francisco in 1852 as one of the early Triad branches in America. A year or two later other offshoots came into existence, the Hsieh I Tong (United Righteousness Tong) and the Tan Shan Tong (Red Mountain Tong). The early tongs recruited their members on a distinctly regional basis. The practice turned the struggle for the dominance of Chinese California at times into a contest for the loyalty of its population. At first the Kwan Ducks were men from Sze Yap, the Hip Yees from Sam Yap, and the Ong Sungs from Hiangshan, the district of the Yeong Wo Company.[66] The frequent use of different names for the same brotherhood disguised its operations. Hatchet men more clearly signified a society's power. Tong wars added to the notoriety of a multitude of emerging splinter groups which testified to the intensity of the struggle for control.

Behind the façade of social clubs and benevolent associations, the secret societies linked together revolutionary groups, fraternities bent on righting alleged or real injustices suffered by its members, and gangs of criminals which controlled gambling, prostitution, and opium smuggling by means of extortion, physical coercion, kidnaping, and murder. The evidence for a continuation in the United States of the Triad Society's traditional revolutionary aims is sketchy during the early decades. However, there appeared at least one news report about a shipment of colt revolvers, disguised as bones, to rebels in China.[67] Long before some of these early secret societies became collectively known as the Gee Kung Tong, a general name for the Triad Society eulogizing itself as the Common Tong, tongs functioned as another instrument of suppression in Chinese California and replaced in their spheres the control system of the district companies.

The coexistence of district companies and tongs within the framework of Chinese California indicated the scope of the control system. Other organizations, guilds and clan associations among them, supervised unregulated sectors or doubled the checks of vital areas. Together they shaped the core of the Chinese world. Under merchant leadership, this invisible world formed a web covering the Chinese in scattered mining camps and crowded city and town quarters. Under the guise of benevolence, powerful cliques exploited the sojourners' loyalty and ruled the legions of indentured emigrants.

Viewed against the set of invisible restraints, the visible confines of the Chinese quarters were extensions of the control system. Chinatowns, however, true to the nature of symbols, merely represented the control without aiming to reproduce the system. A sturdier mortar, composed of district loyalty, filial piety, and fear, kept the stones of their walls in place. The durability of the confine allowed a measure of freedom and license to exist within Chinatown, as escape from a strange world, and as outlet of emotions curbed by forbearance and coercion. Chinatown came to function as safety valve of the control system sustaining Chinese California.

CHAPTER V

WORK CAMP AND CHINATOWN

AN invisible control system based on district loyalty, filial piety, and fear circumscribed the realm of Chinese California and re-enforced the basic allegiances of traders and miners in isolated mountain camps. These sentiments formed a stronger and more effective confine than the bricks and mortar of the walls of the visible world, or the chains of daily drudgery that bound the indentured emigrants. Consequently, the Chinese quarters of the cities needed merely to symbolize the presence of control without duplicating the whole system. They permitted a release for emotions checked by restraint and oppression, and provided a brief retreat from work in an alien environment into a world resembling home.

Long before large numbers of Chinese withdrew from California's countryside in the 1870's and crowded into settlements in urban centers, Chinatowns acquired a vital role as safety valves of the control system.[1] In these quarters, islands of freedom and license within the reach of the lowliest bordered on centers of authority and oppression. In a crude mixture of order and chaos, the headquarters of district companies and tongs neighbored the theaters and gambling halls. The Chinatowns fleetingly admitted indentured emigrants to a life of affluence. Visions of that leisure once had stimulated the sojourners' dreams of success and had prompted them to leave home and risk years of certain hardship in a strange country in the struggle for an uncertain

fortune. The Chinese quarter liberated the indentured emigrants briefly from the shackles of work which debt bondage
placed on their shoulders. For hours the excitement of a
gambling table or the air of abundance pervading one of
the great public festivals elevated them above their lowly
status. These brighter interludes added color and brought
relief from the gray monotony and strict discipline of an
austere world of work.

Descriptions of San Francisco's Chinese quarters in official
reports and newspaper accounts of the 1850's and 1860's
furnish more useful information than the political, sociological, and missionary polemics, or the fantastic tales of
succeeding decades.[2] The Chinatown of popular fancy, if it
ever existed at all, flourished between 1882 and 1906. Some
of the later belletristic sources also give a broader perspective
of the extraordinary life in Chinatown.[3]

The 1850's and 1860's labeled the Chinese quarters in San
Francisco variously. Little Canton and Little China were
two of the appellations in use. However, the name "China
Town" appeared as early as 1853 in newspaper reports.[4]
Sacramento Street, where Chinese had first located canvas
houses in 1849 between Kearny and Dupont Streets, was
called by the sojourners T'ang Yen Gai, *t'ang-jen chieh* —
the Street of the Men of T'ang, Chinese (Cantonese) Street.[5]
The early Chinese occupied scattered localities in San Francisco which were yet a far cry from the later strictly confined
area of Chinatown, roughly encircled by California, Stockton, Broadway, and Kearny Streets, and depicted in the
"Official Map of Chinatown in San Francisco" published
under the supervision of the Special Committee of the Board
of Supervisors in July, 1885.[6] In these pages the term Chinatown has been applied indiscriminately to all Chinese settlements in the United States, without regard for *the* Chinatown. Chinese quarters in urban areas, isolated fishing villages, or stores in distant mining camps, irrespective of size

or location, all harbored the world of freedom, license, and escape which sanctioned their existence.

In mountain villages and mining towns Chinese stores were the focus of life. As soon as several Chinese moved into a settlement, one of them sent to Marysville, Sacramento, Stockton, or some other supply center for the groceries and other wares needed by the colony.[7] These he sold to his comrades without at first discontinuing his regular work. If the colony increased in numbers, he rented a small store and formed a trading company with the assistance of friends, clan association, or district company. Often, a Chinese physician began to dispense medicines from a supply of drugs ranged along one side of the store, and an itinerant barber made it a place of call. In a short time, an auspicious name, goods from San Francisco, and news from the Pearl River Delta made the store the resort of all Chinese in the vicinity.[8]

In time the aspiring merchant hired a cook who at first was available only for banquets but later ran a small restaurant in an annex. Another room housed a couch for opium smokers or a table for gamblers; once a slave girl found her way into the store, another island of freedom and license sprang into existence.[9] On the mining frontier old timers remembered hearing at dusk the call "mei hanna [probably *mo k'un na*]," and took it as a signal for all Chinese who wanted to gamble.[10] Their hunch, essentially correct, did slight injustice to the precise meaning of the invitation, "Not yet to bed." Frequently sojourners from isolated settlements, craving greater diversions than the country store offered, visited larger Chinatowns. In September California farmers came from far and near to Sacramento for the state fair, in October Chinese from the countryside flocked to the capital for their religious festivals.[11] Hardly any of the pictorial advertisements of early California stage lines failed to depict a couple of Chinese traveling on top of the coach.[12] Entire mining companies left their tents, huts, and claims

with the beginning of the rainy season to winter in Chinatown.

San Francisco's Chinatown was similar to those of other
California settlements.[13] Its Chinese population in the 1850's
and 1860's was hardly larger than that of some of the half-
forgotten mining towns, where no traces of Chinese life
have been preserved save the remnants of a general store,
the skeleton of a gambling hall, a dilapidated joss house,
or simply the words China or Chinese which were among the
most popular of California place names derived from nationalities.[14]

Few indentured emigrants ever shook off the shackles of
work for periods longer than a New Year's celebration, a day
in the theater, or a night at the fan-tan table. With the ex-
plosion of the last firecracker, an actor's closing line, and the
loss of the last copper cash, the pressure of the control system brought the sojourners back to their life of service. For
a few hours, the atmosphere of Chinatown had alleviated
their homesickness. Their dreams of freedom, dignity, and
grandeur, released by the visit, vanished rapidly in the ordinary air of Chinese California. Incessant toil and drudgery,
rigid regimentation, and strict supervision again filled their
ordinary world of labor and debt bondage. Less colorful and
exotic than Chinatown, this world of labor has never been
adequately depicted, although it harbored the majority of
Chinese sojourners and formed the setting which gave Chinatown meaning and value.

Mining and railroad construction work absorbed the masses
of indentured emigrants. In both occupations large groups
of laborers could be easily employed, regimented, and controlled. In mining companies and construction gangs agents
of the merchant-creditors applied Chinese California's invisible controls to the world of work. The indentured emigrants' constant drudgery sustained debt bondage in Chinese
California. In the 1850's and 1860's the Chinese drifted also

into other pursuits. They found employment as fishermen, freighters, wood choppers, washermen, gardeners, farm hands, and cooks. The world of control also dominated these occupations, although they attracted far fewer laborers than mining and railroad construction.[15]

The life of service in early Chinese California centered around mining. Various sources frequently registered the number of Chinese miners during the 1850's and 1860's. The Sacramento *Daily Union* estimated on October 10, 1855, that 20,000 out of 36,557 Chinese on the Pacific Coast mined in the California gold region. Thirty thousand out of 48,391 Chinese worked the mines in 1862, according to the calculations of Chinese merchants in San Francisco.[16] By 1873 the Chinese formed the largest single ethnic or national group of miners, Americans included.[17] However, contemporary writers and chroniclers failed almost completely to record the habits of the Chinese miners. The world of regimented drudgery in the mountain camps has to be pieced together from incidental remarks of travelers, the reminiscences of pioneers, newspaper accounts, and scenes preserved in lithographs and on letter sheets.

Missionary reports and news items depict the arrival of Chinese newcomers at San Francisco, their lodging in company houses, and their subsequent dispatch to the mining region. These accounts form the border stones of the mosaic delineating the life of service in California.[18] The Chinese on landing in San Francisco usually remained there but a few days. They "then proceeded by the steamers to Sacramento, Stockton, Marysville, and other points on the Sacramento and San Joaquin Rivers."[19] In these supply centers and in other outfitting posts agents directed the companies of indentured emigrants into the Mother Lode Country, distributing the miners into camps between Mariposa in the South and Downieville in the North. The "portly Chinese Agent, Si Mong, one of our merchant princes," stated the

Stockton *Republican* in describing a supervisor, "is a stout important looking personage, apparently about thirty-five years of age." He is "quite wealthy and dressed in the most approved American fashion . . . , has dispensed with his tail appendage, . . . and has taken unto himself a Mexican lady for a wife, . . . by whom he has one or two children." [20]

The Chinese miner in the foothills of the Sierra retained his blue cotton blouse and his "broad trowsers, his wooden shoes," and "his broad brimmed hat." He wore "his hair close cropped before with a long jet black queue hanging down behind." [21] His concession to Western civilization consisted of working in American-made boots that were always too large for him. As some observers speculated, he probably delighted in gaining a maximum return from his purchase money. The isolation in which he and his countrymen labored in strictly controlled companies strengthened their adherence to their customary way of life. While "traveling in a desolate mountain region" in 1868, Charles Loring Brace "was much impressed by the sad, lonely form of a Chinaman, walking pensively toward a solitary grave, and scattering little papers as he went, . . . his prayers to the spirit of his ancestors and to the departed." [22]

On the banks of the rivers and in ravines, a correspondent of the San Francisco *Herald* found companies of twenty or thirty Chinese "inhabiting close cabins, so small that one . . . would not be of sufficient size to allow a couple of Americans to breathe in it. Chinamen, stools, tables, cooking utensils, bunks, etc., all huddled up together in indiscriminate confusion, and enwreathed with dense smoke, present a spectacle which is . . . suggestive of anything but health and comfort." [23] The Chinese miners enjoyed little ease. If not crowed into abandoned cabins they dwelt in tents and brush huts. In groups of a hundred they banded together in short-lived villages which studded the Mother Lode or occupied camps deserted by white miners. Rice, dried fish, and tea formed the staples of their diet. Pork and chicken represented the luxuries in the life of service in Chinese California.[24]

Ordinarily the Chinese worked only placers with rockers, long toms, and river dams in companies of ten to thirty men who were supervised by bosses.[25] Occasionally the reports of the United States Commissioner noted Chinese hired for quartz operations or employed in several quartz mills "for certain inferior purposes, such as dumping cars, surface excavation, etc." [26] At times the superstitions of the workers prevented the bosses from engaging their companies in types of mining which disturbed the multitude of gods inhabiting mountains, meadows, and rivers. Apart from this limitation, drawings and photos show headmen and crews in any place where other miners left the Chinese undisturbed.[27] The headmen bought the claims and directed the reworking of the deserted diggings, the "scratching," as American miners labeled the desolate placers. "Long files of Chinamen alone break the monotony of the landscape as they scrape and wash the sands in the nearly dry beds of the torrents," Ludovic de Beauvoir observed on his tour through the Sierra Nevada.[28]

The Chinese quickly took to the rocker method of placer mining, Charles Peters noted, and "a line of sluice boxes appeared to be especially adapted to their use." They introduced the Chinese water wheel and the bailing bucket, attached to ropes and manipulated by two men, to clear holes of water. Given a choice, the Orientals continued to use their familiar tools in their own way.[29] Their working methods endeared the Chinese miners to the numerous water companies which found in them faithful customers.

Among the miners "were Chinamen of the better class," J. Douglas Borthwick noted, "who no doubt directed the work, and paid the common men very poor wages — poor at least in California." [30] Charles Peters recorded several colorful episodes in the life of Ah Sam, a Chinese boss, who in

1856 "had a large company of coolies working on Auburn Ravine," near Ophir in Placer County. For twenty-five dollars Ah Sam acquired a log cabin from six Americans who had mined the ground and dissolved their partnership. Some of his men, under his personal supervision, washed three thousand dollars out of the dirt floor of the cabin, thus justifying his speculation that the American miners' practice of clearing their gold dust nightly in a blower before the fire had left the floor covered with particles of gold. However, Ah Sam never admitted to more than three hundred dollars profit. That, he felt, was all he had realized with his scheme, since he subtracted from his gain the twenty-seven hundred dollars that two of his men had cheated him out of. These two members of his company, while Ah Sam was busily looking after the cabin floor, discovered, unknown to him, a nugget worth a little less than three thousand dollars as they were shoveling dirt into his sluice box line a short distance from the cabin. They concealed their find, left at night, and sold the nugget in San Francisco.[31]

The ordinary life of Chinese miners with its regimentation and supervision by headmen precluded such escapades. Extreme cases depicting disciplinary measures were most likely to find their way into the newspapers. At Drytown in Amador County a Chinese miner who had stolen four hundred dollars received twenty-five lashes and lost his queue. When he was returned to his mining company his countrymen whipped him again, cut off his left ear, marched him to San Francisco, and shot him by the road.[32] However, the long chain of uneventful days, filled with drudgery and toil, was more typical of the life of Chinese miners.

The working discipline of the mining companies, enforced by constant supervision, accounted for the mass of conflicting reports about the miners' diligence. At times the authors of these accounts marveled at the laborers' incessant toil, "burrowing like ants in the depths" of river beds and ravines; at other times they criticized the miners' lengthy siestas and gay nights. Now and then the workers openly fought the bosses' discipline because there was " 'too muchee workee and too little payee.' " [33] Outside the reach of the headmen's control the Orientals quickly adjusted the rate of their drudgery to their own standards of industry. Cut off from an alien environment by customs and habits, with the bosses controlling contacts with the settlements, the miners eagerly relied on such diversions as the company of their comrades or the nearby Chinese store provided after the working hours.[34]

Companies of docile Chinese laborers slowly but surely found their way into the "great army laying siege to Nature in her strongest citadel," the construction crews of the Central Pacific building the Western section of the Transcontinental Railroad.[35] Smaller projects prepared the way for and accompanied the ultimate employment of ten thousand Chinese in the completion of the Pacific Railway.[36] In the late 1850's one hundred and fifty of the five hundred hands working on the San Francisco and Marysville Railroad were Chinese, "employed by a Chinese subcontractor." [37] Other early California railroads, such as the Sacramento and Vallejo Railroad, also used Chinese in grading and track-laying. In 1869 one thousand "obedient Chinese toiled like ants from morning to night" on the construction of the Virginia and Truckee Railroad in the Washoe and Comstock mines of Nevada, "spurred on continually by urgent supervisors." [38]

The steady demand for laborers on the Central Pacific Railroad attracted increasing numbers of Chinese. Between 1863 and 1868 many left the mines, and a large portion of them ended up in the construction force. In the mid-1860's Chinese merchants and American firms at San Francisco, such as Koopmanschap & Co. and Sisson, Wallace, & Co., also began to supply groups of laborers directly from China.[39] Agents of the Central Pacific recruited men in the mountain districts of the Pearl River Delta. They paid for outfit and passage, and received in return from each Chinese a promissory note for $75 in United States gold coin, secured by endorsement of family and friends. The contract provided for regular installments, to complete repayment of the debt within seven months from the time the newcomers commenced labor on the railroad.[40] These shipments tripled the figures of Chinese arriving at the San Francisco Custom House in 1868 and 1869 as compared with the four preceding years. Soon the "rugged mountains . . . swarmed with Celestials, shoveling, wheeling, carting, drilling and blasting rocks and earth." [41]

The use of indentured emigrants and contract laborers on the Pacific section of the Transcontinental Railway provided ammunition for the political warfare following the completion of the road. However, the hearings of congressional investigation committees, the arguments of lawyers, and the explanations of company executives and engineers throw little light on the daily drudgeries of the construction crews. The amassed material leaves the impression that politicians, financeers, lawyers, accountants, and engineers alone built the road.[42] The San Francisco earthquake and fire of 1906 destroyed all existing records of the Southern Pacific Company, including those of the Central Pacific Company. Later attempts to restore the files met with little success.[43] There are incidental remarks of travelers, the information in early railroad guides, and the jottings of itinerant newspaper editors, but these sources fall short of the observations of Hemmann Hoffmann, a Swiss student, who worked as Chinese overseer on the Central Pacific near Dutch Flat in Placer County in 1864 and 1865 and whose notes furnish the outline for the following sketch of the life and work of the Chinese construction companies.[44]

Along the projected line of work between Dutch Flat and the Nevada boundary, numerous small huts crowded the camps of Chinese workers. The laborers slept and ate on simple wooden cots. Chinese bosses, working with the overseers, effectively kept discipline in the companies. The extra workers in the compounds enabled the headmen to live up to their contracts and to report a complete company of toilers for work every morning. The extras substituted for those workers who on the previous evening had succumbed to the attractions of Chinese stores in the nearby settlements, but who would doubtless show up again for work in a few days. The replacements also filled the gaps left by comrades unable to shake off the effects of a dissolute night. The headmen received wages for the number of men which they regularly reported, and divided the money among all members of their gang. Groups of twelve to twenty men formed a mess and kept a cook who obtained his provisions from the nearest Chinese merchant. At times the kitchen of the white workers furnished meat for the Chinese rice bowls.

During the long working day of grading and track-laying, the sheer number of Chinese workers compensated for the delay caused by the running conversation which accompanied the laborers' drudgery. The multitude of his comrades enabled the individual worker to interrupt his toil frequently for a sip of tea or the forbidden taste of a small pipe of tobacco. At the mercy of his bosses and headmen, disciplined on the job and in the camp, the worker took every opportunity to minimize the effect of the control. Whenever the slightest obstacle interrupted the routine curious laborers crowded together for a brief dispute over the event.

The masses of laborers on the Pacific Railroad appeared to occasional observers as well regimented gangs and smoothly running working machines. Chinese formed part of the celebrated construction crew which on April 28, 1869, laid ten miles of track in a single day. To one of the editors of the *Alta*, the Chinese railroad workers often seemed "in these dreary solitudes . . . the presiding genius." Regimentation and discipline, however, vanished completely when basic differences between district companies broke into the open. The final days of the construction of the Pacific Railroad brought not only the track-laying feast but also the "Grand Chinese Battle in the Salt Lake Valley" between members of the Sze Yap Company and the Yeong Wo Company.[45]

Annual festivals, celebrated with public spectacles and tradition-honored ceremonies, provided a regular outlet from the rigid controls of the work camp.[46] The atmosphere of the gambling halls, theaters, and other centers of entertainment and diversion quickly released the indentured emigrants from the confines of constant toil and loneliness and gave them a substitute for the missing home. Since the ordinary life of Chinese workers resembled a succession of days of reckoning, their religious festivals furnished a string of holidays. Like their system of control or their methods of work, most of their temporary escapes followed forms familiar from the homeland. Scenes of freedom and license gained significance from the work and drudgery which filled the ordinary days of the sojourners.

The observance of the traditional holidays interrupted the routine. During these celebrations, employers of Chinese mining companies in Mariposa County informed the United States Commissioner of Mining Statistics, the laborers "leave the mines *en masse,* and cannot be induced to work, for sometimes a week altogether." [47] These festivities momentarily linked the world of Chinese sojourners in California with the familiar scenes of the Pearl River Delta. The impressive ceremonies which formed part of the popular cycle of the three festivals of the living and the three festivals of the dead, though Californian in their setting, gave even onlookers the illusion of glimpsing life in villages and towns along the course of the Chu Kiang.[48] Of these six traditional holidays the Dragon-boat festival never took deep roots in Chinese California, while New Year's from the beginning occupied a dominant position as the greatest and gayest occasion of the year.

The first recorded Chinese New Year celebration in the United States on February 1, 1851, only incidentally served the needs of Chinese California. Primarily it enhanced the status of a single individual. Norman Assing entertained as his guests "a number of policemen . . . , many ladies and 'China Boys.'" Within two years, however, the celebration lost its private character and assumed the traits of a "grand holiday . . . , with the moving multitude of Celestials rigged out in their finest toggery." [49] Step by step distinctive features of the holiday emerged until the festival became a California ritual at the beginning of the 1860's.

The blaze and the noise of firecrackers signaled the beginning of the New Year's Festival. For as many as six days the din of the squibs filled the air, except during "quiet hours" established in negotiations between the chief of police and the headmen of the district companies. Gay workers who crowded the roofs of the brick stores with hundreds of packages of explosives at their side, abandoned yearlong restraints and pitched ignited bombs into the crowded alleys. Huge strings of firecrackers, suspended from the balconies of restaurants, temples, and company houses, emitted noise and fumes over the multitude of Chinese dressed in new blue cotton suits. "The Chinese throughout the State have been celebrating their New Year's Day with an energy which does them credit," the *Alta* observed in 1858. "The number of firecrackers burned and the quantity of noise and smoke let loose are beyond calculation," the paper marveled. [50]

The narrow streets presented the appearance of a small-scale bombardment. A pall of smoke covered the freshly cleaned quarter. The aristocracy of Chinatown donned their "costly fur and silk robes," with "black satin pants fitting tightly at the ankles," and "snow-white stockings and heavy sandals, lined or covered with silk or satin," and made their rounds of New Year's calls. Tables laden with the choicest fruits and conserves greeted these special guests. The multitudes flocked into the brilliantly lighted temples, the festively decorated theater, or the cook shops "where swarms were feasting in the highest apparent bliss." In this pandemonium, filled with the explosions of firecrackers, the din of gongs, the music of countless orchestras, and the elated ejaculations of a thousand voices, the mass of Chinese forgot the grey monotony of their work-filled days.[51]

In the spring the Ch'ing-ming, one of the three festivals of the dead, provided an outlet for pent-up emotions. In early Chinese California, the district companies, clan associations, or groups of men on this day visited the tombs of their members and friends to sweep the graves clean. In the course of two decades this "Chinese Feast of the Dead" developed an elaborate ritual. Covering a period of three or four days, the festival centered around a ceremony in the open brick enclosure, or temple, of San Francisco's Lone Mountain Cemetery.[52]

Nearly every party of Chinese visitors announced its arrival with a fusillade of firecrackers before they arranged around each grave roast pigs, oranges, bananas, pieces of fresh sugar cane, and tiny porcelain cups filled with brandy. After the worshipers had burned baskets of varicolored papers and conducted other rites, they collected the offerings again. Exchanging congratulations and laughs with their living friends, each group of visitors traveled back to a sumptuous banquet in Chinatown, the rich merchants in the courtliest hacks, followed by an "express wagon loaded with common laborers . . . while a third would be filled with women of the public class only." In the fall, the Feast of Souls and the Midautumn or Moon Festival marked similar ceremonies.[53]

In addition to these and other fixed holidays, Chinese California relied on a multitude of festivities to disrupt temporarily the monotony and restraint of work-filled days. "Where the purse will admit," Augustus W. Loomis observed in 1868, "but few legitimate occasions for feasting are allowed to pass unimproved." [54] The headman's recovery from a dangerous illness, the safe arrival of travelers, or the opening of a temple occasioned elaborate pageants. Universal gaiety and jollity surrounded weddings as well as funerals. The pompous entombment of wealthy Chinese, formally bewailed by groups of official mourners, Buddhist priests, and honored with an impressive procession, or conducted in American style with a richly trimmed mahogany coffin, first class hearse, and thirty carriages of attendants, contrasted with the feasting and mirth which followed. During fashionable nuptial ceremonies, such as the marriage between Cum Chum of the house of Lun Wo & Co. and Ah Too, or the wedding of Tom Quan of the firm of Hong Yuen & Co. to Lai Nyne, banquets, musical performances, and fireworks for one day excited Chinatown. Smaller weddings bridged the interludes between the great affairs. [55]

The pageants of holidays and ceremonies relied for staging on the available settings. They centered around temples, but included restaurants, theaters, gambling houses, opium dens, and brothels in the less ceremonious yet more popular pursuits of the holidays. In the summer of 1853 the Sze Yap Company constructed the first joss house in San Francisco. It dominated all other temples in Chinese California until the Ning Yeong Company opened a larger temple in August 1864, on Dupont Alley, on a lot in the center of the block formed by Pacific, Dupont, Broadway, and Kearny Streets, paying $4,000 for the lot, $12,000 for the construction, and the enormous sum of $16,000 for furniture and decoration. These two temples maintained their leading position among the eight joss houses existing in 1875 and the thirteen located on the Official Map of Chinatown in 1885. The California Supreme Court preserved the public character of the Buddhist rites in the spring of 1859. The justices decided in their review of John Eldridge *v.* See Yup Company that the court had no power to determine whether " 'this or that form of religious or superstitious worship — unaccompanied by acts prohibited by law — is against public policy or morals.' " [56]

Tucked away in ordinary dingy business blocks of Chinatown, the joss houses suggested only to the Chinese sojourners the splendor and magnificence of the Honam Temple or other edifices in the Pearl River Delta.[57] Several flights of narrow stairs led up to the chambers of the enthroned deities located in the top stories of the buildings to guard the idols against thieves and to insure that nothing used by human hands came above the gods. The first "Chinese church," the Sze Yap's temple, was designed by the San Francisco architect Lewis R. Townsend. Except for the "great" Chinese architect who allegedly supervised the construction of John Parrott's Granite Block in 1852, there is no record of any significant activity by oriental designers in early Chinese California.[58]

The sojourners adapted existing American structures to their cultural needs by adding elaborate balconies, paper or bronze lanterns, richly colored inscriptions, and rows of porcelain pots. Similarly, they substituted their own colorful names for the official designations of Chinatown's thoroughfares.[59] A crude brick building with a tin roof formed the joss house in Fiddletown, Amador County, an ugly adobe box constructed in the Spanish-Mexican manner housed the temple at Dutch Flat, Placer County. Wooden frame structures or log buildings served in other settlements, such as San Andreas in Calaveras County or Weaverville in Trinity County. Only the elaborate interior decoration fostered the illusion of ornate Chinese temples.[60]

Restaurants and theaters furnished the extraordinary life of Chinese California with other focal points during the hours when the religious ceremonies turned into feast days. Every restaurant, from the lowliest soup kitchen to the famous cafés of the rich and the dissolute, held its banquets. Musicians and entertainers, in ravishing, dainty garments, lent excitement to a life void of ordinary diversions. To the accompaniment of brass gong, moon guitar, Tartar fiddle, drums, and cymbals they sang operatic ballads, frequently celebrating the past glory of ancient dynasties. At the stage in which food meant less to the guests than liquor and games, the feasters drank and played and played and drank, and their expressions showed a fierceness usually hidden beneath the mask of placid docility that they assumed under regimentation.[61]

On holidays festive multitudes thronged boxes, pit, and balcony of Chinatown's theaters. Following the actors' lines, the singing, the jugglers' feats, and the music of the orchestra, visitors lost themselves in an illusionary world which their imagination built despite the contrast between the barren stage and the actors' dazzling finery. Long historical dramas seemed as endless as the audience's craving for the extension of the illusion. In such plays as "The Return of Sit Ping Quai [Hsieh P'ing-kuei]" the Chinese sojourners suffered for days the warrior's anguish, endured his hardships, basked in his fame, and finally found their way home with the hero to his virtuous wife.

The familiarity of the onloookers with the content of romances, dramas, and ballads, told and retold by storytellers, facilitated the process. The participants in the eagerly solicited world of fancy squatted on crowded benches in a plain hall. On stage Sit Ping Quai balanced on one table protected by a mighty and impassable torrent from the pursuing Princess Liufa three feet away on another. The spectators' freed imagination, however, conveniently dissolved the reality of their world which lacked similar ready escapes from a daily routine of hardship and oppression.[62]

Year in, year out, regardless of the occasion, Chinatown

provided respite from daily drudgeries. Since the set of holidays barely furnished a legitimate excuse for the enjoyment
of these escapes, their pursuit lay outside of the accepted
cycles of diversion. The visit to a gambling hall, a brothel,
or an opium den added precious hours of freedom to the
life of indentured emigrants who lacked the means for these
entertainments in their homeland. In Chinese California
they saw themselves momentarily admitted to that life of
leisure which in part had motivated them to leave their
native village in search for a fortune overseas. The dreams
of an opium smoker or the dissipations waiting in a house
of prostitution ranked second in attraction to the fascination
which a gambling table radiated.[63] Here, desperate daring
could change the course of a gambler's life with one single
stroke of luck.

Games of chance particularly attracted the men who
existed at the point of no return. Hunting for escapes from
their daily hardships, they readily took solace in a set of
simple games which combined a maximum of thrill with a
constant chance of sudden gain. With the fate of gamesters
continually hanging upon a breath, they fatalistically accepted an adverse verdict of chance. Accustomed to attribute
almost every phenomenon of nature to the intervention of
supernatural powers, the sojourners hardly questioned the
outcome of a gambling game in which chance played a
slightly greater role than it appeared to in the daily course
of their lives. Only a short step separated divination from
gambling, and the circulation of a handbook for calculating
the prices of chances and the prizes for the literary lottery
called "White Pigeon Ticket" suggested an application of the
art.[64]

Lithographs, letter sheets, and broadsides depict scenes in
Chinese gambling houses in early California. Reminiscences,
travelogues, news accounts, and official reports add color to
these contours.[65] Great numbers of silent spectators motion-

lessly observed the gamblers' moves. The voice of a richly dressed singer, the music of an accompanying orchestra, and a view of the exciting scenes compensated these onlookers for their lack of Chinese copper cash to participate in a round of fan-tan, the most popular game.[66] The tension produced by various games served one end: they furnished a sudden escape from confines and anxieties. Between two quickened heartbeats gambling offered an abrupt breath of the diluted air of freedom.

The type of game was unimportant. If somebody took the fan-tan counters away or destroyed the pie-gow [*p'ai-chiu*] blocks, the sojourners would bet on the number of seeds in an uncut orange. While merchants and professional gamblers grew steadily richer from the profits which these means of escape in Chinatown produced, the picture of the losing indentured emigrant appeared again and again. Having paid off his debts and saved for years to return to his family in China, on the eve of his departure the free man might drop into a gambling house, lose his savings in one night, and turn back, with great surface indifference, to begin a life of service again.

In the scheme of control and work Chinatown ensured the drudgery of mining company and railroad construction crews. With major commodities and supplies under their management, the merchant-creditors profited from the sojourners' very existence at a time when the debtors' labor furnished a constant return on the initial investment in indentured emigrants. The mass of lowly workers earned just enough to keep alive their hopes and guarantee their acquiescence to the system, but not enough to free themselves from it. Chinatown also gave these workers in an alien environment the illusion of home.

Chinatown and work camp fulfilled an essential role in Chinese California. However, their significance went beyond the confines of the regimented world in which the small realm of diversion provided only the background for the large domain of work. Chinatown and work camp also furnished the major contacts with the alien world that encompassed Chinese California. The vast variety of reactions to the newcomers crystallized around these vital institutions. Chinatown and work camp provoked incidents of strife and stimulated humanitarian attempts at acculturation as the Americans became aware of the sojourners in their midst.

CHAPTER VI

STRIFE

CHINATOWN and work camp precipitated California's reaction to the newcomers, provoking strife and stimulating humanitarian attempts at acculturation. In isolated mountain regions and in bustling urban centers, Californians reacted to the presence of work camps and Chinatowns with sentiments that ranged from open hostility to overt friendliness.

Both the conflict and the concord stemmed from notions underlying and permeating the structure of California society. The Chinese sojourners were another element, like the Indians, Mexicans, Europeans, and Negroes, to distort the vision of California and they were also another challenge, like all other newcomers to the United States, for the humanitarian concepts of American culture. Strife and acculturation were the opposite poles of the reaction toward the Chinese sojourners, the varied manifestations of which crystallized around work camp and Chinatown.[1] Both reactions existed side by side like the set of conflicting notions sustaining American California.

Historical studies of California or of the Chinese in the United States have sketched the general setting of, or the events leading to, the first major encounter between Americans and Chinese. Charles Howard Shinn traced the disorder in the mines to "evil-disposed" non-Anglo-Saxons while Hubert Howe Bancroft pinned the responsibility for the turmoil on "immoral" Anglo-Saxons.[2] Josiah Royce's discourse in Hegelian dialectic reduced the social struggle to moral and racial issues. He accommodated a generation that viewed "immoral" foreigners and "evil" Americans as causes of the unrest; and he provided a framework for subsequent commentators who also placed the struggle between Californians and foreigners in a purely negative setting.[3]

Mary Roberts Coolidge, in 1909, traced the development of anti-Chinese politics in California to the discontented classes. She attributed the organized antagonism against the sojourners to the "violent race prejudices and political ambitions" of Governor John Bigler.[4] Later observers of California's nativism emphasized the lack of a mature legal machinery, the absence of a core of stable citizens in the mining districts, and the want of such social restraints as family and church. Elmer Clarence Sandmeyer traced the motivation of the anti-Chinese movement in California to economic, moral and religious, and social and political shortcomings.[5] Rodman W. Paul considered the transition from the agitation regarding foreign immigrants in general "to a definite hostility towards one specific race, the Chinese, . . . natural and perhaps inevitable." [6]

Recent studies of nativism in California undermine Royce's assumption that rabble or respectable men derelict in their concern for order instigated the antiforeign actions. The efforts to stabilize California's society and economy in the years from 1849 to 1852, just before the first major clash between Americans and Chinese, suggest that nativism did not originate among dissolute men but among those possessed by and acting from a zeal for order.[7] Newspaper reports, travelogues, and reminiscences, recording the early encounters between Americans and Chinese, show that positive goals motivated the activities which led to the first major clash. The regimented Chinese miners conflicted with California's stand against slavery and posed an obstacle to the building of

the true American state. They endangered Californians' hope
for the realization of their dream about the future.

Work camp and Chinatown provide two vantage points
from which to survey the emergence of California's hostile
reaction. The regimented drudgery of Chinese miners reminded Californians of the slave labor which had troubled
them earlier. The growing Chinese quarters struck observers
as the breeding grounds of immorality which added to the
insecurity and the social disorganization brought on by
rapid physical and social mobility. Long before the filth of
Chinatown raised the ire of Californians, the working methods of Chinese miners had led to clashes between sojourners
and Americans. Long after the work camps in the Mother
Lode had been accepted, Chinatown remained a focal point
of strife.

A running debate among Americans over the nature of
their growing society was always in the background of the
encounter, while the Chinese attempts to incorporate work
camp and Chinatown into American life generally precipitated the struggle. Although the headmen of the companies
succeeded in establishing the work camp in the California
countryside, they failed to integrate Chinatown into the
settlements. The task demanded a choice between the certainty of unceasing strife over Chinatown's filth and immorality and the sacrifice of its essential function as the safety
valve of the control system. The headmen avoided that choice.
They attempted to pacify agitated Americans with token
support of the struggle against Chinatown, a maneuver which
succeeded in protecting its role. However, the strategy made
the quarter's physical and moral conditions appear a part of
the sojourners' second nature. The scheme fixed Chinatown
as the focus of perpetual strife which assumed in the eyes of
Californians the character of an inevitable struggle.

Companies of Chinese miners furnished the initial point
of discord. They raised the specter of Indians and Pacific im-

migrants, of Mexicans, Chileans, Peruvians, and Islanders, who, as lowly bondmen, had dug gold under the supervision of their masters.[8] Extravagant tales told how the heads of Chinese merchant houses in San Francisco manipulated indentured emigrants to their advantage. These stories resembled the wild rumors which earlier had accompanied the penetration of the gold region by wealthy Sonoran merchants who worked their village peons in the mines, sold their provisions profitably, and hurried back to Mexico to invest their gains in securities, while their Mexican workers were left to drift into the mining towns.[9] Hunting for work and undercutting the price of artisan labor, they foreshadowed the trickle of foot-loose and untrammeled Chinese who accumulated in the settlements.

The sight of toiling Chinese mining companies in the ravines and canyons of the Mother Lode kept alive memories of the short step that had separated the work of Pacific bondmen and masters from that of American slaves and their overlords. In the fall of 1851, the editor of the Mokelumne *Calaveras Chronicle* spotted in the vicinity of Jackson "several Chinese camps, with a population of Celestials estimated at two thousand souls." [10] The determined stand of miners on the Yuba River seemed to have been in vain. They had evicted the Texan party of General Thomas Jefferson Green and his Negro slaves from Rose Bar in July 1849, and had prohibited in their mining laws all combinations of masters and servants.[11] This contest, and similar encounters with monopolists and underlings, became meaningless in the face of the Chinese mining villages that dotted the mountain region. Chinatown and work camp negated the determined stand of the California Constitutional Convention against slavery and the presence of free Negroes.[12] The toil of the Chinese indentured emigrants relegated to the realm of empty rhetoric Representative George B. Tingley's philippic in the first legislature. The speech advocated barring from the state immigrants "with habits of life low and degraded, . . . but one degree above the beasts of the fields." [13]

The free laborers in the mines lacked the technical skill and conceptual insight to tackle the dual task of gold mining and state building. As average Americans, at the middle of the nineteenth century, they were familiar with a variety of trades and occupations. Mining, however, was not one of them. Only slowly and hesitantly did the farmers and clerks utilize in their new existence the full measure of Old and New World mining experience.[14] The rush of these miners to the unworked placers in the foothills of the Sierra Nevada was like the movement of farmers to virgin lands of the frontier. In both cases, individuals sought to carve out a livelihood under their own direction with the work of their own hands.

Accustomed to an agricultural society with slaves or free men as alternative forms of labor, the American miners superimposed standards of a free agrarian society upon their young state. They also formulated their apprehensions of the dangers threatening their dream in agrarian terms. Their arguments resembled the objections of farmers to slavery in agriculture: it rendered work dishonorable, drove free farmers from the choicest lands, which then fell into the hands of slave-owning planters. The individualistic miners dreaded competition with slave laborers or with freedmen, which they insisted would drive out free miners who demanded a higher standard of living.

William Shaw, who came from Australia to San Francisco in September 1848, and in the company of a Chinese and a Malay servant mined on the Stanislaus River, vividly recorded the American reaction to his Oriental company. The miners made the presence of his "black confederates . . . a source of complaint," he noticed, "evidently imagining them to be in a state of slavery or vassalage to us, who pocketed the fruit of their labor." Some time afterward, Shaw keenly observed, "this feeling against the coloured race rose to a pitch of exasperation." At several diggings "capitalists had hired numbers of Chinese, Cooleys, and Kanakas, to work for them." The "gang-system was very obnoxious to the Californians, and several parties of that description were abolished; the obligations and agreements entered into being cancelled and annulled by the fiat of the vox populi." [15]

A mass meeting of miners on the Mokelumne River and its tributaries on July 7, 1849, directed the "foreign task-masters and . . . men in their employ" to leave the placers.[16] The growing unrest in the mines stirred the *Alta* belatedly into action. "How can the evil of slavery," the paper thundered almost a year later, "be tolerated in the mines by the thousands of white men, of whom the habits and education of their whole lives have imparted an unconquerable hatred of the institution?" To introduce "slave labor into the mines . . . will be certain cause of violence and bloodshed," the editorial writer could predict comfortably after violence and bloodshed had ruled the day.[17]

One attempt to disentangle the problems of immigration and labor from the slavery question came from Senator Thomas Jefferson Green. The former slaveholder's Foreign Miners' Tax of 1850 aimed at exploiting rather than expelling alien laborers from the mines. The measure intended to aid American mining capitalists by blocking foreign investors through a system of indenture and taxation.[18] The ingenious device failed to pacify disillusioned miners or to fill California's bankrupt treasury. A new phase in the development of mining multiplied the difficulties of individualistic American goldseekers. The danger which Delegate Henry A. Tefft had envisioned during the debates of the Constitutional Convention now really existed. The "labor of intelligent and enterprising white men who, from the want of capital, are compelled to do their own work," no longer produced adequate returns.[19] The resulting struggle set into motion several waves of expulsions.[20] A few years later Friedrich Gerstaecker dubbed portions of the strife "The French Revolution." [21] The conflict broke up large combines of foreign laborers, but also rallied the advocates of contract labor and traders to the defense of foreigners. This was the background for the first major encounter between Californians and Chinese in 1852 when the state legislature again took up the debate whether to curtail or utilize foreign laborers.

The expulsion of foreign workers from the mines ruined the prospects of American entrepreneurs, traders, and speculators. The unrest in the mountain districts shattered the precarious unity of sentiment on which the individualistic miners aimed to build a free society. The struggle between American factions extended into the following decades the vociferous debate about the nature of California. In the middle of 1849, artisans, merchants, mule dealers, and teamsters, because of strong Mexican competition in their own enterprises, had shared the independent miners' widespread antagonism against servile laborers. Now they joined the formerly isolated exploiters of bonded labor in demanding the protection of foreign hands in the mines. While the retreat of the foreigners upset the market for foodstuffs, mining equipment, and land, the entrepreneurs in the southern mines realized that, regardless of all predictions, free American miners followed the attraction of the northern placers and failed to replace the companies of foreign laborers in the tedious dry diggings of the south. Entrepreneurs realized that only foreign laborers would work for one dollar a day and yet bring business to merchants and traders. Former exclusionists turned exploiters, and while they still agreed with the individualistic prospectors that the hordes of depraved foreign laborers endangered the Californian dream, they attempted to steer a moderate course in the waves of expulsion and to find a substitute for the lost labor force.

Docile Chinese seemed ideally suited to provide the way out of this dilemma. They complemented rather than competed with American miners. As early as 1848 a correspondent of the *Californian* suggested that "laborers on contract may be brought from China . . . , who will work faithfully for low wages," if white workers proved too expensive for agriculture.[22] On January 7, 1852, in his only annual message to the California Legislature, Governor John McDougal gave the first official endorsement to the use of Chinese newcomers in projects to settle swamps and flooded lands. He described them as "one of the most worthy classes of our newly adopted citizens — to whom the climate and the character of these lands are peculiarly suited." [23] Two years earlier, at the Monterey convention, McDougal had still wanted Negroes completely excluded from the state in order to prevent the introduction of contract labor by Southerners. He had then feared that planters would free their slaves by binding them to a contract to work in the mines.[24] Now his concern for the countryside's disorder paralleled his advocacy of law and order against the rule of the San Francisco Vigilance Committee of 1851 and explained his toleration of Chinese laborers as a means of pacifying the mining districts and solving the entrepreneurs' labor problem.[25]

A few months later another former exclusionist, perhaps also under the strain of official responsibilities, experienced a similar change in views. On March 6, 1852, Senator George B. Tingley introduced into the California Legislature a bill to legalize contracts by which Chinese laborers could sell their services for periods of ten years or less at fixed wages.[26] Unexpectedly, he fired the opening gun in the first major clash between Californians and Chinese. The dispute emerged primarily as a quarrel between groups of Americans who held diverging notions on the social and economic structure of their rising society.[27] The California debate overshadowed the part of the Chinese in the struggle. By 1859 newspaper reviews purporting to deal with Chinese sojourners merely summarized stages of the American controversy.[28]

The subject of these endless arguments, the Chinese, hardly emerged from their passive role as silent bystanders. With the same surface indifference with which they endured regimentation, they also suffered the consequences of the dispute. During the initial encounter the headmen of the Chinese district companies shunned participation in the open debate. Unfamiliar with, or distrustful of, public opinion and the role of the electorate for the protection of their interests they employed methods of persuasion similar to their customary, or businesslike way of handling other affairs. Only after these attempts had failed did they take public opinion into consideration. They then utilized the Foreign Miners' Tax as a suitable vehicle for their objective: the toleration of Chinese mining companies in the Mother Lode. While groups of Americans continued the dispute and vigorously debated problems touching on the form of their society and economy in defense of their specific interests, the headmen with a few bold maneuvers protected the work of the Chinese mining companies in the foothills of the Sierra Nevada.[29]

The life of Chinese indentured emigrants revolved about three primary objectives: to earn and to save money, to pay off the indenture, and to return home to their families in China for a life of relative ease. The structure of Chinese California and the routine of daily drudgery left no room for humanitarian principles, for tribute to a democratic way of life, or for the inclination to join as a new rivulet the stream of immigration to the United States. The success of Chinese California depended on the possibility of working hundreds of indentured emigrants in easily controlled mining companies. The interests of wealthy merchant-creditors and lowly laborers went hand in hand. They found expression in the schemes of the headmen who worked patiently to convince Californians that the presence of the Chinese benefited the state. The fight over the Tingley bill revealed the Chinese strategy.

The temper of the state foredoomed the Tingley bill to failure. The strong popular opposition to the contract labor law caught the backers of the measure by surprise. A similar assembly bill, introduced by Representative A. R. C. Peachy, had forewarned the countryside. This bill provided for a system of contract labor, under which a Chinese or Pacific Islander would sign away his services for a maximum of five years with California courts supervising the execution of the contract. On the evening of the day in mid-March when Representative Peachy's contract labor bill passed the Assembly, an indignation meeting of the citizens of Sacramento warned "its authors, aiders and supporters in the Legislature that they would be followed to their political graves by the public opprobrium or dissatisfaction." Popular sentiment was overwhelming. The newspapers followed it, and "with a most liberal display of patriotism . . . opened in full cry" against Tingley's bill. Only a few politicians or editors cared to counter the general trend. On April 12, the Senate accepted a motion to postpone consideration of the bill indefinitely by a vote of eighteen to two, its author accounting for half the yea votes. On the same day Senator Paul K. Hubbs introduced a bill "to prevent involuntary servitude." [30]

The strong opposition to the contract labor bills surprised the editorial writer of the *Alta* who had originally anticipated popular indifference to the measure. "If the expressions of opinion which have been made in different portions of the state be an index to the public sentiment," he concluded later, "there can be no doubt that the contract law is generally condemned." In earlier editorials, the *Alta* had given measured approval to the project. Attempts to use Chinese labor in California, the paper stated, had always failed because of "the ease with which all labor contracts could be set aside, the temptations of the mines, and the impossibility of coercion." In the past, labor in California had held the whip hand over capital and discouraged speculative investment. With the number of immigrants now reaching a new height and thereby helping to balance the supply of labor and the demands of capital, the *Alta* cautioned that the "permanent results" of the Tingley bill might not be "of that estimable character which should highly recommend it as a true system for a country like ours." [31]

The *Alta*'s qualified endorsement distinguished its comments from those of the other journals. The San Francisco *Picayune* strongly condemned the "movement . . . to introduce among us a system of modified slavery resembling Mexican peonism." Is "any one so simple," the paper queried, "as to doubt that capitalists will avail themselves of its provisions to import crowds of cheap laborers here to work the mines, . . . to build up a large monopoly, to the injury of men of small means, who do their own work?" The Sacramento *Union* viewed the bill as a possible source for "perpetual riots and difficulties." [32] These frontal assaults silenced such proponents of contract labor as the Stockton *Republican* which suggested the use of Chinese to reclaim tule lands for the cultivation of tea and rice. A year earlier, another Stockton newspaper, concerned about the decline of business in the southern mines, had also valiantly defended the interests of entrepreneurs hit hard by expulsionists, while the citizens of this gateway to the southern mines had been instrumental in the repeal of the first Foreign Miners' Tax.[33]

A vigorous minority report summarized the sentiments of the diggings. Philip A. Roach submitted his views to the Senate nineteen days after the introduction of the Tingley bill. The senator considered free labor the foundation of California's society and the chief hope for its future. His description of the rivalry of white labor with Asians possessing an abnormally low standard of living in American eyes reiterated the fears of delegates at Monterey, who had warned the convention that the economic competition of unpaid slave labor in the gold region would drive out free working miners with a higher living standard.[34] Roach's condemnation of the Foreign Miners' Tax of 1850 as "unjust, unconstitutional, and discriminating" marked his report as an eloquent expression of the independent spirit of the countryside which professed to welcome individual foreigners as free miners but rejected companies of foreign laborers as an attempt to introduce bondage and slavery into California and to give "to capital *the hand and heart of labor.*"

While portions of Roach's report rang true to pioneer declarations against slavery and monopoly, other sections advanced beyond these general arguments and appraised particularly California's labor problem. He recognized the entrepreneurs' plight and accepted the introduction of contract laborers for special projects, such as draining swamps, cultivating rice, raising silk, or planting tea, sugar, cotton, and tobacco, "provided they are excluded from citizenship." Underlying this concession was the optimistic assumption that it would be possible to admit bondmen to special occupations on particular lands without damage to laborers elsewhere. However, Roach did not "want to see Chinese or Kanaka carpenters, masons, or blacksmiths, brought here in swarms under contracts, to compete with our own mechanics, whose labor is as honorable . . . as the pursuits" of "learned professions."

With Chinese contract laborers specifically the report dealt only in passing. Senator Roach warned of the dangers of racial mixture and the threat of pagan beliefs to American institutions. He argued that most nations granted reciprocal equality to Americans. But as "regards the Chinese, we are not permitted to enter within their walls." He took the connivance of Chinese officials in the opium trade as an indication that they would send, "if it be to their advantage, . . . every malefactor in the prisons . . . here as contract laborers." A government, "as skilled in tact as is that of the Celestial Empire, could not fail to perceive the advantage of permitting its criminals to emigrate." [35]

During the following weeks miners' meetings restated these arguments. The repercussions of the debates in the legislature and the press shook the gold region with a series of incidents which expelled Chinese mining companies from the diggings. Miners of other nationalities also suffered from the agitation. Even in 1853 "Mexican bandits," not Chinese serfs, were the target of Californians. The waves of expulsion differed from district to district and group to group. Traders, freighters, and transporters continued to show their interest in the presence of the Chinese. At the height of the agitation, in the middle of April, the *Governor Dana* kept transporting Chinese free of charge from Sacramento to Marysville in company with other passengers to promote the development of Butte County. Yet the same county was the scene of several incidents, among them the row at Atchinson's Bar in which thirty Americans "beautifully whipped" a hundred and fifty Chinese. In September, at the Miners' Convention at Jamestown in Tuolumne County, the delegates from Columbia, Shaw's Flat, and Springfield "voted to retain slave labor in the mines." [36]

Senator Roach's report embodied the basic arguments in the subsequent strife between opponents and defenders of the Chinese. The sojourners undermined the foundations of free society, degraded labor, threatened the tranquillity of the mines, encouraged monopolies, and endangered the California dream. The desire for the rapid development of the state's economy, necessitating a large force of cheap labor, had set off this initial debate about the presence of the Chinese. The specific question of contract labor quickly broadened into the problem of Chinese immigration. Four days after the senate had tabled the contract labor bills, the assembly recorded its opposition to the Chinese in a report of the Committee on Mines and Mining Interests which foresaw the time "when absolute prohibition of entry will be necessary for our own protection." The committee recommended calling the attention of Congress to the problem and instructing "our own Representatives . . . to seek a remedy at the hands of the Federal Government by proper treaty provisions . . . determining here at home to exercise the right of our State sovereignty, and protect ourselves should necessity demand." [37]

The clamor for outright exclusion of the Chinese completed the array of goals which emerged during the first encounter. Over several decades a large variety of measures sought to bring about these ends. Gubernatorial messages, state laws, and decisions of the State Supreme Court hardly approximated the pronounced aims. Popular action only temporarily secured the tranquillity of the countryside. Advocates of human rights, missionaries, and vociferous commercial interests joined the early proponents of contract labor in their defense of the Chinese. The decline in trade with China, which accompanied the demand of exclusionists in 1852, persuaded the Assembly Committee on Mines and Mining Interests as early as March 1853, to reverse its previous opposition to the Chinese. Two years later the receipts from the sale of Foreign Miners' Licenses, purchased almost exclusively by the Chinese, had gained an importance for the state and county treasuries which forced exclusionists to a more moderate position. In April 1855, one attempt to restrict the influx of Chinese by some other means than the Foreign Miners' Tax failed when the California Supreme Court declared unconstitutional a law which set a head tax of fifty dollars on the importation of all persons "who cannot become citizens." [38]

The participants in the debate for nearly two decades continued to rely on the set of arguments which emerged in the first major encounter between Americans and Chinese. New issues entered the dispute in the 1860's. The emancipation of the slaves, the development of particular labor problems in the South and East after the Civil War, the Burlingame Treaty, the completion of the Transcontinental Railroad, and California's increased clamor for federal aid in its struggle with the Chinese question projected the old arguments into a nationwide setting. The intricacies of national politics, which until the late 1860's had played no major role in California party politics, then added new dimensions to the dispute. The formation of the People's Protective Union in 1859, the rioting of San Francisco laborers against the Chinese infiltration of specific industries, the activity of the Anti-Coolie Association, and the work of the Chinese Protective Society all were part of the trend.[39]

On the surface the initial encounter was a discussion between groups of Americans over the presence of Chinese in California. The subjects of the debate rarely entered the fray with their own arguments. In most cases the Chinese endured placidly whatever consequences the debate produced. In some instances they successfully encountered force with cunning. Occasionally they resisted attack outright and prevailed. Under duress they generally vacated their old mining claims and searched out new diggings in much the same way as they submitted to the rigid regimentation of their bosses or died at the hands of highwaymen, robbers, rioters, or lawmen.[40]

In general, regular courts and law officers dealt with the crimes of Chinese thieves, robbers, and murderers which had in themselves frequently the potential for mob action.[41] The perpetual strife, however, made the Chinese ready victims of whim, greed, and cruelty. The Orientals' inability to testify in court facilitated the brutish pranks of city hood-lums. The industry of docile Chinese miners sustained avari-cious tax collectors who let off Chinese with a payment of two dollars instead of four if they did not insist on a receipt.[42] Vagabonds and robbers plundered the Chinese of their sav-ings. The physical affronts ranged from queue-cutting, re-ported as early as February 1851, to the Los Angeles riot which took the lives of eighteen or nineteen Chinese in October 1871.[43]

In part these incidents were the work of unruly men in an unstable society who maltreated anybody as long as they felt stronger than their victim. In part they represented the high-waymen's awareness that plundering a Chinese camp re-quired less daring and involved a smaller risk than holding up a stage coach. In part the encounters thrived on the ex-tension of the frontier spirit which found right and virtue on the side of the stronger fists and faster gun. The incident of the wild steer which raged through the streets of San Fran-cisco in October 1860, rushed the crowd, singled out a Chi-nese, "ran at him full tilt and knocked him down, cutting his head severely," symbolized the course of other clashes.[44] However, from this variety of incidents emerged no Cali-fornian who killed Chinese as methodically as did Three-Fingered Jack Manuel Garcia in the saga of Joaquin Muri-eta.[45]

The fabricator of the Joaquin legend, who designed Gar-cia's peculiar character trait and delineated its consequences in detail, belonged on his father's side to the only racial group on the California scene which consistently showed an inveterate hatred of all Chinese.[46] The polyglot invaders of the sleeping Bucolia evinced a multitude of reactions to the Chinese newcomers. Only with the passage of the Civil Rights Bill did Negro spokesmen in California turn against the Chinese in their newspaper, the San Francisco *Elevator*. "As there is only one step from the sublime to the ridiculous," the *Alta* commented when the *Elevator* called for the prohibition of Chinese immigration in 1866, "so the slave need not travel far to become a tyrant." But the debate in the *Elevator*'s columns in 1869 showed that among Negroes little agreement existed in regard to such an extreme demand.[47] Negroes and Chinese frequented the same dance halls. The Chinese also found other groups sharing their life. Americans entered their employ, Germans occupied their dormitories, tents, and log cabins, Frenchmen sat at their tables, and Mexicans guided their pack horses through the Sierra. All these nationalities intermarried with the Chinese.

California Indians, however, manifested nothing but hostility. The Maidu, the Diggers in contemporary jargon, volunteered their services to tax collectors and tracked down those Chinese miners who had gone into hiding at the first sight of the officials. The Indians, aware of their weakness before the dominant groups, rigorously rejected the even weaker Orientals, and frequently robbed and killed them. At the great Indian Council in Nevada County in the fall of 1854, King Weimah, the head chief of the Grass Valley Indians, objected to his removal to a reservation as long as the Chinese were permitted to remain free in his country.[48] At the time of the council, however, a set of devices already afforded the Chinese in the gold country some protection. They had emerged as result of the Chinese schemes during the initial debate.

The first statement of the struggle purporting to come from the Chinese side received the plaudit of leading California newspapers. Published on April 30, 1852, in reply to John Bigler's special message to the legislature on April 23, the open letter's opposition to Governor Bigler automatically guaranteed its favorable reception by a set of vituperative editors.[49] Editorials, letters to the editors, and a merchant memorial to the legislature took up the cause of the Chinese. Several journals jumped readily at a ghost writer's defense of the Chinese as a splendid excuse to harass California's chief executive. John Bigler suffered the misfortune of encountering hostile chroniclers during his lifetime and unsympathetic historians after his death. However, the image of the scheming politician, capitalizing on the individualistic miners' "blind nativism" and innate hostility to foreigners, no longer explains the events.[50]

Newspaper reports kept the rapidly increasing arrival figures of Chinese sojourners constantly before the public during the debate over the contract labor law in the spring of 1852.[51] They made the governor's demand "to check this tide of Asiatic immigration" more a reflection of the "lively interest among our citizens on the subject" and less an attempt to secure his re-election in the state campaign of 1852 on the strength of anti-Chinese pronouncements.[52] His opponents quickly utilized the Chinese answer to his message to heckle and ridicule the governor. Mockery and derision lowered Bigler's status in New York, London, and Hong Kong.[53] At the moment they failed to affect his position in California.

If his followers among squatters and miners read the "Letter of the Chinamen to his Excellency, Gov. Bigler" at all, they may have wondered about argument and style. In composition and reasoning it resembled more a missionary's sermon and a lawyer's brief than a document which could have come from those Chinese miners whom they knew, or the Chinese merchant princes whom they had seen from afar. The Chinese authorship of the letter is doubtful. Tong K. Achick and Hab Wa, whose names appear at the end of the document, most likely furnished only the factual information on which the reply was based.[54] An appeal to the general public through an open letter fell outside Chinese practice. Leaders of the merchant community in San Francisco may have been connected with this public reply to the governor's message, or with a second memorial, signed by Chun Aching and Tong K. Achick and published on June 6, 1852.[55] Their hearts, however, backed Tong K. Achick's mission to Sacramento to restore the Chinese sojourners again to Governor Bigler's favor.

The envoy of the "Chinese Committee," itself more characteristic of the customary Chinese procedure than an open letter to the general public, presented the governor with "shawls of rarest pattern, rolls of silk of the costliest texture, and some . . . seventy handkerchiefs of the choicest description." He submitted a "votive offering . . . to appease the stern divinity that rules the destinies of the Celestials in California," the editorial writer of the *Herald* caustically remarked. The outcome of the mission revealed the chasm which separated the hostility of the countryside from the pleasantry of politicians. Although Tong K. Achick was amicably wined and dined at the governor's mansion, his friends and the Chinese in the mining districts were made aware of the shortcomings of the customary policy.[56]

The intermezzo furnished the *Herald* with opportunities to harass John Bigler about the disposition of the presents. Subsequent to the mission, Colonel James E. Zabriskie, a Sacramento lawyer, sued Tong K. Achick and Sam Wo & Co. for a fee of five hundred dollars for acting as go-between for the Chinese and the governor. The trial threw light on the manipulations which accompanied the first Chinese memorial. The remonstrance was signed by Hab Wa and Tong K. Achick, but edited by Colonel Zabriskie, and scrutinized by William E. Cornwall, the governor's private secretary. The executive mansion nevertheless turned down the letter because of its immoderate language. In a reply to the *Herald* the Colonel rejected the implication of several newspapers that he "wrote the letters addressed by the Chinese to the Governor." He disclaimed his authorship in terms which made it quite certain that none of the letters had actually been written by Chinese.[57] The publication of the letters in pamphlet form, for distribution in the mines, misled some people at the time and students of the subject in a more recent day into taking the products as genuine Chinese arguments, "reasonable in tone and admirably stated." Only later did the heads of the Chinese companies use open letters to remonstrate with the governor, the legislature, and the people of California, Congress, and the President of the United States.[58]

The testimony of the heads of the Chinese Four Houses before a sympathetic Committee on Mining and Mining Interests in 1853 revealed the nature of the leading Chinese merchants' concern about the wave of expulsion in the mining districts more accurately than the lofty humanitarian sentiments embodied in open letters affixed with Chinese signatures. The restoration of what Governor Bigler had called the tranquillity of the mines was their chief objective.[59] To achieve that end the Chinese spokesmen felt it necessary to bring "the people in the mining counties . . . to believe that the presence of the Chinese among them was a benefit to the country." They dwelt, therefore, only briefly on the growing tendency of the mining counties to ban Chinese from testifying in court, which Chief Justice Hugh C. Murray belatedly sanctioned in 1854 with his opinion that Chinese testimony, like the testimony of Negroes and Indians, was inadmissible as evidence for or against a white man.[60]

The heads of the Four Houses instead took pains to suggest to the committee an increase of the Foreign Miners' Tax if necessary. They recommended collecting the fee as part of the counties' revenue "to create . . . friends among the tax paying citizens . . . or those who would at least be willing to tolerate their people." The Four Houses offered to provide the county tax collector with an interpreter who would "use the authority of the superintendents of the several houses to make the Chinese . . . pay . . . his taxes."

Anxious about the discipline in their mining companies, they worried about the effect on the rate of wages in the event the legislature passed a law requiring those defaulting their miners' tax to perform public labor. Just "as soon and as fast as it can be done without causing great losses," the headmen promised to arrange a more equal distribution of Chinese miners and to re-establish the population balance in the restless counties of the gold region.

With the quick restoration of normal working conditions in the Mother Lode as their principal goal, the headmen assured the committee they would "exert much influence" to "prevent too large an emigration from China" to California. "After our representation last spring," they emphasized, "the emigration ceased almost entirely for many months, and now has only partially revived." [61] Several newspapers at the time had recorded the dispatch of these messages to China but had given no clue to the arguments of those letters which suddenly halted the influx of Chinese. [62] The Hong Kong *China Mail*, publishing Governor Bigler's statement and letters from Chinese in San Francisco to their countrymen, reported that Chinese California's leading men posted a placard in Hong Kong. The handbill stated that Americans had lost their earlier respect for the Chinese because of the increased number of newcomers during the last two years, "many of whom were in filthy state, and on that account were mocked by foreigners and [made] their countrymen ashamed of them." [63]

The strategy of the heads of the Four Houses, outlined in 1853 during the hearings of the Committee of Mines and Mining Interests in San Francisco, succeeded in its broad objectives. The revenue from the Foreign Miners' Tax, paid almost exclusively by Chinese, provided much of the needed regular income for a great number of mining counties, supporting the headmen's assumption that the payment of the tax would ensure Chinese mining companies a measure of toleration which the labor companies of Latins and Europeans had failed to gain. Their position as taxpayers guaranteed Chinese miners a modicum of protection of life and property, and ensured their continued access to the diggings. That the money from the Orientals was welcome, indeed counted upon, is attested to by the alarm with which the mining counties viewed the railroad construction camps in the 1860's. These camps, and the advance of the mines into the Rocky Mountains threatened to draw off Chinese, and thus deplete revenues. Even the collectors of the Foreign Miners' Tax at times "accommodated their demands to the ability" of the companies.[64] The realistic appraisal of the countryside's temper by the headmen preserved the work camp as an institution while abstract arguments about justice, humanity, and the dignity of labor continued to agitate the opponents and defenders of the bondmen.

With the gradual acceptance of the work camp, Chinatown was left as the focal point of strife. Californians initially observed the growth of Chinatown with pride for it came into view almost naturally as part of the bustling port or the rapidly developing supply centers in the interior. The exotic quarter added another gem to California's crown.[65] Favorable comments about Chinese industry and frugality continued to accompany adverse reaction to the development of a distinct Chinese settlement in the heart of San Francisco. The Grand Jury Report for the December term, 1853, regretted finding "a disposition on the part of some inconsiderate persons to annoy, persecute and maltreat inoffensive and industrious Chinamen." The actions of city officials and the complaints of residents directed attention to a series of distinct grievances around which the strife between American communities and Chinatown revolved.[66]

These charges originally encompassed the whole range of tensions which rose from the accelerated growth of San Francisco. They ranged from the laments of bachelors about Chinese washermen to the Recorder's complaints about the problem of administering oaths to feuding Orientals. They covered the Chief Engineer's difficulties with sanitation and fire fighting, and the irritation of residents at hordes of Chinese bathing naked in the back of company houses, "rendering it impossible for the female portion of the families adjacent thereto to have ingress to or egress from their houses, or to remain at their windows." [67] The years reduced the accusations to two basic indictments: the living habits of the Chinese endangered San Francisco's physical health, the vices threatened the moral character of the city. These charges stimulated waves of reform which sought to tackle some of the problems leading to a concentration of filth and prostitution, with crowded residents and gambling visitors, in Chinatown.

The arrival of shiploads of dying Chinese newcomers, another fire endangering the city's growth, reports about the spread of a cholera epidemic around the world and of leprosy in the Chinese quarter, reform groups threatening the tranquillity of municipal corruption, or attempts to erase San Francisco's immorality by purifying Chinatown — these and other calamities, real and imagined, brought on newspaper exposés, investigations, official reports, and court trials. A constant deterioration of the city's affairs seemed to accompany each local catastrophe.[68] High-sounding measures and radical solutions aimed primarily at pacifying the suddenly aroused collective conscience of the city. The re-education of the sojourners to San Francisco standards of living or the relocation of Chinatown in the sand hills surrounding the sprawling town were gigantic undertakings which rapidly exhausted the momentum of each short-lived burst of indignation. Every attempt to alter Chinatown merely impressed deeper on the quarter the stamp of the "rankest outgrowth of human degradation . . . upon this continent," as the report of the Special Committee of the Board of Supervisors

labeled Chinatown in the 1880's.[69] During two decades of
strife Californians came to accept the conditions of Chinatown and regard them as inseparable from the nature of its
inhabitants.

A set of incidents in the 1850's illustrated the emergence of
Chinatown as a constant source of strife. The "fearful mortality" which decimated the Chinese emigrants on the *Libertad* and the *Challenge* during their passage in the summer
of 1854, filled San Francisco with alarm at the possible threat
to the city's health. The arrival of the ships and the quaran-
tine of ailing survivors on Goat Island (Yerba Buena Island)
in the Bay suddenly concentrated public attention on the
modes and conditions of living in the Chinese Quarter. The
disaster among the newcomers had been preceded by newspaper references to the filth and stench in Chinatown. Reports of the spread of the cholera "with alarming rapidity
all over the Western continent" heightened San Francisco's
anxiety about "these offensive dens" furnishing "material
for a sweeping epidemic." The agitation also increased the
old concern over the fire hazard which the wooden Chinese
houses and their primitive cooking facilities represented.
Petitions and letters to the editors of the local journals kept
before the public eye a memorial by Dr. William Rabe to
the Board of Assistant Aldermen "in relation to the Chinese
and their filthy quarters." It initiated the second stage of the
strife.

The memorial inspired members of the Common Council
to a flight of oratory which "left as much light on the question
as before." The Board of Assistant Aldermen asked its Committee on Health and Police together with the memorialist
to investigate the problem. Within a week the group produced a report which described the "different localities
owned by the various Chinese companies" as "the filthiest
places that could be imagined." The investigators found
houses "with hundreds of Chinamen . . . crowded to ex-

cess," who cooked on the floor, without stoves or chimneys, "in a manner similar to our savage Indians." Emphasizing that "these people come here only as hirelings to five . . . companies . . . to die when they cannot serve their task-masters any more . . . , that the women . . . are the most degraded prostitutes, and that the . . . sole enjoyment of the male population is gambling . . . ," and knowing the sojourners "to be foreign slaves to foreign masters, governed by force and religious dread, and kept in terror by a secret society called the 'Triad'," the Committee stamped the Chinese an "unmitigated and wholesale nuisance." Inflamed by the evidence, the investigators recommended a memorial to the legislature and the "immediate expulsion of the whole Chinese race from the city, or at least their removal outside the more inhabited line of streets." However, doubting the Council's legal authority to enact such sweeping measures, they advocated a series of ordinances which required "that the fire laws be vigilantly enforced; that the police and health regulations be rigidly adhered to; and that the Chinese companies be requested . . . to take their immigrants and sick countrymen beyond the limits of the city."

A meeting of a "large number of the most respectable Chinese residents" initiated the third stage of the struggle. A-hing, a San Francisco merchant, presided, representatives of the "five great companies" graced the assembly, Charles Carvalho interpreted, and William Howard, the publisher of the *Golden Hills' News*, acted as secretary, furnishing the Common Council with a report which would have been a credit to any town meeting on the eastern seaboard. The Chinese defense embodied ready promises to alleviate the shortcomings, gave evidence of good intentions blocked by selfish Chinese or white men, and attempted to direct the reform spirit to the gigantic tasks of prostitution and gambling which promised to slow down the movement effectively. The meeting resolved that the five companies erect a hospi-

tal outside the city limits within one month, that "all Chinamen . . . take immediate steps to have their premises
cleared," that "the different buildings kept as boarding
houses by the companies . . . be cleaned and renovated,
and that any excess of boarders injurious to health be immediately removed," and that all fireplaces and kitchens be
fireproofed. The group asked for the appointment of an
inspector by the City Council to enforce these steps so that
"the innocent may not suffer with the guilty," and informed
the Council that a great number of Chinese houses had paid
and still paid one dollar per week "to one Cross, whom they
believe to be a policeman, . . . to clean their . . . quarters," and one more dollar "weekly for protection." The
meeting "respectfully requested" the Council "to suppress
the Chinese houses of ill-fame, and gambling houses," which
the group "considered a great grievance to the Chinese residents."

Disputes of the City Council and the Chinese Committee
filled the final phase of this encounter. They centered around
the working of the ordinance and the realization of the
promises made at the height of the agitation. The measures
brought only minor relief from the problem. The weeks
"when there was some little excitement . . . on the subject
of cholera and . . . the filthy condition" of "these dens of
corruption" had passed. Nothing remained for the editorial
writer of the *Alta* but to regret that "decided action could
not have been . . . put in force." New disturbances agitated the city. On October 7, 1854, Alderman Henry Meiggs
escaped in the bark *America* after the discovery of his extensive forgeries which upset the community.[70] Established interests soon prevailed in favor of the old conditions. Real
estate owners and sublessors, profiting heavily from Chinese
rentals, were a formidable obstacle to all attempts to relo-
cate Chinatown.[71] Variations of this pattern characterized
the struggle over Chinatown's filth for decades to come.

Meanwhile there was a running battle over prostitution. At times the crusade bore aspects of a carnival as when the fire companies of several towns directed their hoses at Chinese brothels "to sweep them clean." [72] A multitude of conflicting interests distorted the dividing line separating the struggling parties. District companies fought tongs over the control of the traffic in Chinese females while San Francisco lawyers battled municipal officials over the rights of procurers and prostitutes. Accounts of murders and kidnapings, street fights and assassinations, escapes and suicides, extortions, and trials peopled with perjurers and false witnesses spiced the endless stream of monotonous reports about the arrests of Chinese prostitutes. Charged with tapping upon the window glass to attract prospective customers, the women regularly failed to appear in court and forfeited their bail of five dollars. By the summer of 1859 the constant struggle had driven the Chinese women "from their former abodes on the public streets and compelled them to reside in alleys and by-streets, away from the public gaze," only to initiate the new phase of Chinese prostitution with highbinders, special policemen, blackmailers, immigration officials, ward politicians, mission workers, and bagnios of slave girls.[73]

Chinatown remained for decades the major center of strife between Californians and Chinese. As a result of a changing economy, other fields of employment took over the function which the mining camp had originally fulfilled. Railroad construction, agriculture, and cigar making absorbed companies of Chinese laborers. Others became house servants, shoemakers, and textile workers. With the shifts in the areas of employment, Chinatown gained significance beyond its role as safety valve of the control system. Attracted by new fields of work, increasing numbers of Chinese swarmed into its teeming quarters and added to its old problems. Compressed within narrow confines, filth and immorality persisted, endangering the health and virtue of the growing state, and they soon came to be regarded by Americans as part of the sojourners' second nature. While precise grievances had caused the original clashes, Californians now viewed their struggle as an inevitable and perpetual conflict. Yet by extending American culture to the Chinese, they also responded compassionately to the suffering humanity in their midst.

CHAPTER VII

ACCULTURATION

CALIFORNIA'S encounter with the regimentation of work camp and the sufferings of Chinatown inspired a series of humanitarian endeavors to expose the Chinese sojourners to the liberating influences of American culture. There were two major aspects to the process of acculturation which paralleled the waves of strife, the response to the humanitarian challenge of hordes of downtrodden newcomers and the Chinese reaction to the strange world which they encountered.

The goals of the Californians and the Chinese differed. The former attempted to extend the blessings of American culture to all Chinese as an answer to the challenge of their humanitarian concepts. The latter ignored the overtures which had little significance for men seeking to make and save money quickly, to pay off their debts, and to rejoin their families. They had left home and entered into a life of bondage in defense of the tenets of their culture. Consequently they rejected values which undermined the meaning of their plight. Most of them merely accepted such products of American culture as hats and shoes; a few adopted whatever promised to bring them closer to their aim.

These discordant goals predetermined the ultimate measure of accomplishment. The growing interest of Americans about China and of the Chinese about California was an incidental result. Californians, inspired by the universal message of the American democratic creed, aimed at reaching all Chinese within the boundaries of their commonwealth.

While their venture fell far short of success in their own state, at times they unhesitatingly sought to embrace *the* Chinese *in toto*. This urge brought about an increasing preoccupation with contemporary developments in the Chinese Empire and in the young field of sinology. In the same way, the gold fever of the Pearl River Delta stimulated Chinese attempts to learn more about California life. It produced not only a local gold rush into hills around Canton in imitation of the California experience, but also a demand for broadsides and maps describing the chances of success in the California Golden Mountain.[1]

Efforts to bring the newcomers into contact with American culture had a large basis of support. The discouraging results of organized drives, sometimes viewed as outright failures in the debate over missionary work, predisposed disillusioned Californians to view the attempt to bring the Chinese into the realm of American culture as hopeless. Yet there were significant results. The discovery that the sojourners were individual human beings aided solitary Chinese in their struggle to break away from the confines of their regimented world and facilitated a modification of their goal. The new outlook that drove home the advantages of acculturation to individual Chinese, added fresh incentive to Californian humanitarian endeavors, and provided the foundation for a measure of good feeling which tended to soften the strife of the 1870's. Its effect on Chinese and Americans revived the process of acculturation when the Chinese problem extended to the national scene.

Philanthropists, missionaries, public officials, and clergymen aimed to draw the sojourners into the realm of American culture. Compassion and enlightened self-interest motivated the work, which was sustained by the concepts of America's destiny and Christian charity. The "China boys will yet vote at the same school and bow at the same altar as our countrymen," the *Alta* predicted on May 12, 1851.

"A young Chinese community will grow up in our mountains," the editor speculated six days later, "so that it is possible in a few years that the Hon. Tchang Whang, Senator from Yuba county, will introduce a resolution into the State legislature, providing for the building of a bridge connecting the Sierra Nevada with the Chinese wall." [2]

In the absence of larger social organizations in the unstable gold rush society, church groups guided the attempts to make the Chinese Americans. The role of the churches grew more prominent as more denominations and missionary societies took part in these organized drives; and that also obscured the broader basis of the ventures.[3] The participation of wide segments of the population in these efforts exposed the entire state to the feeling of futility which resulted from the failure of their endeavors when evaluated against high-sounding aims. The feeling of futility restrained Californians from additional organized efforts until the movement of Chinese into the South and East provided a national basis for the problem.

The California Presbytery, the Presbyterian Board of Foreign Missions in New York, and the Reverend William Speer began the missionary work among the Chinese in California. The Board had sent Speer west in answer to a call from the California Presbytery. He and his wife, the former Elizabeth B. Ewing, arrived at San Francisco on November 6, 1852. This missionary's zeal, his talents as writer and lecturer, and the sketches of sympathetic chroniclers have obliterated the other elements involved. Yet his struggle to establish a Chinese mission church in San Francisco revealed the broader foundation on which the movement rested. A printed charter stressed the wider aspects of the work in its title, "Form of Incorporation of the Chinese Mission For The State Of California, under the charge of the Rev. William Speer, Missionary of the Board of Foreign Missions of the Presbyterian Church in the United States of America." [4]

In his first report from San Francisco, William Speer emphasized that he had "been greeted . . . by persons of all denominations, with great cordiality." A "main interest is taken," he observed, "by the mass of the community in the purposes of my mission." He preached about his task in two churches and addressed the Methodist Conference while several newspapers, "one of them the Methodist organ, . . . published favorable notices." During the initial year of his work Speer encountered "opposition to the mission being permanently Presbyterian." We have had, he informed the Board in New York, "to be more slow + prudent in collecting funds on account of this feeling." The trustees of the Chinese Mission, "composed of Gentlemen from the various evangelical denominations . . . , a majority of whom are from the Presbyterian and Congregational Churches," in later years continued to give evidence for the broad basis of the mission work.[5]

One of the supporters of the Mission remonstrated in November 1853, against the effort of the Presbyterian Board in New York to tighten its control. His letter emphasized the concern of Californians for the mission work regardless of their religious views. Before he came to San Francisco in 1850, Thomas C. Hambly recalled, "and constantly since public opinion was open, active, and earnest for the establishment of a Chinese Mission." In the winter of 1851 the Presbyterian elder himself conducted a bible class for Chinese converts. "With few exceptions nobody seemed to care," he emphasized, "what denomination should first occupy the ground." Even members of his own church favored an independent organization. "Some of these," Hambly explained the attitude, "had been brought up in Congregational churches and had no attachment to Presbyterianism, but from early impressions a strong inclination for voluntary independent associations. These men," the San Francisco attorney insisted, "not only subscribed liberally but labored actively." All denominations participated in the collection of funds, "and perhaps a majority . . . of the amount was obtained from those of no denomination."

Hambly explained San Francisco's urge for an independent Chinese mission. "There is a general repugnance here among all classes," he reasoned, "to being controlled from 'home' as the older states are called." Indeed two months earlier, a letter to the *Alta* had strongly attacked the arrangement and urged San Franciscans not to leave "the management of the Institution . . . to a board . . . thousands of miles away." It is "generally considered," the Presbyterian elder conceded now, "that we are . . . regarded as a restless, uneasy, reckless, speculating people . . . in whose hands nothing can be trusted." Californians, on the other hand, he argued, are inclined to be self-sufficient, prompt, and arrogant. Their state of mind, he concluded, instilled Californians in general with an active concern for the newcomers.[6]

Actually San Franciscans had tackled the task of Chinese acculturation for the first time three years earlier, when a shipment of missionary tracts dispatched by the agent of the American Board of Commissioners for Foreign Missions at Canton reached San Francisco in August 1850. The *Alta* promptly suggested distributing the pamphlets to the newcomers at a public ceremony in the Plaza. The mayor, the "acting Chinese consul," and several clergymen rose immediately to the occasion and conducted the ceremony, witnessed by "quite an assemblage of citizens and several ladies." Trusting Norman Assing's abilities as interpreter implicitly, none of the dignitaries hesitated to address the "China boys."

The newcomers, "dressed in their native holiday suits, with their pigtails nicely braided, . . . presented a perfectly neat and singularly picturesque appearance." When Reverend T. Dwight Hunt, pastor of the First Congregational Church, startled the Chinese with a discourse on life after death, "the idea of the existence of a country where the

China boys would never die made them laugh quite heartily."
In the face of the meeting's obvious success Californians
ignored the finer points of Christian theology. In the prevailing enthusiasm the *Alta* had turned the Reverend Albert
Williams into an old China hand until the pastor of the
First Presbyterian Church informed the paper that "the fact
of a residence in the country and an acquaintance with the
language . . . should be credited to S. Wells Williams," the
author of the first major American study on China published
in 1848.[7]

Public spectacles furnished additional opportunities to
attract the newcomers to symbols of American culture. The
rites commemorating the funeral of President Zachary Taylor opened the round of pageants. The festivities included
regular holidays, such as the Fourth of July and Washington's
Birthday, as well as extraordinary spectacles, such as the celebration of California's admission into the Union, Henry
Clay's funeral obsequies in 1852, the Atlantic Cable Jubilee
in 1858, and, on April 19, 1865, the ceremony following the
assassination of Abraham Lincoln. On the last occasion every
building in San Francisco occupied by Chinese, "from the
temples and the finest mercantile houses to the humblest
washhouse," was "draped in mourning." [8]

Very soon, however, the shallowness of these attempts to
bring the sojourners into contact with outward manifestations of democracy became obvious. The fervor of Californians vanished like the patience with which Chinese had
repeatedly lent an exotic touch to the parades. The general
enthusiasm gave way to the realization that the sojourners'
goal kept the manifest blessings of the American way from
gaining significance in their life.

Although these spontaneous attempts failed to bring the
newcomers under the influence of American culture, the sojourners' misery and paganism continued to challenge California's conscience and zeal. Individual ministers and Fred-

erick Buel, the agent of the American Bible Society, had already attempted to live up to their obligation, and missionary enterprises of other denominations sprang into existence after the emergence of Speer's mission under the auspices of the Presbyterian Board.[9] The groups now rallied in the belief that Providence had placed the Chinese on California soil to be converted and to return to China as native witnesses of the Christian faith.[10] These undertakings fell far short of their goal and as a result led large numbers of Californians to view Chinese acculturation as an unrewarding project.

In February 1853, Speer's mission began its regular preaching service to Chinese in the Presbyterian Church on Stockton Street. Elijah C. Bridgman, Congregational minister and first China missionary of the American Board of Commissioners for Foreign Missions, addressed the assembly. About a year later, on the first Sunday in June, Reverend Speer opened the new chapel with a sermon in Chinese.[11] Four months after this dedication ceremony in San Francisco, the Reverend Jehu Lewis Shuck purchased a lot in Sacramento on Sixth between G and H streets for the construction of a Chinese church.[12] Shuck, an old China hand whose first wife was the earliest female American missionary in the Celestial Empire, had been appointed to work among the Chinese in California by the Board of Domestic and Indian Missions of the Southern Baptist Convention.[13] On the last day of the same year Reverend Edward W. Syle, delegated by the Foreign and Domestic Committees of the Protestant Episcopal Church, arrived in San Francisco. During the preceding summer he had preached regularly in their own language to a handful of destitute Chinese at St. George's in New York City. Bishop William Ingraham Kip welcomed the former China missionary and pledged his cooperation to advance Syle's project.[14]

Catholic missionaries shared in the work but their activities were more difficult to trace. Their efforts also yielded little noticeable fruit and, unlike the Protestants, they failed to preserve the record of their toils for posterity. As members of religious orders or as part of the church hierarchy, the priests' presence was not apt to be noted by others. William Speer at least credited Shuck and Syle for their labor among the Chinese, but his bias blinded him to that of Catholics in an area which he considered his personal domain. His successor mentioned briefly a Catholic priest, "a native of Ningpo," in one line of his correspondence with the Board in New York.[15]

Successive Protestant chroniclers followed Speer's lead. In 1877, Reverend Otis Gibson outlined what had become the classic position for pro-Chinese clergymen in regard to the Catholic Church. The head of the Methodist Episcopal mission work among the Chinese on the West Coast, a onetime missionary at Foochow, Gibson formulated a vigorous attack on Roman Catholicism, Irish workers, and labor unions. During the 1870's the intemperate anti-Chinese utterances of Father James Bouchard, a leading California Jesuit, were taken as the fixed policy of Catholic priests, were projected back into the preceding decades, and were regarded as the established Catholic attitude toward mission work among the Orientals in California. The destruction of the records of the archdiocese in the San Francisco earthquake and fire of 1906 left the beginning of the enterprise in the dark.[16]

The first Catholic missionary to the Chinese in California, Father Thomas R. Cian, or Chan, may have been in San Francisco as early as 1850. Presumably he had just been ordained in Rome and was on his way back to China. Two lines in the *Kim-Shan Jit San-Luk*, the San Francisco *Golden Hills' News*, attest to his presence in 1854. "There is now," they said, "a priest, a Chinese from Hunan province, in San Francisco. He wants to teach the Chinese to learn Jesus' doctrine." The "Romanists imported a priest," Bishop Kip reported in the following year to the Domestic Committee of the Protestant Episcopal Church, "who is a native of China." His statement that Father Cian did not speak any Cantonese dialect confirms the priest's Hunanese origin.[17] These pieces of evidence suggest that Father Cian was working among the Chinese in California at the time of the beginning of organized Protestant mission work.

The Sacramento *Union* recorded Father Cian's first visit to the capital in the summer of 1854. "He has been travelling among his brethren in the interior," the paper related, "and returned . . . from Marysville where he succeeded in making fifteen converts." Father Thomas had "adopted the American costume of a clerical cast," the reporter noted. The missionary, "eminently proficient in Greek, Latin, Hebrew and French, although but slightly acquainted with the English tongue," received high praise for his learning. He "comes from the interior of China," the paper informed its readers, "and is assiduously endeavoring to procure among his countrymen the means to erect a church in San Francisco." The plan never materialized. From 1856 to 1862 the San Francisco *City Directory* lists "Rev. Thos. R. Cian (Chinese)" as assistant at St. Francis on Vallejo Street, between Stockton and Dupont. Father Cian labored at Chinese Camp in Tuolumne County before his departure in 1865 to join the small missionary congregation in Italy to which he belonged. Three years later he died in Naples at the seminary for Chinese missionary priests.[18]

Other Catholics left little trace beyond their names. Father Florian, the Austrian Benedictine Martin Francis Schwenninger, served in northern California from 1853 until his death at Weaverville in 1868. "O how I felt myself to be a true Catholic missionary," Father Florian confided on September 20, 1853, in a letter from Shasta to the Abbot of the Benedictine Monastery of Fiecht, "when in the past fall a Chinese served my Mass." [19]

Only in very rare moments, however, did the work of

Catholic and Protestant missionaries justify any elation about accomplishments. The singlemindedness of purpose which guided actions and interests of the Chinese in California made the sojourners immune, or nearly so, to any Christian message. Equally set in their beliefs and determined to complete what seemed to them the design of Providence, the missionaries doggedly pursued their goal.

The missionary work encountered serious difficulties as the limited nature of their success wore thin the initial enthusiasm of Californians to better the lot of the Orientals. William Speer, supported by a monthly salary of two hundred dollars from the Presbyterian Board, had been able to build his church with funds raised largely in San Francisco. Leading Chinese contributed upward of two thousand dollars. The Board in New York furnished a mortgage of five thousand dollars on which the trustees pledged to pay an annual interest of three hundred and fifty dollars. In Sacramento J. Lewis Shuck profited similarly from the citizens' urge to help. In less than one year he raised all but five hundred and fifty dollars for the construction of a chapel which he dedicated on June 10, 1855.[20]

Reverend Edward Syle was less fortunate. He did not speak Cantonese, and his salary forced him to live at Oakland, eight miles across San Francisco Bay. Facing the prejudices of Bishop Kip and without sufficient support from the local churches, Syle resigned after two years of half-hearted endeavors, never having resolved the problem. In the spring of 1856 he left San Francisco to return to China to his "former field of missionary labor." [21] In the following year Shuck doubled up as pastor of the regular Baptist congregation in Sacramento. "Two very effective Chinese preachers" aided him in his missionary work. He served as Chinese interpreter in courts and weathered financial difficulties on a ranch until he removed to South Carolina on the eve of the Civil War.[22]

The concern of Californians for the missionary work among the Chinese, however, never permitted the central enterprise to collapse. When William Speer vacated his post in San Francisco on account of ill health in 1857, Californians kept urging the Presbyterian Board of Foreign Missions until they sent to California Augustus Ward Loomis, another former China missionary, to continue the mission work.[23]

Observers measured the value of the missionary endeavors in numbers of converted sojourners.[24] The missionaries added to this preoccupation with their concern over legions of well-counted converts. These figures expressed in terms of tens or, at best, hundreds conveyed a false image.[25] They attested a manifestly genuine religious experience which Protestant missionaries required as basis for any conversion. The letters of Speer and Loomis to the Presbyterian Board in New York revealed the degree of scrutiny and reserve with which they viewed new converts.[26] The matter-of-fact tone in which Father Florian accounted for "almost 300 Catholics" among the Chinese in California suggests, as in China, the Catholic approach to mission work.[27] The effect of missionary labor among the Chinese in California, however, went beyond the finer points of theology or the simple facts of arithmetic. The untiring effort was an avenue of acculturation which, regardless of its limitations, touched Chinese as well as Americans.

When the goals of missionaries and sojourners coincided, the labors of the former yielded the greatest return in acculturation. The work of public officials and philanthropists showed the same characteristic. The Chinese utilized writs of habeas corpus and certificates of civil marriage for such conflicting ends as gaining freedom from or enforcing the restrictions of their control system.[28] Their manipulations and schemes paralyzed the plans of magistrates, lawyers, police judges, and law officers to bring Chinese affairs within the reach of American law and justice. Missionaries also saw means designed to reach laudable ends diverted into tools to suit Chinese goals. With only a few Californians able to proselytize in Cantonese and with a lack of interpreters, they faced the necessity of familiarizing their prospective converts with a working knowledge of English. An increasing number of sojourners recognized the advantage of conversing and dealing with Californians in English. Whenever the opportunity arose they flocked into bible classes and mission schools to acquire the rudiments of English grammar but, to the distress of missionaries, no more.

Disheartened missionaries groped for a rationale to explain the rejection of the Word in favor of a few English utterances repeated with parrot-like intensity. They viewed their experience as the by-product of a gigantic racial struggle between Americans and Chinese. The encounter, they concluded, had lowered Christianity to an enemy religion and blocked its road to success.[29] The missionaries faced a dilemma similar to that of the disturbed prophets of the universally desirable American way of life. Rejection of the blessings of their Republic's institutions threatened to invalidate the concepts which had contributed to the image of the country as a refuge for suffering and oppressed humanity. They had to explain the failure of their visions in terms of a cosmic struggle between the forces of light and darkness.[30] Rationalizations of the bewildering experience produced an avalanche of arguments. They stamped the outcome of the encounter as an inevitable process, stifled new attempts at acculturation, and obscured the actual effects.

However, behind the barrage of rhetoric, at times heavily inspired by the debate about the irrepressible conflict over Negro slavery, individual cases of acculturation appear as the tangible results of the encounter. During the actual strife in California Chinese spokesmen needed the aid of missionaries to deal with American politics. William Speer frequently lobbied at Sacramento for the headmen of the district companies.[31] His successor, refusing "to get mixed up in any political matters," arranged for the representation of the companies in the state capital by a San Francisco lawyer, after the headmen had reminded him of Speer's services.[32]

The regular mission work attracted Orientals as pupils, teachers, elders, translators, colporteurs, and hangers-on and brought them into contact with American life. These men formed the core of the Chinese mission followers. Several of them had been in China in contact with such opposite representatives of the mission movement as James Legge and Issachar J. Roberts.[33] In dress and habits members of this group evidenced their exposure to American norms and values. The constant turnover among the mission followers indicated that the influence of the new culture never substituted a different goal for the expected return to China.[34] It also brought new men into the picture who took over the vacated positions in the hierarchy of mission followers and continued the sojourners' contact with aspects of American culture.

The motley array of mission followers enjoyed a certain measure of freedom from the regimentation of Chinese California. Homeward bound sailors and plantation workers drifted to California by way of New York or the West Indies. Others reached the United States in the employ of returning missionaries. Still others had made their way to the New World with the aid of philanthropists but had taken a less auspicious road than Yung Wing, a native of the Pearl River Delta who became the first Chinese to graduate from an American college when he received a bachelor's degree at Yale in 1854.[35] A few served their years in the work camps of the Mother Lode. On visits to San Francisco they were recognized as former assistants of such towering figures in the China missions as Charles Gutzlaff and George Smith. In time even a relative of Liang A-fa, apparently the first ordained Chinese Protestant minister, graced the group.[36]

A missionary's apprehension about one of the men suggested the group's state of religious conviction. "Five years in the mines, away from religious associates and . . . churches," Augustus W. Loomis suspected, "has not tended his growth in grace." [37] However, years of struggle among Californians deepened these sojourners' familiarity with American culture more than the preaching of missionaries or the admonitions of orators. Separated from the mass of their countrymen, acculturation actually offered them advantages. They surprised Californians with their skillful adaptation of Western technical inventions, political concepts, and dress habits.

San Franciscans marveled at the miniature steamer built by Lam Tai Sam, a former fireman on the *Pluto* of the East India Company. They delighted in the men's shrewd evaluation of politics.[38] They gazed at the fashionable Western dress of an ironworker or shuddered at the sight of a drifter dying in the street, whose body, "indifferently dressed in American clothing," remained unclaimed by the companies.[39] In 1861 a Chinese printer, who had learned his trade from Richard Cole in the London Mission's Printing Establishment at Hong Kong during the 1840's, found his way as pressman into the shop of the Placerville *El Dorado County Daily Union*.[40] The later traces of these men disappear with their return to the Pearl River Delta. However, the presence of returned Christians from California induced the American Board in 1883 to reopen its own stations at Canton and Hong Kong which the Congregationalists had transferred to the Presbyterians on their removal to Shanghai.[41] Beyond the financial support which trickled regularly into villages of Kwangtung, the American experience of these sojourners had some impact on their native districts. Suggestively, the same generation in the Pearl River Delta saw the birth of K'ang Yu-wei, Sun Yat-sen, and Liang Ch'i-ch'ao.

During their years in the United States some members of the group acquired a degree of Western learning as translators for banking firms, merchant houses, and stage lines, as well as in the role of factory hands and house servants. They supplemented their knowledge through incidental bits of schooling picked up over the years. None of the five or six Chinese whose names appeared between 1819 and 1825 in the register of the Foreign Mission School of the American Board of Commissioners for Foreign Missions at Cornwall, Connecticut, made their way to San Francisco. Laisun, another Chinese boy who studied for two years at Hamilton College at the expense of the ABCFM and the Maternal Association of the City of Utica in the late 1840's returned also directly to China.[42]

California itself, however, offered a variety of instruction for the sojourners. In addition to the missionary efforts, the municipality of San Francisco, churches, and individuals provided elementary education in regular schools, evening instruction, Sunday Schools, or bible classes. These facilities satisfied the limited interest in formal education which the routine and the regimentation of Chinese California permitted. The "Summary of a Report of the First Public School, San Francisco, . . . Kept in the Baptist Church," listed in 1851 one Chinese among 106 foreign pupils from 13 different countries; the report of the Happy Valley Free School, "Kept in the Chapel of the Howard Street Presbyterian Church," mentioned one Chinese among 75 students from nine countries.[43]

The limited number of schools frequently misled observers to believe that missing facilities hampered acculturation more than the sojourners' lack of interest. While the City of San Francisco appeared ever ready to close down its Chinese school because of insufficient funds and Sacramento by-passed Shuck's petition for a Public Chinese School, the newcomers' reaction indicated that their limited goal, not the absence of facilities, kept them out of the class rooms. The "prejudices of cast and religious idolatry are so indelibly stamped upon their character and existence," the 1861 report of the San Francisco Superintendent of Common Schools conveniently emphasized, "that . . . they take but little interest in adopting our habits, or learning our language or institutions." [44]

The few students, however, gained insights which went beyond the subjects of reading, writing, and spelling taught during the regular class hours. In December 1860, members of the Public Chinese Evening School presented Preceptor Lanctot "with a gold watch." The present struck a reporter as "a timely memento of regard and a fitting testimonial of their advancement in civilization." [45] In the same year the tenth annual report of the San Francisco Superintendent of Common Schools listed 77 Chinese pupils in public classes. Four years later the number had increased to 199, with about thirty in regular attendance. "One of the most active students," a journalist noticed during his visit, "is a man of forty years or over." [46]

The establishment of a Methodist Episcopal Mission at San Francisco in 1868, the formation of Congregational and Baptist missions, and the organization of a Chinese Young Men's Christian Association by the Presbyterian Mission in 1870 paralleled the growth of Chinese schools.[47] A new institute which Reverend Gibson opened at San Jose attracted about seventy "scholars, most of whom [were] grown-up boys and men," while "nearly one hundred persons . . . volunteered to assist as teachers." With the visit of the Congressional Committee of Ways and Means to the Chinese school in the chapel of the Howard Street Presbyterian Church a series of "grand reviews" reached their climax. These students sang "Beautiful River," as had others when local church groups, lodges, and fraternal organizations inspected their classrooms. This time, however, the merchant Fung Tang translated the address not of a clergyman but of a congressman from Tennessee.[48] The visit marked the dawn of an era in which the process of acculturation would no longer be a California task but interwoven with the affairs of the nation.

Various efforts to draw the sojourners into American culture through personal contacts increased the concern about China and the Chinese in California. Through articles, public lectures, and the communiqués of merchant houses, Californians widened their knowledge about the sojourners and their homeland. Leading newspapers satisfied some of the interest with reports, quoted from Hong Kong and Shanghai journals, and letters of their correspondents.[49] The missionaries to the Chinese in California, regular clergymen, and itinerant China missionaries, on their way to the eastern states or their stations in the Middle Kingdom, formed the major source of information. They utilized lectures, church conferences, and sermons as a convenient mode of conducting fund raising campaigns for their work.

This narrow purpose at times influenced their interpretation, as William Speer's addresses indicate. Speer's work as lecturer was long unrivaled. He began to speak to churches, tract societies, library associations, and assemblies on the subject of mission work immediately after his arrival in California and soon extended his lecture program to general topics of Chinese life. The progress of the Taiping Rebellion and Commodore Matthew C. Perry's Japan Expedition aroused new interest in the Far East, and Speer was repeatedly called upon by committees of citizens to discuss such thorny questions as "The creed and sentiments of the Patriots [Rebels] — The probable result of the Revolution to the Chinese people, to the continent on which they dwell, and to the United States." He tackled a wide range of topics, many of which later appeared in his *Oldest and Newest Empire*.[50]

The publication of Chinese newspapers in California spurred the growing curiosity about Chinese culture, and engendered a respect for the Oriental, evidently on the un-

warranted assumption that, since most Californians de-
ciphered their own journals, all sojourners were also able to
read the pages filled with characters. "There are several
Chinamen here," the editor of the Columbia *Gazette* in
Tuolumne County marveled, "who speak English and Spanish fluently, while . . . they all, without an exception, are
able to read and write their own difficult language." [51] From
the beginning of the contact the sojourners' spoken and written language had been the object of editorial humor, rivaled
only by the journalists' remarks about Chinese music. With a
set of fictitious "Chinese Letters" the *Pioneer* caricatured
Chinese prose style and thought.[52] In their confused reports
covering mysterious Chinese affairs newsmen apologized to
their readers for all shortcomings with the hint that they
spoke only "what Mrs. Partington would call broken China."
They compared the typographical appearance of the lithographed characters in Chinese newspapers with the crawling
of a spider out of an ink bottle over a sheet of white paper.[53]

Early in the San Francisco contact with the newcomers,
English language newspapers used lithography to reproduce
the foreign characters in advertisements and in reports describing the inscription on a Chinese grave. They paid
special attention to commercial guides on China. Later
journals published crude conversation aids and noted the
appearance of books printed in Chinese characters. Richard
Cole's Hong Kong printing, from newly founded type, of an
arithmetic book, which he presented to the *Alta* in February 1853, struck the editor as conducive "more to speedier
and better acquaintance with that people than any other
thing." In the summer of the same year the paper greeted
Samuel Wells Williams' *Middle Kingdom,* the first major
American study on China, initially printed in 1848. In 1854
the *Alta* noticed a Chinese dictionary published at Boston.
The compiler, Stanislas Hernisz, M.D., "late attache to the
U.S. Legation in China," had opportunely taken up residence

in San Francisco. The editor felt that the volume promised an opportunity for serious occupation with the Chinese language and enabled "the Chinese to become acquainted with our language," the "only means of elevating and enlightening them." In 1872 the American Tract Society published a small volume of *English and Chinese Lessons* based on the linguistic experience the Reverend Loomis had gained in China and California.[54]

The first Chinese newspaper in California, *Kim-Shan Jit San-Luk*, the San Francisco *Golden Hills' News*, appeared at the end of April 1854, most likely on the twenty-eighth of the month and three San Francisco newspapers greeted the newcomer on the following day. The first copy promised the regular appearance of the four-page paper on Wednesdays and Saturdays. William Howard of the San Francisco firm of Howard & Lersner published the sheet; F. Kuhl lithographed the Chinese characters.[55] Number 9 of the paper, issued by Howard & Hudson, appeared on Saturday, July 8, 1854, indicating that *Kim-Shan Jit San-Luk* had quickly turned into a weekly. Single copies sold at twenty-five cents, the monthly subscription coming to seventy-five cents. The number of characters determined the advertising rate: each insertion under twenty-five characters cost $1, under fifty characters $2, with three cents per character for each character above fifty. Generally written entirely in colloquial Cantonese, incidental California news and advertisements of sales and auctions predominated. On June 18, 1854, the San Francisco *Golden Era* announced the "establishment of a post office for the benefit of the Chinese . . . by the publishers . . . Messrs. Howard and Hudson."

An editorial in English had become an established practice by June. One of these, "Is There No Help For The Chinese In California," was reprinted in the *Alta*.[56] An English editorial in a July issue held forth on "The Fourth of July and The Chinese Race." The "National Festival this year in San

Francisco," it asserted, "has given additional evidence of the faith and adaptation of the Chinese race to the creed of Republicanism." [57] These English editorials established a practice which other Chinese newspapers in California followed. While indictments of the abrogation of civil rights in California and hopeful announcements of the acculturation of Chinese in politics and religion filled the English section of the papers, the Chinese pages remained on the level of a commercial bulletin, evidently more suited to the particular interest of the literate sojourners than the lofty pronouncements of the editorials. Edward C. Kemble's laconic remark that "it did not live long," summed up the history of the *Golden Hills' News*.[58]

The Sacramento *Chinese Daily News* inspired equally little comment; it disappeared without a significant trace less than two years after its first appearance in December 1856. A few brief references attest to its short-lived existence. "Except for the heading and the date," one notice described Fletcher E. Webster's publication, "it is all printed in Chinese." The "small sheet of one side" resembled "somewhat the side of a tea-chest." Another report mentioned lithography as the reproduction process and listed Ze Too Yune, alias Hung Tai, as editor. A few years later a story in the Sacramento *Bee* related that Hung Tai, "formerly editor of the Chinese Daily News," had established a school in Sacramento for the instruction of Chinese children "in their own and the English languages." [59]

The San Francisco *Tung-Ngai San-Luk, or Oriental*, was the early Chinese newspaper in California which gained most attention. After almost two years of planning, its first issue appeared on January 4, 1855. "The American population of this State," editor William Speer declared in the Prospectus, has "felt strongly the want of a newspaper to connect them with the Chinese." The missionary continued by outlining the objectives: to disseminate information about the Chinese in California, to furnish intelligence from China, to promote the spread of Christianity, and to afford an advertising medium for the mutual benefit of Chinese and Californians.[60]

A contemporary compilation of San Francisco periodicals registered the *Oriental* as number twenty-two on the list. "In Chinese and English," the remarks read, "by Rev. Wm. Speer. Commenced Jan. 4, 1855, weekly at $5 per annum; in Chinese tri-weekly, at $12 per annum: size 14 x 20 inches. Religious and literary." Many of the Chinese issues were distributed gratis. Consequently after a few months the sequence of publication dropped to a weekly and monthly basis. F. Kuhl also lithographed the characters of the *Oriental*'s Chinese edition since the purchase of a font of Chinese type from Hong Kong failed to materialize.[61] Whitton, Towne & Co. printed the English text of the weekly edition of four pages on one side of the sheet, the lithographed characters appeared on the reverse.

Editor William Speer, from the outset, was "conscious of but partial qualification for the work." [62] He filled the columns of the English edition with his own writings and with a motley array of excerpts from learned journals, missionary periodicals, foreign and domestic newspapers, and sermons. Frequently only the advertising sections with a "Chinese Directory" and the names of doctors, barbers, washermen, brokers, and merchants, or the notices of the Chinese Mission House, threw light on the life of the Chinese in California.

Lee Kan superintended the Chinese edition as Speer's assistant. Having received an English education at Hong Kong under the care of an American missionary, or in the Morrison Mission School, Lee Kan made a public profession of Christianity only many years after his editorship. Ira M. Condit's reminiscences, published about forty years after the disappearance of the *Oriental*, contain a photograph of Lee Kan still in traditional Chinese dress.[63] While working for

Speer, and later, Lee Kan functioned as interpreter and agent of American merchants.

The Chinese sections of the *Tung-Ngai San-Luk*, written in colloquial Cantonese, abounded in incidental bits of foreign news centering around South China. California items and advertisements were selected from developments significant to the paramount goal of the Chinese, with little or no attention to explanations of the American political system or the intricacies of California life. Only now and then did a Chinese parable serve as filler.

William Speer's zeal accounted for the difference between the *Oriental* and the two other early Chinese newspapers. With the departure of the missionary from California in 1857, the *Oriental* came to an end after but two years of existence. The silence in which the most important of the early Chinese journals faded from the scene, unlamented by other newspapers, suggested its limited influence. Californians referred to the Chinese papers at times as items of curiosity or sent copies back east in much the same spirit in which they had earlier surprised their relatives with nuggets.[64] The fact that the United States remained without any Chinese newspaper until the middle 1870's emphasized also the indifference of Chinese California to the journals.[65]

Though the Speer newspaper expired, other factors were at work to link Chinese and Americans. The better known interpreters of courts, of district companies, and of express offices, from John Marcel, Charles Carvalho, and Ah Tong in San Francisco to James Hanley at Chinese Camp, continued to bring together sojourners and Californians. They were favorites of newspaper editors. Whenever Charles Carvalho ran into difficulties through his highhanded way of shaping and aiding the course of justice among the Chinese, the reports of the *Alta* credited his version of the story.[66] Americans upheld these fragile contacts with Chinese California even if they led only to the ruling hierarchy of merchant princes and never reached the legions of indentured emigrants.

As one result of these contacts, Californians were even willing to learn from China. Quoting a passage from Evariste Regis Huc's *Travels in Tartary, Thibet, and China,* the editor of the *Alta* thought, perhaps in anticipation of the Second Vigilance Committee, that the famed traveler's description of popular tribunals in the Celestial Empire in reaction to governmental neglect and corruption furnished "a timely hint to us San Franciscans." [67] The prevailing American concepts had equated the Chinese with beasts of the field or elevated them to representatives of a venerable, yet outdated civilization. Now Californians came to view the Chinese also as representatives of popular government. The new interest in the sojourners' civilization and their political institutions assured a degree of benevolent attention to the limited attempts of individual Chinese to gain the civil rights which law and custom kept from them.

Two major restrictions touched the Chinese in California. Law barred them from becoming citizens and suspended their right to testify in court for or against Caucasians. The bulk of indentured emigrants failed to recognize the severity of these restrictions which hardly affected their goal. Only a few realized the advantages of citizenship and the value of their testimony in court. Not one became a citizen through a California court. During a trial and the debate following Governor Bigler's special message in 1852 two Chinese merchants in San Francisco, Nissum and Norman Assing, boasted of their right to be in California, asserting that they were American citizens and Christians from Charleston, South Carolina.[68] Their names, however, did not appear in the Charleston *City Directory* or in the archives of the South Carolina Historical Society.

In the face of California's experience with Indians, slaves, and free Negroes the barriers of law and custom remained insurmountable during the early decades of the contact between Chinese and Americans. "We are of the opinion," the *Alta* formulated the basic objection, that the Chinese "are neither free nor white," and "if there were no other objections to their becoming free citizens, this alone would be sufficient." We "believe," the editor confessed, "that it is well to cultivate feelings of amity and friendly intercourse with them as far as it can be done on their own ground." [69] These concepts also provided a footloose society with a measure of stability. They divided the polyglot hordes of gold hunters into those eligible to become citizens and others seemingly barred from the privilege. The distinction provided a conveniently legalistic framework for the continuous imposition of the Foreign Miners' Tax upon the Chinese.

Very few sojourners attempted to become citizens during the 1850's and 1860's. With the outcome of the argument predetermined, their applications for citizenship only furnished California lawyers with opportunities to practice their powers of reasoning without damaging their practice.[70] For the vast majority of Chinese, citizenship remained unattractive since it did not speed the accomplishment of their goal. Only when they modified their aim and when the restrictive consequences of the strife in the 1870's blocked the free intercourse between California and Kwangtung, did possession of citizenship become important because then it enabled its bearer to visit his family in China and to return at will.

The struggle of certain Chinese for civil rights underlined again the individual basis of acculturation. Early Californian attempts to bring the sojourners into the realm of American culture had been in all-encompassing terms. Only a few Chinese, however, responded because it furthered the attainment of their goals. The majority remained aloof. Significantly, even the lowliest miner adopted American boots for his work. Only certain members of particular professions, operating outside the confines of their world, adopted Western techniques and at times bridged the gulf between Americans and Chinese.

Conservative Chinese merchants accepted a measure of Western business procedure. They proposed to create their own merchants' exchange. Their contributions to schools, fire companies, police, and public charities emulated the community services of other successful men. The Chinese also set an often cited example for business ethics. Their standards differed sharply from those of a rapidly growing economy in which spectacular failures had led to a deterioration of standards. When the San Francisco County Court discharged the Chinese merchant Wong Jan from his liabilities in the summer of 1864, the *Alta* noted "the case was the first instance of a Chinaman applying for discharge as an insolvent in an American court." The members of the firm of Hong Kee & Co. who suddenly absconded to China five years later leaving debts to San Francisco merchants of $14,000 shattered the image of the honest Chinese merchant.[71]

Very few Chinese artists appeared in California although *objets d'art* were in vogue from the beginning of the contact. "The avidity with which these curiosities are bought up on the occasion of public sales, has given . . . impetus to this particular trade," the *Alta* described the beginning of the fashion in 1850.[72] In the fall of 1866 Lai Yong, a portrait painter, opened a studio at room No. 70 of the Stevenson House. Having practiced his profession for a number of years at Canton, "he produced portraits strikingly accurate in detail . . . The photograph is not more faithful in these particulars," an admiring reporter noted.[73] The 1860's became the decade of Chinese physicians. During this period they gained a foothold in San Francisco while the Chinese restaurants, which had been "in the earlier days . . . the resort of all nations and classes, nearly disappeared." The few remaining restaurants were "exclusively patronized by the Celestials." In November 1858, a reporter spotted the shingle of Dr. Wo Tsun Yuen. "From the fact that the 'Dr.' has a sign in Roman letters," the journalist concluded, "we may presume that he is desirous of having American customers." In 1865 Dr. Li Tai Po, the leading Chinese medical wizard of his generation in San Francisco, announced "that his practice has become so extensive that he is under the necessity of employing an interpreter." [74]

Contacts between Californians and Chinese merchants, mission followers, restaurateurs, physicians, artists, and washermen, brought steadily increasing segments of sojourners into contact with elements of American culture. Providing another avenue of acculturation, personal acquaintance eroded the dominant image of hordes of bondmen that Americans had formed of the newcomers, slowly dissolved it, and led to the discovery of the sojourners as individual human beings.[75] The emergence of the Chinese as distinguishable individuals, their transition from exotics or freaks into persons, paralleled the degree to which the standard "John" of speech, letters, and stage began to turn into a character of flesh and blood. A few months after Bret Harte had traced the particular ways of Ah Sin in his poem, "Plain Language from Truthful James," a dime song book of the New York publishing house of Beadle and Adams greeted "John Chinaman, Esquire." [76]

The new concept and the sojourners' modification of their goal undermined the structure of Chinese California. Together with the advance of the mining frontier into the Rocky Mountains, the changing California economy, the completion of the Transcontinental Railroad, and the movement of Chinese into the South and East as a result of labor problems after the Civil War, they contributed to the demolition of the most oppressive features of the control system. The discovery of the sojourners as individuals and the extension of the Chinese problem to the national scene regenerated and expedited the process of acculturation.

CHAPTER VIII

AFTERMATH: FROM SOJOURNERS TO IMMIGRANTS

FOR two decades the boundaries of the mining region in the foothills of the Sierra Nevada were also the limits of Chinese California. That area harbored the mass of sojourners. An invisible control system, sustained by devotion to the family, permeated this isolated world. Neither strife nor acculturation fundamentally weakened the controls of the clan organizations, district companies, tongs, and guilds.

Other factors, however, stimulated the movement of Chinese into the Rocky Mountains, the South, and the East and helped demolish the oppressive control system. The national diffusion of the problem expedited acculturation, facilitated by the discovery, through personal contact, of the Chinese as individuals.

The problem became national as a result of the sojourners' outward movement. Labor companies brought the newcomers to the South and East under circumstances which influenced the outlook of those sections toward the Orientals. As the wave of Chinese surged beyond California, the effect on the country was wide and various. Each region which encountered the Orientals reacted in its own way. The confrontation upset humanitarians, confused politicians, and altered the existing notions about the Chinese. The call for Chinese hands in the fields and on the railroads of the South handicapped the Democrats in the East and the West in their stand against Negroes and other colored people. With Chinese strikebreakers threatening the domestic tranquillity of the East, Radical Republicans re-examined their views of racial equality. Northern workingmen, who had shown little concern about Negro slaves in the South, quickly revised their opinions with the arrival of the Chinese in their midst. The spectacle of Southern planters arguing against the importation of Chinese field hands, of Northern industrialists condemning the use of Chinese strikebreakers, of spokesmen of the freedmen favoring the sojourners, and of editors of labor papers hailing the newcomers' arrival revealed the infinite possibilities of the question as a political issue.

A vociferous debate among Americans accompanied the eastward movement. To the sojourners it mattered little whether they accumulated their savings as gold miners in California, field hands in Louisiana, or shoemakers in Massachusetts. Nor did it distress their merchant-creditors as long as the laborers earned the money to pay back the indenture. Nevertheless, both groups preferred California. For the former, it spelled home through the presence of friends, the comforts of Chinatown, and the proximity of their native land. The latter increasingly resisted sending labor companies into the industrial East where their presence created foci for hostile sentiment.

In the 1850's the gold rushes in Oregon and British Columbia were a prelude to the expansion of the mining frontier into the Rocky Mountains. The new discoveries began an intensified Chinese contact with the entire country. The vast extension of the regimented world was also the beginning of the system's decline. Although the control machinery followed the sojourners to their new destinations, their separation from the basis of Chinese life in the United States increased their dependence on the American world for supplies, diversion, and work.

With the movement of the Chinese into the Rocky Mountains and their arrival in the South and East, they made contact with unfamiliar groups of Americans. Metropolitan centers attracted individual Chinese who realized that the United States furnished ways of existence outside the confines of work camp and Chinatown. The discovery contributed to a modification of the sojourners' traditional goal; some began to accept a life in the United States as permanent and gave up the struggle to return to China. The altered outlook closed one era and opened another during which the stranded sojourners became immigrants.

Some Chinese had earlier made contact with the Pacific Northwest. In 1788 fifty Cantonese formed part of Captain John Meares's fur trading post on Nootka Sound. There, Chinese carpenters and blacksmiths built a two-story house and a sailing vessel of fifty tons.[1] In the following spring Captain James Colnett sailed the *Argonaut* from China to establish a settlement at Nootka and trade for fur on a large scale. He listed twenty-nine Chinese among his men: seven carpenters, five blacksmiths, five bricklayers and masons, four tailors, four shoemakers, three sailors, and one cook. In July the Spaniards captured the captain and the crew. The Chinese remained in the Northwest as captives until November when they were shipped to San Blas south of Mazatlan. Six Chinese deserted in Mexico where their countrymen had gathered for decades as a result of the regular runs of the Manila Galleons or China Ships. Upon Colnett's release in July 1790, the others returned with the *Argonaut* to the Northwest by way of California, and to Canton in the following March.[2]

The discovery of gold in the Rogue River country and the establishment of regular steamer connections between San Francisco and Portland in 1851 drew the Chinese vanguard into Oregon Territory. The steerage of the *Columbia* accommodated sojourners on the new run to replace avid white miners who had abandoned placers in Southern Oregon in their hunt for richer gulches. Tradition placed the date of the

Chinese quarters in the old mines at Kerbyville, Josephine County, before 1855. The "Chinamen are about to take the country," the writer of a private letter informed the readers of the Portland *Weekly Oregonian* in 1857. "There are from one thousand to twelve hundred" in Josephine County, he added, "buying out the American miners" and "paying big prices for their claims." [3] In the following year the gold rush to the Fraser River in British Columbia brought the entire Pacific Coast within reach.

In the spring of 1858 a "Chinese ambassador" returning from the Fraser River informed the heads of the Five Companies in San Francisco and also the general public about conditions in the mining region. His report described a rich country with miners taking gold out "by the bucketful." Inflamed by these statements, "numbers of Chinese pressed forward with the throngs that shook the wharves of San Francisco in June and July." [4] However, the abandoned claims left behind in the Mother Lode by white miners rushing North opened new opportunities for Chinese mining companies within their established realm in California and kept small the actual number of departing Chinese. Merchants again played the leading role in the migration. In 1864, in behalf of their countrymen, they greeted a newly arriving British governor with "Us be here from year 1858." In answer to the administrator's query, Lee Chang of Kwong Lee & Co. stated that about two thousand Chinese lived on Vancouver Island and in British Columbia, of whom the vast majority engaged in mining. [5]

The sojourner's movement into the Pacific Northwest approximated the pattern of Chinese migration to California and established the framework for the advance into the Rocky Mountains. Control over the newcomers remained in the hands of the San Francisco merchant princes. Commercial agents and storekeepers, in constant contact with the headquarters of their district companies, directed the eastward movement. Within a short period they were recognized in their new surroundings as official spokesmen of their countrymen.

The work of a ditch company attracted the first large group of Chinese to Nevada Territory in the summer of 1855. Fifty sojourners crossed the mountains and dug a thirty-mile trench to divert the water of the Carson River to the placers in Gold Canon.[6] At the end of the decade the silver rush to the Nevada mines brought a stream of Chinese wood hawkers, laborers, cooks, and laundrymen to Washoe. After a few years some continued to pass on through Carson City en route to Montana.[7] The discovery of gold near Lewiston in 1860 led the Chinese vanguard into Idaho. Soon they were "crowding every one out of house and home at Idaho City" and filling up Boise County.[8] A decade later the Boulder *County News* registered the presence of forty-five Chinese in Colorado's capital.[9]

The construction of the Transcontinental Railroad speeded the eastward movement of Chinese into regions theretofore untouched. The feats of docile Chinese construction crews became legendary. Long before guests, journalists, and officers of the Twenty-first Regiment accorded James H. Strowbridge's Chinese foreman three rousing cheers as a public tribute to the construction companies during the ceremony at Promontory Point, some Southern planters had perceived the possibility of using these workers to solve their labor problems.[10]

Labor difficulties had earlier prompted William C. Kelly to bring the only group of Chinese into the ante-bellum South. One of the inventors of the Bessemer iron refining process, Kelly objected to working Christian Negroes as slaves in Kentucky where few whites were willing to do the low labor of an iron factory. Born and raised in Pittsburgh, he had absorbed antislavery sentiment before coming to Eddyville where it was also bad business to contract laborers from slaveholders who required compensation for hired Negroes if they escaped North across the nearby Ohio River. In 1854 Kelly obtained ten Chinese through a New York or Philadelphia tea house to take the place of Blacks at the Suwanee Furnace and Union Forge in Lyon County. Dissatisfied with slave labor generally, he was pleased with the results of his experiment and arranged to import fifty more Chinese. The plan did not materialize and little is known of the undertaking. The 1860 census of Lyon County enumerates, "Jim Fo, age 26, occupation forgeman, born, China, PeKing," and his wife, "Louisa Fo, age 20, born Kentucky." Jim Fo is the only person mentioned with a birthplace in China. The census taker may have added "PeKing" to the information with the same degree of certainty that clerks the world over once considered all Americans to hail from New York. Since Kelly himself was no longer listed in the 1860 census he may have taken his laborers with him to other furnaces.[11]

Among the various schemes for solving the Southern dilemma after Appomattox was one to import another racial group engaged in menial labor in order to bring recalcitrant freedmen to terms. When the South failed to attract European immigrants, a test of the Chinese project became attractive. Industrious and cheap, easily dominated politically, Chinese laborers seemed also ideally fitted to hasten the South on its road to industrialization and political emancipation.[12] The importation of sojourners into the South foreshadowed the use of Chinese labor companies in strike-ridden factories of the East, and extended the debate over these people beyond the West.

Various Southern regions contributed their particular rationales to a new agrarian philosophy. They advocated two ways for overcoming the difficulties of adapting former slaves to tenantry on the planters' terms. "Small farms and white labor or large farms and coolie labor may save the land," the editor of the Franklin *St. Mary's Planters' Banner* in the Sugar Bowl summed up the alternatives. With the coming of the Chinese "the tune . . . will not be 'forty acres and a mule,' " a Kentucky editor warned the freedmen, "but . . . 'work nigger or starve.' " Some Alabama planters, suspicious of free Negro labor, advocated the importation of Chinese field hands and railroad workers. "Either African or Chinese labor would have to be used" in the cultivation of rice, some South Carolinians felt, "inasmuch as only persons of these two races could sustain the trial" of the climate.[13]

The question of introducing "Chinese labour on our plantations in the place of Negro labour," which had become "hopelessly unmanageable, . . . interested us all very much," Frances Butler Leigh recorded in her journal in 1869. There "seemed to be a general move in this direction all through the Southern states," the lady planter observed. Not being willing to see half her property "uncultivated and going to ruin for want of labor," she, together with her neighbors, agreed "to try the experiment" on her rice plantation near Savannah.[14] During his visit in South Carolina, "Mr. Joseph," a Chinese labor importer from San Francisco, "received letters . . . from . . . planters . . . anxious to make arrangements to secure Chinese labor before the planting season commences," the Charleston *News* reported.[15] "Let the Chinamen come," a series of editorials in the New Orleans *Picayune* urged the deep South, and the letters of the paper's special correspondent from California assured the readers that the Chinese "will be a success on the Southern plantation."[16]

The Chinese Labor Convention at Memphis, in July 1869, sought to consolidate various schemes which aimed at preserving the traditional Southern labor system by substituting Chinese hands for Negro slaves. In mid-June planters from the lower Arkansas River had taken the initiative and formed the Arkansas River Valley Immigration Company to bring Chinese laborers into the state. Incorporated under the general acts of the state, it had a former governor, a general, a colonel, and a captain among the directors. At its first meeting the group subscribed stocks to the amount of two hundred and thirty bales of cotton. Having established a home office at Pine Bluff, the planters sent Captain George W. Gift with letters of credit directly to China and authorized him to bring back one thousand laborers. The former Lieutenant Commander in the Confederate Navy had served before the war as a midshipman in the Pacific Squadron, a clerk in California land offices, and a banker in Sacramento, and would later return West as editor and proprietor of the Napa *County Courier*. In 1869 the example of Arkansas electrified the deep South. The people of the Wonder State "have set the ball in motion, will the people of Tennessee, Mississippi and Alabama be backwards?" a Memphis paper queried anxiously.[17]

On July 13, 1869, two hundred delegates from Tennessee, Mississippi, Louisiana, Alabama, Georgia, South Carolina, Kentucky, Missouri, and California gathered in the Opera House of Tennessee's largest city "to follow the noble example of our Arkansas friends." Having chosen Isham G. Harris, Confederate governor of the state, as permanent president, the planters, landowners, and financiers listened to a series of enthusiastic reports endorsing the project. The Transportation Committee stressed that Chinese could be brought from California to Memphis by rail in lots of five hundred for fifty gold dollars each.[18]

The delegates' zeal influenced the reporters who covered the proceedings. The newsmen's glowing stories reflected the mood of the assembly. The reports glossed over the admonitions of the Hawaiian Commissioner of Immigration in a letter to the convention and stressed the encouraging figures furnished by Tye Kim Orr. This Chinese commercial agent had turned his talents to importation schemes after a scandal cut short his career as evangelical leader of a Chinese settlement in British Guiana and brought him to Lafourche parish in Louisiana. He assured the delegates that the sojourners "would easily become successful workers of Southern soil," but urged "the importance of carefully selecting them from the agricultural classes and the artisans of the interior" of Kwangtung. The Hawaiian Commissioner's letter had also emphasized the "striking difference in Chinese laborers . . . and . . . the importance of a careful and experienced personal selection." [19] These sober statements did not dampen the delegates' enthusiasm while they settled down to their major task: to wait for Koopmanschap and to hear from his own lips the account of his recruitment and importation of Chinese laborers.

The name Koopmanschap wielded magical power in the South. The three syllables, resembling a crude transliteration of Chinese characters, startled planters and financiers. Koopmanschap occupied the dreams of landowners and politicians and captured the imagination of editors and readers. The name became synonymous with Chinese importation schemes. Reiterated, its ring alone seemed almost to guarantee success. "Isham G. Harris and his fellow conspirators," a California paper exaggerated, "bring together their conventions, leave the ploughshare in the furrow, lay down the shovel and the hoe, and wait for Koopmanschap." The merchant "heard the Macedonian cry from Memphis and agreed to treat with them if they would call a Convention on the 13th of July . . . And so the rice fields of Louisiana and the tar buckets of North Carolina are all waiting for Koopmanschap." [20]

Cornelius Koopmanschap, the man, was a mystery to the delegates and the general public. He is still one today. Obituaries provide only a sketchy outline of his activities. Their tenor caused immediate comment in 1882 after Koopmanschap's death in Rio de Janeiro where he was negotiating the importation of Chinese laborers into Brazil. "Our naïve newspapers print long necrologues as if he had been a famous man," the editor of the San Francisco *Abendpost* marveled. He informed his colleagues that "said Koopmanschap was one of the most notorious slave traders" who had deserved a rope around his neck for shipping German laborers from San Francisco to Hawaii as well as for his dealings in the Chinese. A balance between this condemnation and the more usual editorial admiration may be struck by drawing on the report of the United States Consul General in Rio de Janeiro, the Marriage Register of Notre Dame des Victoires in San Francisco, and the records of a Dutch village.

About forty years old at the time of the Memphis Convention, Cornelius Koopmanschap was born in Weesperkarspel near Amsterdam on February 13, 1828. The gold rush brought the young man to California, perhaps by way of the Netherlands East Indies and China, a route not unlikely in view of Koopmanschap's later business connections in the Orient. After 1850 he resided in San Francisco as an importer of Chinese goods, listed in the *City Directory* and newspaper advertisements as a commission merchant, at times with Henry F. Edwards as partner. For a number of years in the early 1860's the *Directory* registered his wife, Desiré Touchard Koopmanschap, as proprietress of the Union Hotel. Born in 1823 at Laon, her French background was at times too readily extended to her husband and explains the references in newspapers to his "French-Hebrew descent." Their marriage in 1859 was sanctioned by the Catholic Church in 1872 when Archbishop Joseph S. Alemany of San Francisco granted a dispensation to the non-Catholic Koopmanschap. The merchant probably then became a convert, as the celebration of a high mass at Notre Dame des Victoires "for the repose of the soul of Cornelius Koopmanschap" suggests.

Information on his business operations is sparse. While the

California Police Gazette presented Koopmanschap as "a rich merchant living at Hongkong," his membership in the San Francisco Union Club attested to his residence and eminence in California. Only at the height of Koopmanschap's popularity in the South did a newspaper for once convey the essence of his activity: "He quietly pursued his course undisturbed." Gradually, in consequence of the constant arrival of Chinese, the house of Koopmanschap "was reinforced by more or less passenger traffic" and operated an agency for the North China Marine Insurance Company. The merchants' connections with Chinese firms established him in the 1860's as the leading contractor and importer of Chinese laborers. Thomas King, who at times also tried his hand at the trade, testified at the hearings of a congressional committee in 1876 that he had met Koopmanschap "in China several times" arranging new shiploads of contract laborers.[21]

Koopmanschap told the Memphis Convention that his house had imported 30,000 Chinese into California who "have been employed on railroads, in mining, in agriculture, and as domestics." He explained to the delegates that Chinese could be induced to come from San Francisco into the South for about twenty dollars a month, but that they could be obtained much cheaper in China, on five-year contracts at ten to twenty dollars a month. Koopmanschap's warning that Chinese laborers were "not at all times reliable unless security is exacted," and that they "will take service with others" when offered higher wages did not diminish the delegates' zeal for the project. The convention agreed to raise a million dollars to further the plans. Passenger agents quickly sensed the possibilities of the importation schemes for their railroad lines and offered round-trip tickets to San Francisco "to any agent who may go to assist immigrants in reaching the Valley of the Mississippi via the Union Pacific Railroad."[22]

However, as quickly as it had gained momentum, the

movement collapsed. It left but few Chinese on Southern soil and the stormy debate that followed the sudden cessation of the speculation left its mark on the national scene. Southern and Western Democrats, although in urgent need of an alliance, divided on the issue. Ex-Confederates embarrassed their party friends in California by advocacy of Chinese labor. The appearance of the Ku Klux on the Pacific Coast, harassing employers and teachers of Chinese, deepened the gulf.[23] Alarmed at the turn of affairs in the South, some Democratic papers tried to ease the tension. The Sacramento *Reporter* published a letter purporting to have been written in Memphis. Its author declared that the scheme of importing Chinese to the South was the work of "carpet-baggers from New England and Middle States" and that he yet had to learn of a single Democrat who favored the movement.[24] Radical Republicans, aroused by all manipulations aimed at restoring the rule of the former master class in the South, began to consider concessions to the California demands for Chinese restriction laws as a means of keeping this pivotal state in the camp which controlled Washington politics. Northern humanitarians who had just liberated the Negro hesitated to embrace the sojourners. Facing the problem of absorbing four million slaves, Horace Greeley felt that the Chinese arrived at an inopportune moment in the South.[25]

In the South the debate was equally confusing. When the state of Tennessee passed into the control of the Democrats in 1870, the conservatives were as eager to encourage immigration as the Radicals. However, although the legislature incorporated the Mississippi Valley Immigration Company, one clause provided that "nothing in this Act shall be so construed as to authorize the importation of Chinese into Tennessee." Opposition to and defense of the scheme failed to divide Southerners according to the interest of their groups. Some planters attacked and some Negroes defended the project, thus obscuring the line between the camps.

Other Southerners rejected the scheme because it aimed at supplanting Christian Negroes with heathen Chinese who "despise your Bible, deride your God, and hate your religion." After all, the editor of *De Bow's Review* indignantly responded to the *Picayune*'s "flippant paragraphs" supporting the scheme, "the great end for which the South fought was not cheap cotton. It was for her own social system and the right to direct it." [26]

The complexity of the discussion did not disguise the fact that the measure "was only prevented by the want of means of the planters." Even Koopmanschap's magic failed to make the impoverished South attractive to Chinese sojourners. The "struggle for the monopoly of the Southern coolie trade . . . between the descendants of the original Yankee slave traders, the original Southern slave drivers, and Dutchmen with unpronounceable names," which a satire in the New York *Herald* envisioned, never materialized. With California able to offer higher wages than the South, "the Chinamen are evidently in no hurry to come here," the *Picayune* closed the episode, and "there is no need . . . of exciting either our fears or our expectations about them." [27]

Whereas the Memphis Convention had hoped for many thousands, only a trickle of Chinese found their way into the region. Railroad construction work attracted most of them. Six hundred Chinese built portions of the Alabama and Chattanooga Railroad in the winter of 1870.[28] The failure of the company contributed to Koopmanschap's bankruptcy petition of May 1872, when he could not liquidate his assets of $160,000 in railroads bonds and $100,000 in notes given by Chinese for allowances and passage money, while laborers and storekeepers in Alabama demanded $260,000. His obituaries credited Koopmanschap with the importation of twelve hundred Chinese to construct a line in Georgia. The company failed, so the story went, owing the laborers $113,000. Koopmanschap lost about $80,000 by

sending the workers back to China according to the agreement.[29] On January 8, 1870, at Gretna across the river from
New Orleans, the steamer *Mississippi* landed two hundred
and fifty Chinese employed by General John G. Walker for
the Houston and Texas Railroad. Their three-year contracts
secured the workers twenty dollars a month and the headmen
forty. "At present the price of Chinese labor will not justify
the planter in employing Chinese," a reporter of the *Picayune*
reflected while covering the transfer of sojourners into the
box cars of the Louisiana and Texas Railroad for their trip
to Galveston and Houston.[30]

Chinese laborers worked the cane fields of Louisiana for
a few years, some having been brought over from Cuba in
1866. Later, colonies of Catholic Chinese from the Philippines reached the Sugar Bowl. They soon deserted the plantations and became independent fishermen and truck farmers
for the New Orleans market. The contract for a group of Chinese on one plantation in 1870 specified twenty-six days of
labor at $14 a month in gold, with daily rations of two pounds
of fresh meat, two pounds of rice, and a third ounce of tea.
Late in the fall of 1871 the Chinese house of Fou Loy & Co.
of New Orleans and San Francisco advertised to bring fifteen
hundred laborers from China at $22 a month. Three planters
paid $48,000 for 178 sojourners. Within a year the Chinese
broke their contracts and accepted other work at higher
wages. A Mississippi planter managed to keep twenty-five
sojourners for three years. In Georgia Frances Butler Leigh
and others engaged seventy Chinese through an agent to
work rice fields on General's Island. The Leighs leased a
neighboring island "to an energetic young planter, who . . .
brought down thirty Chinamen to work it." Captain Gift returned from China to Arkansas with six hundred and fifty
laborers only to see them desert the cotton fields at the first
opportunity. About a hundred others went from California
to Jefferson County in the eastern part of the state. Each was

offered as inducement an allowance of a half pound of opium monthly. The cost of the drug was said to be one of the reasons for the planters' abandoning the experiment and most of the Chinese drifted back to San Francisco. Others never went further south than St. Louis where their influx led to the establishment of a Sunday School on Eleventh and Locust Streets "for the instruction of the young of that race" in 1869.[81]

American and Chinese agents arranged the importation of Chinese into the South. The contract agency which facilitated the sojourners' expansion beyond the boundaries of California had appeared during the Chinese advance into the Rocky Mountains. The headmen of the district companies in San Francisco and the storekeepers in the mountain camps had handled the distribution of Chinese mining companies throughout the claims in the Mother Lode. The increased use of Chinese laborers in construction work and the building of the Transcontinental Railroad required the presence of Chinese companies at set dates in work camps along the surveyed route. The race to complete the road put a premium on reliable and punctual labor and created a set of American and Chinese agents. They contracted Chinese workers in San Francisco for specific tasks, or shipped them directly from Hong Kong to wherever their labor was needed. Planters and railroad builders carried the process one step further at the peak of the demand for labor. They sent their own emissaries to California and China to fill their particular needs.

These projects, which aimed at bringing freed Negro plantation workers to terms, also intended to use Chinese in the struggle between capital and labor. The adaptation of the Chinese importation system to labor warfare occasioned the first movement of Chinese sojourners to the East. In three places, North Adams, Massachusetts, Belleville, New Jersey, and Beaver Falls, Pennsylvania, entrepreneurs contracted for Chinese laborers in San Francisco as a weapon against striking American workers.[32]

North Adams had expected the event for days. Finally, on June 13, 1870, two "emigrant cars" rolled into the railroad depot of the small Berkshire hill town. On that Monday, thousands surrounded the station and lined the street leading to Calvin T. Sampson's factory. The strikebreakers had arrived. Seventy-five "pig-tailed, calico-frocked" Chinese debarked and hobbled on wooden shoes to the bunks of their barracks in the rear of a plain, three-story brick structure, the "Model Shoe Factory." When Sampson's frightened mystery weapon in his fight against the Secret Order of the Knights of St. Crispin had finally disappeared behind the well-guarded factory gate, the thirty extra policemen in civilian clothes, the excited spectators, and the pastor of the Congregational Church "were profoundly grateful that the entrance had been effected without bloodshed." The "celestial shoemakers" were a "spectacle which nobody wanted to miss even long enough to stoop for a brickbat." On that Monday night, the Oriental population of Massachusetts more than doubled.[33]

A newspaper report had directed Calvin T. Sampson's attention to the successful use of Chinese laborers in a San Francisco shoe factory.[34] The story furnished the manufacturer with the decisive weapon in the final round of his fight against the Crispins, in 1870 the largest organization of workingmen the United States had known. In the spring of that year he sent George Chase to California with instructions to contract for seventy-five Chinese, but in later years, in a conversation with a British traveler, Sampson himself took credit for the trip to the West.[35] Sampson's superintendent made contact with the San Francisco factory owner, and in turn met the agent of an importer of Chinese laborers who, after investigating Sampson's credit for two days, wrote the contract. The workers were to be paid twenty-three dollars a month for the first year, the agreement stipulated, and twenty-six for the second and third years. Ah Sing, their English-speaking foreman, received sixty dollars monthly. The workers clothed and boarded themselves. The San Francisco house agreed to replace any laborer unfit for the project and to pay a forfeit of twenty-five dollars. Sampson pledged to forward to San Francisco the body of any worker who died in his service for ultimate return of the bones to China. Only when the seventy-five Chinese actually came east on the newly completed Transcontinental Railroad did the people of North Adams realize why Sampson's superintendent had mysteriously left town for a business trip to San Francisco.[36]

The vanguard of the Chinese stunned the East. Their arrival confused politicians and clergymen, industrialists and labor leaders, editors and poets. They distracted General Joseph Roswell Hawley from the favorite pastime of Radical Republicans who aimed at curbing Democrats by keeping alive the hatred of the Civil War, and he interrupted his "waving the bloody shirt" long enough to greet the newcomers in the grand tradition of the Fourth of July oration. "With the flag over our heads and the New Testament in our hand," the former governor of, and future senator from, Connecticut thundered, "bid them come." Their arrival tested the Radical Republicans' view on the equality of races and their arguments against slavery and in favor of Reconstruction. Wendell Phillips discarded the prewar humanitarianism that had permeated his fight against the peculiar institution when he came out against the presence of Chinese in Massachusetts.[37]

Senator Henry Wilson, a former shoemaker and ardent antislavery crusader, and Representative Benjamin Butler, conscious of the workingmen's vote, formed a center of Eastern opposition to the sojourners. "We shall see Sambo and Patrick shaking hands on a common platform — 'Down with the Chinese!,' " the *Alta* predicted from a distance. Northern

Democrats also wanted the labor vote but were handicapped by Southern Democrats who speculated on replacing the emancipated slaves in their fields with Chinese laborers. The *Nation*, with apparent delight, recorded the details of the public embarrassment. The reaction of the nine thousand people in the Berkshire community toward the "first colony of Asiatics that ever settled in New England" has received less attention than "those sounding but utterly empty phrases which Massachusetts politicians are accustomed to laugh at in their sleeves when sitting on the platform behind Gen[eral Nathaniel Prentiss] Banks." [38]

The American, Irish, and French-Canadian Crispins accepted the Chinese strikebreakers in North Adams as equals. The union members primarily used established trade union weapons to combat the rigorous entrepreneur's fifth column. They usually invoked the solidarity of workingmen against the haughty might of capitalists. In previous battles such techniques had worked successfully. The non-Crispin workers hired by Calvin T. Sampson as strikebreakers in 1868 were two years later loyal members of the local lodge. Imported scabs from the shoe manufacturing center of North Brookfield were no more than off the train before the Crispin local had dissuaded them from going to work. Extending the solidarity of the workingmen to the Chinese laborers, the strikers attempted to organize a local Chinese lodge of Crispins that would agitate for wages of two dollars a day. The undertaking failed. While the Chinese labored in the assembly and the pegging room, former Crispins and greenhands found that working in other departments of the factory was better than not working at all.

"Chinese lodges will come in due time when enough Chinamen are collected together in any given place," the *Nation* commented, "but the prospects appear not to be immediately flattering at North Adams." For Washington Gladden, the pastor of the town's Congregational Church who was to reach prominence as critic of the American industrial society in the same decade, "the self-restraint of the working-people . . . was a cause of gratitude." Although the Chinese shoemakers continued to live in the community for several years, "there was very little disposition to interfere with them; they were permitted to go and come without insult or annoyance." Philanthropists cared for the Chinese, and "various well-meant endeavors to teach them the English language and fit them for self-support and citizenship were promptly set into operation." Gladden regarded North Adams' reaction to the Chinese as "an encouraging instance of the absorbent power of good sense and good will in an American community, in dealing with an acute case of social inflammation." [39]

Although the people of North Adams accepted the Chinese in their midst, their veiled animosity contrasted with the professional enthusiasm of the reporters of *Harper's* and *Scribner's*. The citizens themselves needed missionaries more than the Chinese, a correspondent of a leading religious weekly concluded after a visit to North Adams. "They've no business here," one woman had told him, "everybody hates 'em but Mr. Sampson, and he worships 'em more than he does his Maker." The Chinese "don't take part in the government," another agreed, "they've no wives or families. They don't mean to stay here. They only come to get money — our money." [40] With the exception of the handful of good Christians who taught the Chinese on Sundays to read and write and the visitors who came to watch the teachers, the people of North Adams saw little of the strangers. The workers made modest purchases in town. On Sundays some wore black American suits, and others entertained their Sunday School teachers at dinner. Only hesitantly did the Chinese leave the confines of their regimented world.

California's attitude toward slavery had shaped the West's encounter with the sojourners. The strange workers in mining and construction companies, governed by the invisible control system of Chinese California, resembled slave gangs and were a constant threat to the California dream. Their regimented world heightened the insecurity of an unstable society that lacked the safety of settled ways on which one of Massachusetts' most northerly manufacturing towns met the newcomers. However, the Crispins' failure to convert the Chinese strikebreakers in North Adams turned Eastern workingmen into determined opponents of Chinese labor and ardent advocates of Chinese exclusion.

The applause for Calvin T. Sampson, who had lived up to the New England image of the self-reliant man by resisting "intimidation and violence" and triumphing "over every obstacle that hindered the development of his prosperity," drowned the resolutions of indignation meetings.[41] Denouncing the Chinese as servile and their presence as intended to degrade the American workingmen, Eastern laborers felt their world threatened not by the resemblance of the Chinese to slaves but by the deadly weapon which these docile workers put in the hands of reckless entrepreneurs. The use of sojourners as strikebreakers alarmed the Eastern workingmen.

When Captain James B. Hervey set out to repeat Sampson's coup in Belleville, New Jersey, "it was deemed advisable" that the entry of the Chinese into the Passaic Steam Laundry "should be made under the cover of night," owing "to the threats of violence against the imported laborers made by a gang of roughs . . . , who had heard of the approach of the 'coming man.'" From morning till night of Tuesday, September 20, 1870, the two cars of the train which brought the sixty-eight Chinese down the Erie Railroad were detained at Port Jervis, in New York's Orange County, at the northernmost tip of New Jersey. It was just midnight when the Chinese marched into the silent streets of Belleville, a few miles north of Newark on the Passaic

River, and were "assigned to safe . . . quarters in one of the laundry buildings." A high board fence, "erected immediately around the works," prevented "any intercourse between the Chinese and too curious visitors." A reporter of a Newark paper hours later found his way into the Chinese quarters in several rooms of the upper story of the factory. All newcomers wore the Chinese upper garment of blue muslin, American felt hats, and Chinese shoes. They readily converted the downstairs kitchen into a "sort of barber-shop and dressing room." Their presence made Captain Hervey the object of contempt of Eastern workingmen.

Captain James B. Hervey had sailed the seven seas before he settled down at Belleville with a comfortable little fortune in the middle 1850's. He soon doubled it through speculation in land and started the Passaic Steam Laundry which washed five hundred dozen shirts per week. At first the Captain engaged "practical laundrywomen," but since he could not get along with them he retained only a dozen, and went regularly to Castle Garden, the landing depot for immigrants on The Battery at the southernmost tip of Manhattan, where he secured batches of newly arrived German and Irish girls who were able to do second rate work after a few weeks of training. The two groups had quarreled continuously, and during the eighteen months before the arrival of the Chinese the Captain employed only "Irish women of the Catholic persuasion." However, "most of the young ladies," the Captain complained, were above work and departed as soon as they got thirty dollars in their hands. "Out of every hundred new hands at least sixty" left "after learning the business, either to get married or to take out jobs." Whenever the laundry girls noticed that their employer had a large contract to fill, they promptly demanded higher wages and went on strike. In July 1870, the Captain took "the hint of the Massachusetts shoe-manufacturer," and set out for San Francisco to contract Chinese laborers.[42]

George T. Casebolt, in later years Hervey's business partner and eventually the sole owner of the Passaic Steam Laundry, at the age of ninety-three remembered that he negotiated the initial Chinese contracts in San Francisco.[43] It is more likely, however, as contemporary news stories reported, that Hervey himself secured the laborers "through the principal Chinese agency in San Francisco." The three-year contract guaranteed each Chinese twenty gold dollars per month. As in North Adams, they provisioned and clothed themselves. Hervey boarded his European recruits who received ten dollars monthly for two months, after which they netted between twenty and thirty dollars per month. Within six months the pay of an industrious girl amounted to fifty dollars a month clear of board and lodging. Hervey's female employees took the arrival of the Chinese laborers in stride. "Out of the one hundred women only sixteen" left their places, and twelve "were glad enough to be taken back before night." [44]

Captain Hervey received several threatening letters. One note informed him of his impending assassination if the Chinese were not discharged before the first of October. An indignation meeting attracted about two hundred Bellevillians and four carriage loads of mechanics from Paterson. They listened to addresses by Democratic politicians, "kept constantly demanding some practical way of abating the nuisance and persistently refused to take the political stone tendered them for bread," according to the report of a staunch Republican newspaper. After the speeches Belleville settled down to the task of living with the Chinese. The first Chinese New Year celebrated in the village found all sojourners working as ironers. The laundry's need for laborers continued to plague Captain Hervey. In the following months he continually increased the number of Chinese. Ah Bong, the headman better known as Charlie Ming, went back to San Francisco and several weeks later returned with fifty-two recruits, increasing to 172 the total number of Chinese employed in the laundry. When Charlie Ming was on the point of returning to China, the Newark paper still reported the arrival of new laborers at the laundry which eventually employed three hundred Chinese.[45]

The Eastern encounter with Chinese on the Passaic, as well as on the Hoosic and the Beaver rivers, repeated the development in California on a reduced scale. Against the background of a running debate on the presence of Chinese in Belleville in local newspapers, some citizens set out to discover the newcomers. A missionary of the Methodist Episcopal Church, just returned from his station at Foochow, led the way. With a series of lectures Reverend Stephen L. Baldwin enlightened congregations on the social habits and customs of the Chinese. The illness of two laundry workers, their misery and anxiety, brought Bellevillians into contact with the therapy of a Chinese physician. Opportunely he had been discovered in neighboring New York City after the patients refused to submit to a diagnosis by a white doctor. The elaborate Chinese funeral pageant of Zing Sing, at which the Reverend S. P. Dally, a Methodist clergyman, officiated, impressed onlookers with the genuine grief of Chinese mourners. His observations led one reporter to conclude that "death raises the same feelings in the breast of the heathen as in the Christian." The first celebration of the Chinese New Year in Belleville permitted an additional glance at the customs of the isolated laundry workers.[46]

Eight months after their arrival "Captain Hervey's boys" went "about the village with the most perfect freedom, . . . unmolested and even treated with marked kindness." Hervey, however, kept assuring the public that only the lack of suitable workers forced him to continue to employ Chinese. The Newark *Advertiser* linked the burning of a hat factory in Woodside to the bitter feeling against the proprietors created by the rumor among the workers "that

Chinamen were to be employed in the factory." A Sunday School, started "by some of the prominent citizens of the village" one year after the arrival of the first Chinese in Belleville, provided a safer meeting ground than the work shop. Within a year "many of the scholars," assisted by twenty teachers from different churches, "made great progress in reading and writing" and manifested a "deep interest in spiritual matters." They delighted Reverend Bergfels, the Superintendent of the Chinese Sabbath School, with the gift of a silk banner bearing the inscription in Chinese characters, "Boys of the Province of Canton Go for Jesus." In turn Reverend Alfred Taylor pleased the Chinese with his definition of eternity as "great big much time." At the anniversary exercises the number of students had increased from fifteen to sixty, with an average attendance of thirty-five. A short time later the members of the Chinese Sunday School presented their superintendent with a "handsome gold ring." [47]

When Ah Young, "importer of Chinese labor" and "successor to Koopmanschap," visited Belleville in December 1872, to arrange for renewing the contracts which were to expire in a few months, several Chinese had found employment outside the Passaic Steam Laundry. House servants had spread the example of Chinese industry and docility in New Jersey. As independent washermen the sojourners moved into Hackettstown and Newark, and started the development which in later years led George T. Casebolt to claim "that the Chinese barracks of the Pacific Steam Laundry gave way to the Chinatowns of Newark and New York." At least one of the Orientals ventured to follow his Irish girl into New York City only to be arrested for disorderly conduct after he chose the noon train in which to declare his feelings. [48]

Within a decade the Chinese experiment at Belleville, as well as the one at North Adams, had run its course. A multitude of factors accounted for the disappearance of the Chinese enclaves. When their contracts expired, many of the homesick sojourners returned to China to face the future complacently, fortified with their savings. Others found work outside the restrictions of Chinese labor companies. Contractors in San Francisco felt reluctant to dispatch additional workers into industrial areas where American laborers were likely to be hostile to their presence. The panic of 1873 contributed to keeping the animosity in bounds, by making any further experiments with Chinese laborers in the East costly, unprofitable, and unnecessary gambles. Along the windows of factories white workingmen lined up again who did not ask for a three-year contract, the deposit of a security in San Francisco, and a round-trip ticket from the Sacramento to the Hudson.

The coming of the Chinese to Beaver Falls, Pennsylvania, on July 1, 1872, followed the pattern established in North Adams and Belleville. From New Orleans, and not from San Francisco, that Sunday evening came the seventy Chinese whom John Reeves marched the four blocks from the depot to the factory of the Beaver Falls Cutlery Company. Superintendent Reeves, the secretary and treasurer of the cutlery, had tried in vain to contract Chinese laborers in San Francisco. He found the sojourners "well contented with conditions in California" and reluctant "to leave their countrymen and journey so far into the interior of a strange land." Although he had the assistance of mission workers and manufacturers employing Chinese in California, the emissary from Pennsylvania remained unsuccessful. Reeves finally learned that a company of Chinese laborers had completed grading the route of a projected railroad in the vicinity of New Orleans. Accompanied by an interpreter he hurried south and hired the entire gang.

The cutlery, in the valley of the Beaver River, about three and a half miles from its confluence with the Ohio River, faced labor problems similar to those of Sampson's shoe factory and Hervey's laundry. The business year 1872 had opened with a promising outlook and the workers struck for higher wages. Concessions kept production going for a short time until new demands caused another shutdown. Frequent strikes continued to disrupt the work until someone, inspired by the examples of North Adams and Belleville, suggested replacing the strikers with Chinese hands. A couple of years earlier the ownership of the joint-stock company had passed into the hands of the Harmony Society which from nearby Economy had in 1865 laid out the lots for a manufacturing center at the site of Beaver Falls. The Economites, however, did not formulate the policy of the management. The suggestion seems to to have come from a minister of the Methodist Protestant Church who for years had been actively interested in Chinese mission work. Joseph W. Knott, accountant and bookkeeper of the cutlery during the Chinese experiment, believed in later years that Jacob Henrici, a trustee of the Harmony Society, and Henry T. Reeves, the president of the company, had also envisioned this solution to the problem.

The members of the Harmony Society formulated their defense on March 1, 1873, in their reply to a delegation of citizens from Beaver Falls to Economy who had protested "against the employment of Chinese laborers in the works." The Society refused to accept any responsibility for the importation of the laborers. The members emphasized that only one director represented their interest on the board of the company. "The directors of the Company," they stressed, "without our knowledge as a Society, entered into a contract" with "three hundred Chinese laborers for a time of four years." As a result of this move, the Society argued, the works employed one hundred and twenty white residents of Beaver Falls in addition to one hundred and ninety Chinese. The Economites felt that the Chinese enabled the cutlery again to fulfill its major task: to provide employment for the residents whom the Harmony Society had attracted to Beaver Falls. However, as long as the Chinese remained, the animosity continued. When several pastors and their congregations feared that the establishment of a Chinese mission would antagonize the workingmen, the Harmony Society backed the Presbyterian Church financially in attempts to improve the welfare of the Chinese.

The Sunday School, as in North Adams and Belleville, again bridged the gulf between the two worlds. Many Chinese took a lively interest in the entertainments, strawberry festivals, and oyster suppers of the Presbyterian Church. During the time of the Chinese New Year the sojourners reciprocated, filled baskets with tea and delicacies, and visited the homes of their friends and Sunday School teachers. They regularly patronized the principal confectionery and became fond of ice cream. The majority of the Chinese laborers carried silver or gold watches; some possessed diamond rings purchased from local merchants. Predominantly, however, their cultural life turned around their traditional festivals and elaborate funerals. A tea store, run by the Chinese interpreter, formed the center of their social life. Here they received their pay, and here they purchased their clothes, opium, and tea. When a new interpreter joined the company he brought with him his wife, the only Chinese woman to come to Beaver Falls. At times the affairs of the sojourners kept the citizens' ears buzzing. For a while "Pretty Joe" provided the town with a love story before his departure for Philadelphia where he became a merchant. In 1877, the last of the Chinese went home. Groups of workers had already left from time to time, but the remainder departed in a body with their fare to San Francisco paid by the Cutlery Company.[49]

The Chinese disappeared from the three locations leaving hardly a trace. In most cases the bones of their dead countrymen had gone back to China before them. But these encounters produced a lasting heritage in the growing antagonism of Eastern workmen for the Chinese. The impact of the three experiments with Chinese strikebreakers came to overshadow the humanitarian concern which the East once accorded the newcomers. In the 1780's the beginning of the China trade had now and then brought Chinese sailors and traders into the harbors of the Atlantic seaboard. Their sometime destitute conditions aroused the pity of merchants in Baltimore and Philadelphia. Later, jugglers and players, tumblers and acrobats appeared on Broadway. Chinese museums in Philadelphia, Boston, and New York furnished a more intimate view of the mysterious empire which received increasing attention as a result of the establishment of missionary and diplomatic contacts. They supplemented the curios which had found their way from China to the Atlantic Coast in the sea chests of captains, supercargoes, and sailors. Mixed marriages cemented the early bonds. "Many Chinamen in New York . . . have gone the way of matrimony with their elephant-eyed, olive-skinned contemporaries," *Harper's Weekly* described the marriages between Chinese cigar vendors and Irish apple women in 1857. A few years later the New York *Times* found most keepers of Chinese boarding houses married to Irish or German girls.[50]

The importation of Chinese strikebreakers into North Adams, Belleville, and Beaver Falls disrupted the sympathetic attitude which the East had shown to Chinese drifters for many decades. The three experiments stamped the sojourners as economic threats to Eastern workingmen and politicians. Laboring men came to regard Chinese as a danger to their livelihood without having previously shared the preoccupation of Californians with slavery or having experienced their fear of the resemblance between Chinese laborers and slaves. The reaction in the East paralleled the growing feeling in the West which now, because of the changing California economy, viewed Chinese laborers also as an economic threat.

The pressure from their constituents linked the interests of Eastern and Western politicians and elevated the Chinese question to a national issue.

Different influences conditioned the sentiments that molded Eastern and Western attitudes toward the Chinese. The expediencies of politics transferred into law the sections' combined opposition to the sojourners. The convenient alliance obliterated the distinctions between Western and Eastern reactions to the Chinese. Its rationale interpreted the emerging Chinese question as the necessary result of economic, social, and moral laws directing the destinies of nations. This explanation obscured the initial opposition's limited nature. While California's attitude toward slavery had shaped the Western reaction against Chinese, the experience of the Pacific Coast indicated that the sojourners as such hardly formed an economic threat. The Orientals menaced the workingmen's welfare only in particular economic settings such as the three strike-ridden factories of the East. However, there the Chinese represented no social problem as they did in California.

The politicians' manipulation of the new national issue produced a series of federal laws which restricted the coming of Chinese to the United States. Their schemes accompanied two decades of violence which saw the sand-lot riots in San Francisco and the Rock Springs massacre. The extension of the Chinese issue to the national scene also solidified the humanitarian efforts at acculturation. In coming to the Atlantic Coast the Chinese exchanged the web of local prejudice in the West for the restricted economic rivalry of the East. While the invisible control system accompanied the sojourners beyond the Rocky Mountains, its effectiveness deteriorated. Without the network of Chinatowns and stores, the sojourners relied for their diversions and provisions at first on facilities provided by the humanitarian concern or the business sense of Easterners. The Chinese quarters which later came into prominence in the East appeared only as an extension of San Francisco's Chinatown.

The increasing awareness that the United States offered the possibility of living outside their regimented world of work camp and Chinatown encouraged individuals to abandon the control system. The attractions of such metropolitan centers as New York, Philadelphia, Boston, and New Orleans lured sojourners from their familiar path. Together with the impact of the Western world on the bonds of filial piety and familism, the new insights into American life began to modify the sojourners' goal. A small but ever-increasing number of Chinese came to view the United States as a country in which they could live, marry, and raise children. Living in America began to be accepted as a substitute for the traditional aim of returning to China. This change initiated the laborious process which transferred a slowly increasing number of the legion of sojourners into Chinese immigrants.

Until then, their goal had set the Chinese apart from other immigrants and excluded them from the privileges and obligations of newcomers who came to the United States as permanent residents. The sojourners intended to make and save money quickly, and to return to China to a life of ease with the family which their drudgery had maintained. In the clutches of debt bondage or under contract to labor companies, they became docile subjects of bosses and headmen, still directed in the United States by the dictates of the Chinese world, sustained by a control system based on family loyalty and fear. The sojourners shouldered the burden of daily toil in an alien environment in defense of their own system of values. They rejected new standards, and clung to their culture to give meaning to the ordeal.

The sojourners' goal influenced the American reaction. Their world raised up specters that challenged American values. The work camps which regimented anonymous hordes of laborers resembled gangs of Negro slaves. The control system extended debt bondage and despotism to the United States. Chinatown, which harbored indentured emigrants in dilapidated structures, suggested filth and immorality as the sojourners' second nature. These images impressed themselves firmly on Americans and determined the reaction toward the Chinese even after the sojourners had abandoned their traditional goal for the promise of a life defined no longer in terms of mere survival, but of liberty.

GLOSSARY OF CHINESE
CHARACTERS

GLOSSARY

THE romanization, usually an approximation of the Cantonese pronunciation, follows the form most commonly found in the sources. In some cases variants are given in brackets.

Anping 恩平
Bow On [Pao-an] 寶安
Chak Kai [Ch'ih-ch'i] 赤溪
Chew Mui [Ch'ao-mei] 潮梅
Chew Yick Kung Shaw [*chao-i kung-so*] 昭一公所
chia 家
Chin Shan 金山
Ch'ing-ming 清明
Chiu Chin Shan 舊金山
Chu Kiang 珠江
Chung Wah Kung Saw 中華公所
Chung Wah Wui Kun 中華會館
fan-tan [*fan-t'an*] 番攤
Fang Ta-hung 方大洪
Gee Kung Tong 致公堂
Haiping 開平
Hakka [*k'e-chia*] 客家
Hiangshan [Heungsan, Chung Shan] 香山，中山
Hohshan 鶴山
Hop Wo Wui Kun 合和會館

Hu-men 虎門

Hwang Ngantung [Huang En-t'ung] 黃恩彤

hui 會

hui-kuan 會館

Hung-chin-tsei 紅中賊

Hung-men Hui 洪門會

Hung Shun Tong 洪順堂

Hsia-Erh Kuan-Chen 遐邇貫珍

Hsieh I Tong 協義堂

Hsin Chin Shan 新金山

hsin-k'e 新客

Hsin-ta-lu yu-chi chieh-lu 新大陸遊記節錄

I Hing Tong 義興堂

Kauming 高明

Kim Shan [Chin Shan] 金山

Kim-Shan Jit San-Luk 金山日新錄

Kong Pan Yee 公班衙

kongsi 公司

k'u-li 苦力

Kwangchau [Kong Chow] 廣州

Kwang Tek Tong 廣德堂

kung-so 公所

kung-ssu 公司

Langfang Kongsi 蘭芳公司

mei hanna [probably *mo k'un na*] 沒睏那

Nanhai 南海

Ng Yap 五邑

Ning Yeong Wui Kun 寧陽會館

pie-gow [*p'ai-chiu*] 牌九
Punti [*pen-ti*] 本地
Pwanyü 番禺
Sam Yap 三邑
Sam Yap Wui Kun 三邑會館
San-ho Hui 三合會
Sanshwui 三水
San-tien Hui 三點會
Sinan [Sanon, Sunoan] 新安
Sinhwui 新會
Sinning [Toi Shan] 新寧，台山
Sit Ping Quai [Hsieh P'ing-kuei] 薛平貴
Sze Yap 四邑
Sze Yap Wui Kun 四邑會館
Shauking 肇慶
Shunte 順德
Tan Shan Tong 丹山堂
tang 黨
T'ang Yen Gai [*t'ang-jen chieh*] 唐人街
Tanka [*tan-chia*] 蛋家
Tong [*t'ang*] 堂
T'ien-ti Hui 天地會
Tungkwan [Tung Gwoon, Tung-kuan] 東莞
Tung-Ngai San-Luk 東涯新錄
Tseng Wang-yen 曾望顏
tsu 族
wai 圍
Wui Kun [*hui-kuan*] 會館

Yan Wo Wui Kun 人和會館
Yap Si Kongsi 葉氏公司
Yee 余
Yeh Ming-ch'en 葉名琛
Yeong Wo Wui Kun 陽和會館

SOURCES

SOURCES

CONVENTIONAL sources for this history of the Chinese in the United States are limited. Illiterate or poorly educated, the sojourners left few written records of their experience. Scarcely any descendants tell their story in America. The fire of 1906 destroyed the physical remains of the center of their world, San Francisco's old Chinatown. However, other material offers rich perceptions and brings to life the era of these silent sojourners.

The following is not an exhaustive bibliography. It does not even include all items cited in the end notes. As in the case of the evidence for each chapter, detailed documentation for primary sources and secondary materials can be found in the writer's dissertation, Bitter Strength: A History of the Chinese in the United States, 1850–1870 (Harvard University, 1962), in the archives of Widener Library.

Missionary letters and newspaper reports were the most important sources of information. They depict the emigrants' homeland, their passage to California, and their life in the United States. The attempt to verify the broad outlines of the emerging picture and to fill in details led to the inclusion of many other sources of possible significance.

The geography and the social life of the Pearl River Delta attracted the attention of missionaries who found outlets for their restricted zeal in sympathetic reports. Their writings are preserved in the Papers of the American Board of Commissioners for Foreign Missions (Houghton Library, Harvard University), as articles in the twenty volumes of the *Chinese Repository* (Canton), and in printed journals, reminiscences, and memoirs. They throw light on facets of daily life hardly treated in Chinese gazetteers, the learned compilers of which obviously looked more into their books than beyond the yamen walls. Other Americans verify the observations of missionaries. The Dexter and Appleton Manuscripts (Baker Library, School of Business Administration, Harvard University) contain impressions of early American traders in China who did not have the literary ambitions of William C. Hunter, *Bits of Old China* (2nd ed., Shanghai, 1911) and *'Fan Kwae' at Canton* . . . (2d ed., Shanghai, 1911), or Robert B. Forbes, . . . *Reminiscences* (Boston, 1878). William Wightman Wood, *Sketches of China* . . . (Philadelphia, 1830), Osmond Tiffany, Jr., *Canton Chinese* . . . (Boston, 1849), and Harriet Low, . . . *Journal* . . . (Boston, 1900), refreshingly view the scene from the vantage point of curious travelers.

The correspondence of the Presbyterian Board of Foreign Missions (Presbyterian Historical Society, Philadelphia) contains the reports of missionaries to the Chinese in California who had already worked on mission stations in the Middle Kingdom. William Speer, *Oldest and Newest Empire* . . . (Hartford, 1870), the first Presbyterian missionary to the sojourners, combined his insight into their homeland and a rare familiarity with their institutions in the United States. Letters of other ministers to the Foreign and Domestic Committee of the Protestant Episcopal Church found their way into the *Spirit of Missions* (New York). Memoirs of later missionaries, Otis Gibson, *Chinese in America* (Cincinnati, 1877), and Ira M. Condit, *Chinaman* . . . (Chicago, 1900), add little to the picture. The recollections of preachers and pastors and the histories of California churches deal only in passing with the newcomers. John J. Manion's accounts of tongs (Bancroft Library, University of California), penned while he was head of the San Francisco police's Chinatown detail between 1921 and 1946, further an understanding of the Chinese societies.

Measured reports and judicious editing make the Hong Kong *China Mail* the most valuable Western language newspaper in the Far East. The San Francisco *Alta* occupies the same position on the Pacific Coast. A variety of other California journals, ranging from the Sacramento *Placer Times* to the San Francisco *California Police Gazette*, and the Bancroft Scraps, the newspaper clippings in the Bancroft Library, balance and supplement its reports. The *Alta* and the San Francisco *Herald* are particularly useful for their regular reprints of news items from smaller papers. These journals cover the expanse of the Mother Lode, from the Mariposa *Gazette* in the south to the Downieville *Sierra Citizen* in the north. The New Orleans *Picayune*, the North Adams *Transcript*, the Newark *Advertiser*, and the New York *Nation* help trace the movement of sojourners into the South and the East. Frederick Rudolph, "Chinamen in Yankeedom: Anti-Unionism in Massachusetts in 1870," *American Historical Review* (New York), 53:1–29 (October 1947) depicts the background at North Adams. Beaver Falls, Pennsylvania, yields a manuscript by Charles Reeves May (Carnegie Free Library, Beaver Falls) to tell part of the story.

The few preserved copies of Chinese newspapers published in the United States during the 1850's are disappointing for the purpose of this investigation. Directed at the Chinese in California, or at readers acquainted with their mode of life, they lack almost completely any direct description of the sojourners' world. Their incidental information, advertisements, and business directories compensate in part for this shortcoming and enrich the data gained from *City Directories* of various California towns.

Magazines were of secondary importance, with the exception of the *Journal of the Indian Archipelago and Eastern Asia* (Singapore) which illuminated the world of Chinese sojourners in Malaysia. Helpful for a broad view of life and work in Chinatown and countryside were *Hesperian, Hutch-*

ings', Overland, and *Pioneer* in San Francisco; *Harper's Weekly* and *Monthly, Hunt's, Leslie's,* and *Scribner's* in New York; *Atlantic, Gleason's,* and *Littell's* in Boston; *Lippincott's* in Philadelphia; and *De Bow's* in New Orleans.

Public documents became storehouses of information on the newcomers after one penetrated the unimaginative compilations and the façade of polemic attached to the evidence. *Senate Rept. 689,* 44 Cong., 2 Sess., stands out among the congressional documents, flanked by the California Senate reports of 1876 and 1878 on *Chinese Immigration,* and *House Mis. Doc. 5* and *House Rept. 572,* both 46 Cong., 2 Sess. The *Report of the Royal Commission . . .* (Ottawa, 1885) conveniently incorporates into its findings some results of these investigations. The statements on emigration by British officials in China, collected in the *Parliamentary Papers,* supplement the despatches of American consuls. Among the latter, *Senate Ex. Doc. 99,* 34 Cong., 1 Sess., is of importance for aspects of the passage.

It was the State of California, however, that was particularly concerned with the sojourners. The *Journals of the California Legislature,* the *Statutes* of the various sessions, and the *Reports* of the California Supreme Court contain such crucial documents as the testimony of the headmen of the Four Houses before the Committee on Mines and Mining, *Appendix to Assembly Journal,* 4 Sess., 1853. The *Municipal Reports* of the San Francisco Board of Supervisors do not go beyond the extensive coverage which the leading California newspapers extended to the affairs of their metropolis. However, the "Report of the Special Committee" in the Appendix of the *Municipal Reports for 1884–85,* published also as part of William B. Farwell, *Chinese at Home and Abroad* (San Francisco, 1885), reproduces a valuable map of Chinatown.

Among other contemporary material two groups of sources stand out; one, a limited number of pamphlets, rich in information and saturated with polemic, the other, the seemingly unlimited number of Western Americana. Most letters, journals, travelogues, and reminiscences sooner or later reveal a chapter, a paragraph, or a line on the Chinese. Their authors include such strange bedfellows as Henryk Sienkiewicz, "Chinese in California . . . ," *California Historical Society Quarterly* (San Francisco), 34:301–316 (December 1955) and Charles Peters, by no means the last of a number of "honest miners" who put to paper his *Autobiography* (Sacramento, [1915]).

The classics of the field do not disappoint. Keen observations and a flair for well-rounded scenes are combined in William Shaw, *Golden Dreams* . . . (London, 1851); Alexandre Holinski, *La Californie* . . . (Bruxelles, 1853); Frank Marryat, *Mountains and Molehills* . . . (New York, 1855); Hinton Helper, *Land of Gold* . . . (Baltimore, 1855); Friedrich Gerstaecker, *Californische Skizzen* (Leipzig, 1856); J. Douglas Borthwick, *Three Years* . . . (Edinburgh, 1857); Horace Greeley, *Overland Journey* . . . (New York, 1860); Albert D. Richardson, *Beyond the Mississippi* . . . (Hartford, 1867); and Samuel Bowles, *Our New West* . . . (Hartford, 1869).

Many other accounts are equally rewarding, but are surpassed by a number of less literate products which ploddingly detail phases of Chinese life: Pringle Shaw, *Ramblings* . . . (Toronto, [1856?]); Israel Joseph Benjamin, *Drei Jahre* . . . (Hannover, 1862); Albert S. Evans, *À la California* . . . (San Francisco, 1873); Hemmann Hoffmann, *Californien* . . . (Basel, 1871); Caroline C. Leighton, *Life* . . . (Boston, 1884); and John Carr, *Pioneer Days* . . . (Eureka, California, 1891). The volumes of the *California Historical Society Quarterly* contain the journals of Charles E. DeLong and the recollections of Edwin A. Sherman and other useful letters and reminiscences. Among the numerous well-known accounts of visitors to San Francisco, Liang Ch'i-ch'ao, *Hsin-*

ta-lu yu-chi chieh-lu [Selected Records of Travels in the New Continent] (Shanghai, 1936), occupies a unique position by virtue of the light he sheds on the social structure of the sojourners' world on the eve of transition.

The life stories and portraits of five Chinese assassins make the *Murder of M. V. B. Griswold* . . . (Jackson, California, 1858) the most valuable of all the pamphlets. These sketches expand similar information found in newspaper reports and furnish biographical detail on sojourners sketchily provided in later reminiscences, such as those of a journalist, Yan Phou Lee, *When I Was a Boy* . . . (Boston, [1887]); a minister, Kin Huie, *Reminiscences* (Peking, 1932); a ghost writer, Hamilton Holt (ed.), "Life Story of a Chinaman," . . . *Undistinguished Americans* . . . (New York, 1906), 281–299; or alluded to in a biography, Pardee Lowe, *Father* . . . (Boston, 1943), and an autobiography, Jade Snow Wong, *Fifth Chinese Daughter* (New York, 1950). William Speer's prolific pen produced several pamphlets. His *Humble Plea* . . . (San Francisco, 1856) gives particulars on the financial affairs of Chinese merchant princes. This insight is matched only by Stewart Culin whose brochures on secret societies and social customs make him one of the few perceptive observers of the sojourners' world.

Joaquin Murieta, John Rollin Ridge's penny dreadful of 1854, increased awareness of the wealth of evidence beyond the narrow realm of historical sources. The *Songster* (New York, 1871) of the House of Beadle and Adams suggested a new dimension for the investigation. Pieces of belles-lettres, Chester B. Fernald, *Cat and Cherub* . . . (New York, 1896), and William Norr, *Stories* . . . (New York, [1892]), gave a broader perspective of the extraordinary life in Chinatown. Even the fantastic tales of Alfred Trumble, *Heathen Chinee* . . . (New York, [1882]), and Walter J. Raymond, *Horrors* . . . (Boston, [1886?]), were helpful. They quite clearly demonstrated the limitations of these would-be exposés.

There is no satisfactory history of the Chinese in America. A pioneer study, Mary Roberts Coolidge, *Chinese Immigration* (New York, 1909), is dated but useful for details on the anti-Chinese movement. Dr. Coolidge's unrestrained sympathy for the Chinese urges a re-evaluation of the collected facts. Elmer Clarence Sandmeyer, *Anti-Chinese Movement in California* (Urbana, 1939), only partly balances the distorted perspective. Rose Hum Lee, *Chinese in the United States* (Hong Kong, 1960), an illuminating sociological survey, suffers from inadequate historical sections. The scope of S. W. Kung, *Chinese in American Life* (Seattle, 1962) is too broad, that of Ping Chiu, *Chinese Labor in California* (Madison, 1963), too narrow, but the latter details with statistics the newcomers' involvement in the economy.

William Speer set the general tenor for blindly sympathetic accounts of the Chinese associations with a series of articles in the *Oriental, or Tung-Ngai San-Luk*, in February and March 1855. Over the decades they have inspired legions of writers. The true apologia is of more recent date, William Hoy, . . . *Six Companies* . . . (San Francisco, [1942]). The opposite approach is equally frequent and unsatisfactory. It is exemplified in an account of San Francisco, Benjamin E. Lloyd, *Lights and Shades* . . . (San Francisco, 1876); a pamphlet, G. B. Densmore, *Chinese* . . . (San Francisco, 1880); and an article, Charles Frederick Holder, "Dragon in America . . . ," *Arena* (Boston), 32:113–122 (August 1904).

Most surveyors of the sojourners' world delighted in glimpses of an exotic scene and missed the significance of their delineation. Eng Ying Gong and Bruce Grant, *Tong War* . . . (New York, 1930), show their hazy notions of history by discussing the emergence of early tongs "right after the Civil War, during the California gold rush." Carl Glick and Hong Sheng-hwa, *Swords of Silence* . . . (New York, 1947), ignore Chinese secret societies in California before the turn of the century. Alexander McLeod, *Pigtails and Gold*

Dust . . . (Caldwell, Idaho, 1947), indiscriminately mixes facts and fancy. Richard Dillon, *The Hatchet Men* (New York, 1962), continues to stress the colorful story.

Most studies of Chinatown pay homage to the bizarre aspects of the quarter. A few, such as Arnold Genthe and Will Irwin, *Pictures* . . . (New York, 1908), touch on its more essential function. A collection of telegrams which were sent by Chinese in 1874 and edited by Albert Dressler, . . . *Chinese Chatter* (San Francisco, 1927), provides insight into a Chinatown of the Mother Lode. George R. MacMinn, *Theater of the Golden Era* . . . (Caldwell, 1941), and Lois Rodecape, "Celestial Drama . . . ," *California Historical Society Quarterly*, 23:97–116 (June 1944), competently document the Chinatown stage.

The studies of overseas Chinese in Southeast Asia furnish a framework for the American evidence. Barrington Kaye, *Upper Nankin Street* . . . (Singapore, 1960), a sociological analysis of certain households in present-day Singapore, recalls living conditions in the American Chinatown of the past. Representative of the other background material are Gustave Schlegel, *Thian Ti Hwui* . . . (Batavia, 1866); Victor Purcell, *Chinese in Malaya* (London, 1948); and Leon F. Comber, *Chinese Secret Societies in Malaya* . . . (Locust Valley, New York, 1959). A review article, in answer to the last-mentioned study, accused Mr. Comber of plagiarism, Wong Lin Ken and C. S. Wong, "Secret Societies in Malaya," *Journal of Southeast Asian History* (Singapore), 1:97–114 (March 1960). Whatever the merits of the case may be, ironically, the student of the field ought to be thankful for Mr. Comber's investigation in part precisely because he utilizes the findings of W. L. Wynne, *Triad and Tabut* . . . (Singapore, 1941), published for the official use of the Singapore government only.

The pertinent volumes of Hubert Howe Bancroft's *Works* overshadow the numerous other general histories of Western states. Franke Soulé, *Annals* . . . (New York, 1855) occupies the same position among the municipal histories. Lucile Eaves, *History of California Labor Legislation* . . . (Berkeley, [1910]), and Ira B. Cross, . . . *Labor Movement* . . . (Berkeley, 1935) have not yet been surpassed in wealth of detail. Eldon Griffin, *Clippers and Consuls* . . . (Ann Arbor, 1938) probably never will be. Rodman W. Paul, *California Gold* . . . (Cambridge, 1947) dispels the nostalgic concept of the miner's life. James D. Hart, *American Images* . . . (Berkeley, [1960]) does the same for the legendry of Spanish California. Franklin Walker, *San Francisco's Literary Frontier* (New York, 1939) and *Literary History* . . . (Berkeley, 1950) and Louis B. Wright, *Culture on the Moving Frontier* (Bloomington, 1955) perceptively portray the intellectual life of California. Leonard Pitt, "Beginnings of Nativism . . . ," *Pacific Historical Review* (Berkeley), 30:23–38 (February 1961) adds new insight in a field earlier delineated in part by Rodman W. Paul, "Origin of the Chinese Issue . . . ," *Mississippi Valley Historical Review* (Cedar Rapids) 25:181–196 (September 1938).

Few sojourners have yet received biographical treatment; others intimately connected with their world also have escaped attention. Charles Carvalho and Cornelius Koopmanschap are cases in point. A study of Catholic priests in Northern California, Henry L. Walsh, *Hallowed Were the Gold Dust Trails* ([Santa Clara], 1946) and a biography, John Bernard McGloin, . . . *James Bouchard* . . . (Stanford, [1949]) suggest work yet to be done among Protestant clergymen. Two instructive articles, Robert Seager II, "Denominational Reaction . . ." *Pacific Historical Review* (Berkeley), 28:49–66 (February 1959) and Lionel U. Ridout, "Church, Chinese, and Negroes . . . ," *Historical Magazine of the Protestant Episcopal Church* (New Brunswick), 28:115–138 (June 1959), partly fill the gap.

NOTES

NOTES

CHAPTER I. Delta of Contrasts

1. "Report of the Joint Special Committee to Investigate Chinese Immigration," *Senate Rept. 689*, 44 Cong., 2 Sess., 444–476. The spelling of Chinese proper and place names follows the transcription in the sources. When the local dialect deviates considerably from the familiar rendition, the Wade-Giles version of the Mandarin has been added for clarification. The form of a name that has found its way into the second edition of Webster's *New International Dictionary* is always preferred. The Chinese characters of the settlements can be found in George Macdonald Home Playfair (comp.), *The Cities and Towns of China, a Geographical Dictionary* (2nd ed., Shanghai, 1910).

2. Oscar Lewis and Carroll D. Hall, *Bonanza Inn: America's First Luxury Hotel* (New York, 1939), 19–29, 116–118.

3. Augustus Ward Loomis to Walter Lowrie, December 15, 1859, Correspondence of the Presbyterian Board of Foreign Missions (microfilm, Presbyterian Historical Society, Philadelphia); San Francisco *City Directory*, 1872, 407, 881; [Presbyterian Board of Foreign Missions], *Jubilee Papers of the Central China Presbyterian Mission. 1844–1894. Comprising Historical Sketches of the Mission Stations at Ningpo, Shanghai, Hangchow, Soochow and Nanking, With a Sketch of the Presbyterian Mission Press* (Shanghai, 1895), 3, 4, 9; Ira M. Condit, *The Chinaman as We See Him and Fifty Years of Work For Him* (Chicago, 1900), 97–100.

4. John Ledyard, *A Journal of Captain Cook's Last Voyage to the Pacific Ocean, And in Quest of a North-West Passage, Between Asia & America; Performed in the Years 1776, 1777, 1778, and 1779* (Hartford, 1783), 199–201.

5. Josiah Quincy, ed. *The Journals of Major Samuel Shaw, The First American Consul at Canton* (Boston, 1847), 163–164, 217, 219.

6. Artists depicting the scene supplement the verbal picture, James Orange, ed. *The [Sir Catchick Paul] Chater Collection, Pictures Relating to China, Hongkong, Macao, 1655–1860; With Historical and Descriptive Letterpress* (London, [1924]).

7. Francis L. Hawks, ed. *Narrative of the Expedition of an American Squadron to the China Seas and Japan, Performed in the Years 1852, 1853, and 1854, Under the Command of Commodore M[atthew]. C[albraith]. Perry, United States Navy, By Order of the Government of the United States*, 3 vols. (Washington, 1856), I, 133.

8. W[illiam]. W[ightman]. Wood, *Sketches of China: With Illustrations from Original Drawings* (Philadelphia, 1830), 34–38.

9. William Maxwell Wood, *Fankwei; or, the San Jacinto in the Seas of India, China and Japan* (New York, 1859), 266–267; [Elijah C. Bridgman], "Notices of Hongkong; shape and circumference of the island; names of places, distances, &c.," *Chinese Repository* (Canton), 12:435–437 (August 1843).

10. David Abeel, *Journal of a Residence in China, and the Neighboring Countries; With a Preliminary Essay on the Commencement and Progress of Missions in the World* (2nd ed., New York, 1836), 63–71; J[eremiah]. B[ell]. Jeter, ed. *A Memoir of Mrs. Henrietta Shuck, The First American Female Missionary to China* (Boston, 1849), 93–95; Elma Loines, ed. "Harriet Low's Journal, 1829–1834 (much abridged by Katherine Hillard, 1900)," *The China Trade Post-Bag of the Seth Low Family of Salem and New York* (Manchester, Maine, 1953), 110–198.

11. [Elijah C. Bridgman], "Topography of the province of Canton: notices of the islands from the border of Fukien to the frontiers of Cochinchina," *Chinese Repository*, 12:483 (September 1843).

12. Francis Warriner, *Cruise of the United States Frigate Potomac Round the World, During the Years 1831–1834* (New York, 1835), 193–194; "The Approach to Canton," *Harper's Weekly* (New York), 2:165 (March 13, 1858).

13. [Samuel Wells Williams], "Pagodas in and near Canton: their names and time of their erection," *Chinese Repository*, 19:537–538 (October 1850).

14. William Speer, *The Oldest and the Newest Empire: China and the United States* (Hartford, 1870), 79–80, 82–83.

15. Osmond Tiffany, Jr., *The Canton Chinese, or the American's Sojourn in the Celestial Empire* (Boston, 1849), 130–144.

16. Rev[erend]. P[eter]. Parker's Journal, Papers of the American Board of Commissioners for Foreign Missions, South China, 1831–1837 (Houghton Library, Harvard University).

17. Charles Nordhoff, "The Merchant Vessel," *Nine Years a Sailor: Being Sketches of Personal Experiences in the United States Naval Service, The American and British Merchant Marine, and the Whaling Service* (Cincinnati, 1857), 219–221.

18. Edmund Roberts, *Embassy to the Eastern Courts of Cochin-China, Siam, and Muscat; In the U. S. Sloop-of-War Peacock, David Geislinger, Commander, During the Years 1832–3–4* (New York, 1837), 89–93.

19. [Elijah C. Bridgman], "Description of the City of Canton," *Chinese Repository*, 2:145–160 (August 1833), 2:193–211 (September 1833), 2:261–264 (October 1833), 2:289–303 (November 1833).

20. [Samuel Wells Williams], "Illustrations of men and things in

China: angling for frogs; trials of strength; economy of Chinese workmen; quadrating cash, from a Private Journal," *Chinese Repository*, 10:473 (August 1841).

21. [Elijah C. Bridgman], "Climate of Canton and Macao," *Chinese Repository*, 1:488–491 (April 1833); George B. Cressey, *Land of the 500 Million, A Geography of China* (New York, 1955), 78–79.

22. S[amuel]. Wells Williams, *The Middle Kingdom; A Survey of the Geography, Government, Education, Social Life, Arts, Religion, &c., of the Chinese Empire and Its Inhabitants*, 2 vols. (New York, 1848), II, 29–32.

23. [Samuel Wells Williams], "Course of the Chu Kiang, or Pearl River," *Chinese Repository*, 20:105–110 (February 1851), 113–122 (March 1851).

24. Journal of Mr. E[lijah]. C. Bridgman, ABCFM Papers, South China, 1831–1837.

25. [Elijah C. Bridgman], "Kwangtung Tung-chi, or a general Historical and Statistical Account of the province of Canton. Kwangtung Tungseng shuitau Tu, or map of the entire province of Canton," *Chinese Repository*, 12:309–327 (June 1843).

26. Journal of James G. Bridgman, ABCFM Papers, [Canton], Amoy, Siam, Borneo, 1820–1846; [Elijah C. Bridgman], "Description of the city of Canton: number and character of its inhabitants; its commerce; walks around the walls and into the adjacent country; ingress to the city; note to the governor from Sir John Francis Davis; trip to Fuhshan, [fifteen miles west-southwest of Canton]; effects of the late war; different dialects; a missionary station," *Chinese Repository*, 15:57–68 (February 1846); [James G. Bridgman], "Notice of a trip to Fuhshan, in a Chinese fast-boat, on the twelfth of March, 1847. Written for the Repository by one of the visitors," *Chinese Repository*, 16:142–147 (March 1847).

27. Liang Ch'i-ch'ao, *Hsin-ta-lu yu-chi chieh-lu* [Selected Records of Travels in the New Continent] (Shanghai, 1936), 113; David Te-chao Cheng, *Acculturation of the Chinese in the United States; A Philadelphia Study* (Philadelphia, 1948), 21.

28. [Elijah C. Bridgman (trans.)], "A discourse warning and advising the simple people to appreciate life. By Hwang [Ngantung, Huang En-t'ung], the governor and acting literary chancellor of the province of Kwangtung (or Canton)," *Chinese Repository*, 14:437 (September 1845); Rev. Mr. [R.] Krone, "A Notice of the Sanon District Read before the Society, February 24th, 1858," *Transactions of the China Branch of the Royal Asiatic Society* (Hong Kong), Part VI (1859), 71–105; [Edwin Stevens], "Clanship among the Chinese: feuds between different clans near Canton; substitutes for those who are guilty of murder; republicanism among the clans," *Chinese Repository*, 4:411–415 (January 1836).

29. [Thomas Francis Wade (trans.)], "Tsang Wang-yen on the Origin of the [Triad] Rebellion [in Kwangtung]," George Wingrove Cooke, *China: being 'The Times' special correspondence from China in the years 1857–58* (London, 1858), Appendix, 433–445; Yung Wing, *My Life in China and America* (New York, 1909), 53–55; L[eon]. F. Comber, "The Triad Society in China," *Chinese Secret Societies in Malaya; A Survey of the Triad Society from 1800 to 1900* (Locust Valley, New York, 1959), 19–31.

30. "The Hakka War (Reprint from [the Hong Kong] *China Mail*)," Shanghai *North China Herald and Market Report*, June 29, 1867, 133; Rev. R[udolph]. Lechler, "The Hakka Chinese," *Chinese Recorder and Missionary Journal* (Shanghai), 9:355 (September–October 1878); William C. Hunter, *Bits of Old China* (2nd ed., Shanghai, 1911), 82–106.

31. [William C. Hunter], *The 'Fan Kwae' at Canton before the Treaty Days, 1825–1844. By an old Resident* (2nd ed., Shanghai, 1911), 64–73; Robert B. Forbes, *Personal Reminiscences* (Boston, 1878), 143–145.

32. Ssu-yu Teng, *New Light on the Taiping Rebellion* (Cambridge, 1950), 37, 49–60; Eugene Powers Boardman, *Christian Influence Upon the Ideology of the Taiping Rebellion* (Madison, 1952), 11–18.

33. [John Robert Morrison (trans.)], "Memorial showing the daily increase of enervation and degeneracy in the province of Kwangtung," *Chinese Repository*, 6:592–605 (April 1838).

34. Hu Hsien-chin, *The Common Descent Group in China and Its Function* (New York, 1948), 95–100.

35. Yan Phou Lee, *When I Was a Boy in China* (Boston, [1887]), 17–25; Fong Kum Ngon, "The Chinese Six Companies," *Overland Monthly* (San Francisco), 23:519–521 (May 1894); Hui-chen Wang Liu, *The Traditional Chinese Clan Rules* (Locust Valley, New York, 1959), 1–7. For comments on the use of the term "clan" as the rendering of the Chinese character *tsu* turn to Morton H. Fried's review of Dr. Liu's study in the *Journal of Asian Studies* (Ann Arbor), 19:74–75 (November 1959).

36. Literally "Southern Ocean," the term applies to the whole area of Southeast Asia with Chinese settlements in the broadest sense of the word.

37. Victor Purcell, *The Chinese in Southeast Asia* (London, 1951), 1–53.

38. Pardee Lowe, *Father and Glorious Descendant* (Boston, 1943), 4.

39. "Letter from Fou Sin to his Father & Brother," [T. A. Springer & Co., Printers], *Murder of M[artin]. V[an]. B[uren]. Griswold, By Five Chinese Assassins; Together with the Life of Griswold, and the Statements of Fou Sin, Chou Yee, and Coon You, Convicted and Sentenced to be Hung at Jackson* [California], *April 16, 1858. Also — A*

History of the Murder, as Made up from the Testimony Elicited at the Coroner's Inquest, and the Trials. Illustrated with Correct Likenesses of the Murderers (Jackson, 1858), 25–26; *Hsia-Erh Kuan-Chen* [Gathered Gems from Far and Near] (Hong Kong), II (January 1, 1854), 5b–7b. The missionaries to the Chinese in California, William Speer and Augustus W. Loomis, in their reports to the Secretary of the Presbyterian Board of Foreign Missions in New York between 1853 and 1865, constantly regret the return of the Chinese members of the mission church to their families; Correspondence of the Presbyterian Board of Foreign Missions. See also Warner Muensterberger, "Orality and Dependence; Characteristics of Southern Chinese," *Psychoanalysis and the Social Sciences* (New York), 3:50–53 ([1951]).

40. Ta Chen, *Emigrant Communities in South China; A Study of Overseas Migration and Its Influence on Standards of Living and Social Change* (New York, 1940), 59.

41. Virginia Heyer, "Patterns of Social Organization in New York City's Chinatown," unpub. diss. Columbia University, 1953, 16.

42. Hamilton Holt, ed. "The Life Story of a Chinaman," *The Life Stories of Undistinguished Americans As Told by Themselves* (New York, 1906), 287–288; Ju-k'ang T'ien, *The Chinese of Sarawak: a Study of Social Structure* (London, [1953]), 9–10.

43. [Elijah C. Bridgman], "Walks about Canton: . . . . laborers standing in the market place. Extracts from a private journal," *Chinese Repository*, 4:193 (August 1835).

44. Hong Kong *China Mail*, April 27, 1848; Hong Kong *Overland Register and Price Current*, May 25, 1849; Russell & Co. to William Appleton, April 22, 1849, June 19, 1850, Dexter Manuscripts, Appleton to George D. Carter, February 5, 1849, Appleton Manuscripts (Baker Library, School of Business Administration, Harvard University); E[rnest]. J[ohn]. Eitel, *Europe in China; The History of Hongkong from the Beginning to the Year 1882* (London, 1895), 273.

CHAPTER II. American California

1. John C. Ewers, ed. *Adventures of Zenas Leonard, Fur Trader* (Norman, [1959]), 89–93. See also Henry R. Wagner, *The First American Vessel in California; Monterey in 1796* (Los Angeles, 1954).

2. John Bidwell, *In California Before the Gold Rush* (Los Angeles, 1948), 50.

3. [John C. Frémont], "A Report of the Exploring Expedition to Oregon and North California, in the Years 1843–'44," *Sen.* [Misc.] *Doc. 174*, 28 Cong., 2 Sess., 245.

4. Edwin Bryant, *What I Saw in California: Being the Journal of a Tour, By the Emigrant Route and South Pass of the Rocky Mountains, Across the Continent of North America, the Great Desert Basin, and*

Through California, in the Years 1846, 1847 (Philadelphia, 1848), 241–244.

5. San Francisco *Alta California*, October 31, 1850.

6. Milo Milton Quaife, ed. *The Diary of James K. Polk During His Presidency, 1845 to 1849*, 4 vols. (Chicago, 1910), IV, 374–376.

7. William H. Ellison, ed. "Memoirs of Hon. William M. Gwin," *California Historical Society Quarterly* (San Francisco), 19:2–3 (March 1940).

8. [Daniel Webster], *The Writings and Speeches of Daniel Webster*, 18 vols. (Boston, 1903), X, 83.

9. Earl Pomeroy, "California, 1846–1860: Politics of a Representative Frontier State," *California Historical Society Quarterly*, 32:291–302 (December 1953).

10. Dorothy O. Johansen, "A Tentative Appraisal of Territorial Government in Oregon," *Pacific Historical Review* (Berkeley), 18:485–499 (November 1949).

11. Bayard Taylor, *El Dorado; or, Adventures in the Path of Empire*, 2 vols. (London, 1850), I, 139.

12. Monterey *Californian*, September 5, 1846.

13. *House Ex. Doc. 17*, 31 Cong., 1 Sess., 707.

14. Thomas J. Green, "Report on Mines and Foreign Miners," *California Senate Journal*, 1 Sess., 1850, Appendix S, 493.

15. *Alta*, March 5, 1852. See also J. S. Holliday, "The California Gold Rush Reconsidered," K. Ross Toole *et al.*, eds. *Probing the American West* (Santa Fe, 1962), 35–41.

16. Oscar Handlin, "Introduction," Charles Reznikoff, (trans.), *Three Years in America, 1859–1862, by (I[srael]. J[oseph].) Benjamin*. 2 vols. (Philadelphia, 1956), I, 26.

17. Emerson Daggett, ed. *History of Foreign Journalism in San Francisco*. [Work Projects Administration], *History of Journalism in San Francisco*, 3 vols. (San Francisco, 1939), I, i.

18. Franklin Walker, *A Literary History of Southern California* (Berkeley, 1950), 21–22.

19. Richard Henry Morefield, "Mexicans in the California Mines, 1848–1853," *California Historical Society Quarterly*, 35:44 (March 1956).

20. James D. Hart, *American Images of Spanish California* (Berkeley, [1960]), 32.

21. San Francisco *California Star*, March 11, 1848.

22. Alban W. Hoopes, *Indian Affairs and Their Administration, With Special Reference to the Far West, 1849–1860* (Philadelphia, 1932), 35–68; William Henry Ellison, *A Self-Governing Dominion. California, 1849–1860* (Berkeley, 1950), 137–166. See also Sherburne Friend Cook, *The American Invasion, 1848–1870*, vol. III of *The Conflict Between the California Indian and White Civilization*, 4 vols. (Berkeley, 1943), and John Walton Caughey, ed. *The Indians of Southern California in 1852;*

The B. D. Wilson Report and a Selection of Contemporary Comment (San Marino, 1952).

23. San Francisco *Californian*, March 15, 1848.

24. Helen Tunnicliff Catteral, ed. *Judicial Cases concerning American Slavery and the Negro*, 5 vols. (Washington, 1937), V, 330.

25. *Statutes of California*, 1852, 77.

26. San Francisco *Herald,* December 29, 1851.

27. *Alta*, February 18, 1853.

28. San Francisco *California Police Gazette,* August 26, 1865.

29. John C. Parish, ed. "A Project for a California Slave Colony in 1851," *Huntington Library Bulletin* (Cambridge), 8:171–175 (October 1935).

30. Lucile Eaves, *A History of California Labor Legislation: With an Introductory Sketch of the San Francisco Labor Movement* (Berkeley, [1910]), 91.

31. San Francisco *Daily Evening Picayune*, February 11, 1852.

32. *Herald*, April 16, 1852.

33. Rev. J. C. Simmons, *The History of Southern Methodism on the Pacific Coast* (Nashville, 1886), 55–62.

34. Sacramento *Daily Union,* January 9, 11, 12, 27, February 11, 12, 13, 1858; *Alta*, February 14, March 6, 7, 1858; Delilah L. Beasley, *The Negro Trail Blazers of California* (Los Angeles, 1919), 78–83. See also William E. Franklin, "The Archy Case: The California Supreme Court Refuses to Free a Slave," *Pacific Historical Review*, 32:137–154 (May 1963).

35. *Ex parte* Archy, 9 Cal. 147.

36. *Union*, February 12, 1858; *Alta*, February 14, 1858.

37. Donald E. Harris, "The Issues of the Broderick-Gwin Debates of 1859," *California Historical Society Quarterly* 32:313–325 (December 1953).

38. George D. Lyman, "Introduction," *California As It Is & As It May Be, Or a Guide to the Gold Region. By F[elix]. P[aul]. Wierzbicki, M. D.* (San Francisco, 1933), xx-xxi, xxix.

39. Carl I. Wheat, ed. *California in 1851; The Letters of Dame Shirley*, 2 vols. (San Francisco, 1933), I, 79.

40. George R. MacMinn, *The Theater of the Golden Era in California* (Caldwell, 1941), 86.

41. Franklin Walker, *San Francisco's Literary Frontier* (New York, 1939), 13.

42. Eliza W. Farnham, *California, In-Doors and Out; or, How We Farm, Mine, and Live Generally in the Golden State* (New York, 1856), 108.

43. Louis B. Wright, "Culture and Anarchy on the Pacific Coast: the Age of Gold," *Culture on the Moving Frontier* (Bloomington, 1955), 123–167.

44. Handlin, "Introduction," Reznikoff (trans.), *Three Years in America*, I, 22–23.

CHAPTER III. The Coming

1. The extent of the early Chinese contact with Southeast Asia is summarized in Purcell, *Chinese in Southeast Asia*, 11–30.

2. Persia Crawford Campbell, *Chinese Coolie Emigration to Countries within the British Empire* (London, 1923); Watt Stewart, *Chinese Bondage in Peru, 1849–1874* (Durham, 1951).

3. C[harles]. R[alph]. Boxer, "Notes on the Chinese Abroad in the Late Ming and Early Manchu Periods, Compiled from Contemporary European Sources (1500–1750)," *T'ien Hsia Monthly* (Shanghai), 9:448 (December 1939).

4. Berthold Laufer, "The Relations of the Chinese to the Philippine Islands," *Smithsonian Miscellaneous Collections* (Washington, [September 13], 1907), 248–284; J[an]. J[ulius]. L[odervijk]. Duyvendak, "Chinese in the Dutch East Indies," *Chinese Social and Political Science Review* (Peking), 11:1–13 (January 1927); Purcell, *Chinese in Southeast Asia*; G. William Skinner, *Chinese Society in Thailand: An Analytical History* (Ithaca [1957]); Comber, *Chinese Secret Societies in Malaya.*

5. [Shanghai *Chinese Miscellany* (trans.)], *The Chinaman Abroad: or a Desultory Account of the Malayan Archipelago, Particularly of Java; By Ong-Tae-Hae* (Shanghai, 1849).

6. Purcell, *Chinese in Southeast Asia,* encompassed the extent of scholarship on overseas Chinese at the middle of the twentieth century. Since 1951 additional studies have appeared. Some of these monographs touched on, but none treated, the system of indentured emigrants in detail. Ju-k'ang T'ien, *The Chinese of Sarawak*; Donald Earl Willmott, *The National Status of the Chinese in Indonesia* (Ithaca, 1956); Skinner, *Chinese Society in Thailand*; Comber, *Chinese Secret Societies in Malaya*; Richard J. Coughlin, *Double Identity; The Chinese in Modern Thailand* (Hong Kong, 1960); Donald Earl Willmott, *The Chinese of Semarang; A Changing Minority Community in Indonesia* (New York, 1960); Lea E. Williams, *Overseas Chinese Nationalism; The Genesis of the Pan-Chinese Movement in Indonesia, 1900–1916* (Cambridge, 1961). Ng Bickleen Fong, *The Chinese in New Zealand; A Study in Assimilation* (Hong Kong, 1959) alludes to the role of the credit-ticket system in the passage to New Zealand.

7. Charles Gutzlaff, *Journal of Three Voyages Along the Coast of China, in 1831, 1832, & 1833, With Notices of Siam, Corea, and the Loo-Choo Islands* (London, 1834), 165–168.

8. Ta Chen, *Chinese Migrations, With Special References to Labor Conditions* (Washington, 1923), 12–13.

9. John Crawfurd, *Journal of an Embassy from the Governor-General*

of India to the Courts of Siam and Cochin China; Exhibiting a View of the Actual State of these Kingdoms (London, 1828), 412.

10. [Johan Hendrik Croockewitcz], "De Tinmijnen van Malaka," *Tijdschrift voor Nederlandsch Indie* (Zaltbommel), XIII (November 1851), 301–302; "Notes on the Chinese of Pinang," *Journal of the Indian Archipelago and Eastern Asia* (Singapore), 8:2–3 ([January–February]), 1854).

11. Siah U Chin, "The Chinese in Singapore; General Sketch of the Numbers, Tribes, and Avocations of the Chinese in Singapore," *Journal of the Indian Archipelago and Eastern Asia* 2:285–287 ([May] 1848). For a biographical sketch of Siah U Chin [Seah En Chin] see Song Ong Siang, *One Hundred Years' History of the Chinese in Singapore* (London, 1923), 122–123.

12. G. F. Davidson, *Trade and Travel in the Far East; or Recollections of Twenty-one Years Passed in Java, Singapore, Australia, and China* (London, 1848), 46.

13. George Windsor Earl, *The Eastern Seas, or Voyages and Adventures in the Indian Archipelago, in 1832–33–34, Comprising a Tour of the Island of Java — Visits to Borneo, the Malay Peninsula, Siam, &c.; Also an Account of the Present State of Singapore, with Observations on the Commercial Resources of the Archipelago* (London, 1837), 369; [Siah U Chin] "Remittances by Chinese Immigrants in Singapore to Their Families in China," *Journal of the Indian Archipelago and Eastern Asia*, 1:35–37 ([January–February], 1847).

14. J. Hunt, "Sketch of Borneo, or Pulo Kalamantan (Communicated, in 1812, to the Honorable Sir Thomas Stamford Raffles, late Lieutenant-Governor of Java)," Henry Keppel, *The Expedition to Borneo of H. M. S. Dido for the Suppression of Piracy. With Extracts from the Journals of James Brooke, Esq., of Sarawak (Now Agent for the British Government in Borneo)* (New York, 1846), appendix IV, 391–392.

15. John Crawfurd, *History of the Indian Archipelago; Containing an Account of the Manners, Arts, Languages, Religions, Institutions, and Commerce of Its Inhabitants*, 3 vols. (Edinburgh, 1820), I, 135, III, 183.

16. J. H. Moor (comp.), *Notices of the Indian Archipelago, and Adjacent Countries; Being a Collection of Papers Relating to Borneo, Celebes, Bali, Java, Sumatra, Nias, the Philippine Islands, Sulus, Siam, Cochin China, Malayan Peninsula, &c.* (Singapore, 1837), 9.

17. E[lihu]. Doty and W[illiam]. J. Pohlman, Journal of a Tour on the Island of Borneo [in the districts of Sambas and Pontianak], November, 1838, Journal of Messrs. [William] Youngblood and [Elbert] Nevius [of Travels in Western Borneo in March, 1840], [Elbert Nevius and William Youngblood], Journal of a Tour to Mandoor [thirty-five miles north of Pontianak] and Sandak [in April, 1840], ABCFM Papers, Borneo Mission, 1838–1844, I; Elihu Doty to Rufus Anderson,

April 13, 1841, Journal of Rev. E. Doty at Sambas, May 21, 1839–April 3, 1840, ABCFM Papers, Borneo Mission, 1838–1844, II.

18. C[oenraad]. J[acob]. Temminck, *Coup-D'Oeil Général sur Les Possessions Néerlandaises dans L'Inde Archipélagique*, 3 vols. (Leiden, 1847), II, 169.

19. *Alta*, March 8, 1852.

20. *Senate Rept. 689*, 44 Cong., 2 Sess. For other official publications, connected with or based on this report, turn to "Views of the late Oliver P. Morton on the character, extent, and effect of Chinese immigration to the United States," *Senate Misc. Doc. 20*, 45 Cong., 2 Sess.; [California Senate], *Chinese Immigration. The Social, Moral, and Political Effect of Chinese Immigration. Testimony Taken Before a Committee of the Senate of the State of California, Appointed April 3d, 1876* (Sacramento, 1876); [California Senate], *Chinese Immigration; Its Social, Moral, and Political Effect. Report to the California State Senate of its Special Committee on Chinese Immigration* (Sacramento, 1878); *House Misc. Doc. 5*, 46 Cong., 2 Sess.; *House Rept. 572*, 46 Cong., 2 Sess.; [Canada, Royal Commission], *Report of the Royal Commission on Chinese Immigration; Report and Evidence* (Ottawa, 1885). Samuel E. W. Becker criticized the report in the *Catholic World* and attacked the committee in a pamphlet, *Humors of a Congressional Investigating Committee. A Review of the Joint Special Committee to Investigate Chinese Immigration* (Washington, 1877). See also Augustus Layres, *Critical Analysis of the Evidence for and against Chinese Immigration, As elicited before the Congressional Commission* (San Francisco, 1877).

21. For an example turn to William Speer, *China and California; Their Relations, Past and Present. A Lecture, in Conclusion of a Series in Relation to the Chinese People, Delivered in the Stockton Street Presbyterian Church, San Francisco, June 28, 1853* (San Francisco, 1853), 13–16; "What are Coolies?" San Francisco *Oriental, or Tung-Ngai San-Luk*, January 11, 1855; *An Humble Plea Addressed to the Legislature of California, In Behalf of the Immigrants from the Empire of China to this State* (San Francisco, 1856); "Democracy of the Chinese," *Harper's New Monthly Magazine* (New York), 37:839–848 (November 1868); *Oldest and Newest Empire*, 462–492; *Alta*, April 2, 1857; *Herald*, July 14, 1853, December 8, 1855.

22. *Alta*, September 6, 13, 20, 27, October 4, 11, November 22, 29, 1849. For a recent sketch of Chinese miners in one of the Australian colonies see Geoffrey Serle, *The Golden Age; A History of the Colony of Victoria, 1851–1861* (Melbourne, [1963]), 320–335.

23. William Redmond Ryan, *Personal Adventures in Upper and Lower California, in 1848–9; With the Author's Experience at the Mines*, 2 vols. (London, 1850), II, 266–267.

24. "Journal of Occurrences: . . . emigration of Chinese to America . . . ," *Chinese Repository*, 19:510–511 (September 1850).

25. *Alta*, March 23, 1851; *Herald*, March 25, 1851.

26. *Alta*, February 21, 1855, May 16 (quoting Stockton *Argus*) 21 (Stockton *Argus*), 1859, September 2 (Stockton *Republican*), December 5 (Stockton *Republican*), 1860.

27. The role of junks in the Chinese emigration to Southeast Asia is briefly discussed in Purcell, "A Note on Chinese Junks," *Chinese in Southeast Asia*, appendix II, 677–681. Richard Halliburton's attempt to sail and motor the *Sea Dragon* from Hong Kong to San Francisco seems to have failed at the end of March 1939. No trace of the junk was found. [Richard Halliburton], *Richard Halliburton, His Story of His Life's Adventure, As Told in Letters to His Mother and Father* (Indianapolis, [1939]), ix, 433. Every junk discovered adrift or stranded on the Pacific Coast proved to be Japanese. Charles Wolcott Brooks, *Japanese Wrecks, Stranded and Picked up Adrift in the North Pacific Ocean, Ethnologically Considered, as Furnishing Evidence of a Constant Infusion of Japanese Blood among the Coast Tribes of Northwestern Indians* (San Francisco, 1876), 7.

28. Howard M. Chapin, "The Chinese Junk Ke Ying at Providence," *Rhode Island Historical Society Collections* (Providence), 27:5–12 (January 1934). The San Francisco newspapers followed the movements of the junk attentively, *Star*, June 19, September 11, December 11, 1847, January 8, March 4, 1848; *Californian*, May 24, 1848. For a view of the vessel see reproduction no. 48, Fred. J. Peters, (comp.), *Clipper Ship Prints, Including Other Merchant Sailing Ships, by N. Currier and Currier & Ives* (New York, 1930).

29. *Star*, February 5, 1848; *Californian*, February 9, 1848; *Alta*, March 15, June 7, July 2, November 8, 1849.

30. *Alta*, June 14, 1849, April 29, 1850, February 24, May 22, 1852.

31. *Alta*, April 23, 1852, June 6, 1860. In 1862, announcing the arrival of the *Swordfish* in thirty-six and a half days, the *Alta*, more accurately, gave thirty-four days for the trip of the *Challenge* in 1852. *Alta*, February 18, 1862.

32. *Herald*, April 29, 30, 1853.

33. *Herald*, December 26, 1855.

34. *Alta*, January 3, 1860.

35. *Alta*, January 1, February 20, 1867; Ernest A. Wiltsee, *Gold Rush Steamers of the Pacific* (San Francisco, 1938), 308.

36. *Herald*, June 12, August 17, 1852.

37. Eldon Griffin, *Clippers and Consuls; American Consular and Commercial Relations with Eastern Asia, 1845–1860* (Ann Arbor, 1938), reviewed in detail the American commerce with China during the period.

38. Frank Soulé, John H. Gihon, and James Nisbet, *The Annals of San Francisco; Containing a Summary of the History of the First Discovery, Settlement, Progress, and Present Condition of California, and*

a Complete History of all the Important Events Connected with Its Great City: To Which Are Added, Biographical Memoirs of Some Prominent Citizens (New York, 1855), 419.

39. For the leading position among Western firms which Cornelius Koopmanschap gained in the traffic of Chinese emigrants during the eighteen sixties see *Alta*, January 15, 1863, July 15, 30, 1869; New York *World*, July 21, 1869; New York *Evening Post*, July 20, 1869; New Orleans *Daily Picayune*, July 14, 15, 28, August 6, October 2, 4, 14, 1869, January 6, 8, 9, 1870.

40. *Herald*, August 17, 1852.

41. *Alta*, January 3, 1858.

42. *Alta*, June 3, October 30, 1853.

43. *Alta*, September 18, 19, 1853, June 27, 29, July 1, 1854; *Herald*, September 17, 1853, October 18, 1855.

44. *Herald*, August 17, 1852, May 9, 1854, May 7, 1856; *Alta*, May 16, June 27, 1854.

45. San Francisco *Daily Evening News and Evening Picayune*, January 28, 1854.

46. Peter Parker to Daniel Webster, March 27, 1852, *Senate Ex. Doc. 99*, 34 Cong., 1 Sess., 119–120.

47. *Alta*, April 25, 1852; *Herald*, February 11, 14, 1856.

48. Speer, *Humble Plea*, 7.

49. Eitel, *History of Hongkong*, 259.

50. *Herald*, August 17, 1852.

51. John Haskell Kemble, ed. "Andrew Wilson's 'Jottings' on Civil War California," *California Historical Society Quarterly*, 32:222, n.1 (September 1953); *Herald*, March 13, 1852.

52. *China Mail*, April 3, 1860.

53. For an account of the *Tinqua*, owned by the firm of Olyphant and Sons, see *Herald*, March 29, 1853.

54. Charles V. Gillespie, Vigilance Committee (MS, Bancroft Library), 1; Hubert Howe Bancroft, *History of California*, 7 vols. (San Francisco, 1888), VI, 83, VII, 336; William Heath Davis, *Sixty Years in California. A History of Events and Life in California; Personal, Political, and Military* (San Francisco, 1889), 571.

55. Russell H. Conwell, *Why and How. Why the Chinese Emigrate, and the Means They Adopt for the Purpose of Reaching America. With Sketches of Travels, Amusing Incidents, Social Customs, &c.* (Boston, 1871), 125; Stewart, *Chinese Bondage in Peru*, 17.

56. *Star*, February 5, 1848; *Californian*, February 2, 9, 16, 1848. On account of the gold fever the *Californian* discontinued publication on May 29, 1848. The *Star* followed suit on June 14, 1848. The *Star*, May 20, 1848, described deserted San Francisco.

57. *Star*, April 1, 1848.

58. *Alta*, March 22, June 30, August 2, 31, October 18, December 10, 1849.

59. *Alta*, March 19, 1851, February 17, March 26, July 23, 1852; *Herald*, May 12, 1851, March 26, April 18, June 12, 1852. Mary Roberts Coolidge, *Chinese Immigration* (New York, 1909), 498–504, and Elmer Clarence Sandmeyer, *The Anti-Chinese Movement in California* (Urbana, 1939), 16–21, offer compilations of the annual arrival figures for the following years. For 1883–1943 see the tables in S. W. Kung, *Chinese in American Life; Some Aspects of their History, Status, Problems and Contributions* (Seattle, 1962), 92–93, 100–101.

60. The mode of coming received no attention in the secondary accounts discussing the Chinese in the United States. Conwell, *Why and How*, 212–223, formed the exception and gave a sketch of Chinese life on one of "those palace steamships owned by the Pacific Mail Steamship Company."

61. *Herald*, June 7, 1852; *Alta*, January 3, 1857, January 3, 1860.

62. "Report of the Commercial Relations of the United States with all Foreign Nations," 4 vols., *Senate Ex. Doc. 107*, 34 Cong., 1 Sess., III, 638; Hosea Ballou Morse, *The International Relations of the Chinese Empire*, 3 vols. (New York, 1910–18), I, 292.

63. George Thomas Staunton (trans.), *Ta Tsing Leu Lee; Being the Fundamental Laws and a Selection from the Supplementary Statutes of the Penal Code of China; Originally Printed and Published in Pekin, in Various Successive Editions, Under the Sanction, and by the Authority, of the Several Emperors of the Ta Tsing, or Present Dynasty* (London, 1810), 543–544.

64. William Alexander Parsons Martin, *A Cycle of Cathay; or China, South and North, With Personal Reminiscences* (New York, 1896), 161.

65. Morse, *International Relations of the Chinese Empire*, I, 504–506.

66. Cecil Clementi, *The Chinese in British Guiana* ([Georgetown, British Guiana], 1915), 82–86. Harley F. MacNair, *The Chinese Abroad, Their Position and Protection; A Study in International Law and Relations* (Shanghai, 1926), 1–27, gives details of the legal aspects of Chinese emigration.

67. Lee, *When I Was a Boy in China*, 96–97.

68. *Alta*, February 17, March 29, June 12, 1852, July 23, 1854; *Herald*, May 12, 1851, May 16, June 12, 1852, September 8, 1856; *Senate Ex. Doc. 99*, 34 Cong., 1 Sess., 102–103, 178–179; *House Ex. Doc. 123*, 33 Cong., 1 Sess., 83–85; Adam W. Elmslie [British Consul at Canton] to Dr. John Bowring, August 25, 1852, *British Parliamentary Papers, 1852–53*, 68:7–8 [263].

69. Kin Huie, *Reminiscences* (Peking, 1932), 12.

70. *Herald*, August 27, 1854; Hemmann Hoffmann, *Californien, Nevada und Mexico. Wanderungen* [March 1864–June 1867] *eines Polytechnikers* (Basel, 1871), 49; J[ames]. O'Meara, "The Chinese in Early Days," *Overland Monthly* (San Francisco), III (2nd s., May, 1884), 480; W. Pember Reeves, "Preface," Campbell, *Chinese Coolie Emigration*, xi-xii.

71. Harry Parkes, "General Remarks on Chinese Emigration," *British Parliamentary Papers, 1852–53*, 68:26 [263].

72. *Alta*, August 3, 1860.

73. *Alta*, June 10, 1850. See also the bill of lading for the *Louisa Baillie, Alta*, June 14, 1850.

74. *Alta*, September 11, 1854, January 3, 1857.

75. Thomas Greaves Cary, Chinese in California — Clipper Ships (MS, Houghton Library), 14; *Alta*, February 25, 1865.

76. M[atthew]. F[ontaine]. Maury, *Explanations and Sailing Directions to Accompany the Wind and Current Charts* (Washington, 1851), 309.

77. *Alta*, April 9, 1858.

78. [Pacific Mail Steamship Company], *A Sketch of the Route to California, China and Japan, via the Isthmus of Panama. A Useful and Amusing Book to Every Traveler* (San Francisco, 1867), 95.

79. Kemble, ed. "Andrew Wilson's 'Jottings' on Civil War California," *California Historical Society Quarterly*, 32:222, n.1 (September 1953).

80. Huie, *Reminiscences*, 22.

81. Andrew Wilson, in the latter 1850's editor of the Hong Kong *China Mail*, described his experiences with Chinese emigrants on a trip to California in a letter published in the *China Mail*, July 11, 1861. See also Kemble, ed. "Andrew Wilson's 'Jottings' on Civil War California," *California Historical Society Quarterly*, 32:213–214 (September 1953).

82. Dr. John Bowring to the Earl of Malmesbury, May 17, 1852, *British Parliamentary Papers, 1852–53*, 58:2 [263]; *Senate Ex. Doc. 99*, 34 Cong., 1 Sess., 119–165, containing a "Translation of an original contract between Captain [Leslie] Bryson and Chin Suy," 162–163; Hong Kong *Friend of China*, April 28, 1852; *China Mail*, April 29, 1852; *Overland Register*, May 18, 1852; *Herald*, June 28, 30, July 1, 20, August 15, October 19, 1852; *Alta*, June 29, July 20, 1852; Earl Swisher, ed. *China's Management of the American Barbarians; A Study of Sino-American Relations, 1841–1861, With Documents* (New Haven, [1953]), 199–203.

83. *Herald*, September 9, 1854 (quoting *China Mail*).

84. *Herald*, July 20, 21, 22, 23, 24, 25, 26, 27, August 8, 12, 13, 15, 17, 19, 21, 22, 24, 26, 27, September 4, 16, 22, 23, 28, 30, October 9, December 29, 1854; *Alta*, July 21, 22, 27, 28, 29, August 1, 4, 12, 15, 17, 18, 19, 24, 26, September 1, 11, 20, 21, 22, 23, 24, 27, 28, October 7, 8, 1854; Dorothy M. Huggins, (comp.), *Continuation of the Annals of San Francisco, Part I, From June 1, 1854, to December 31, 1855* (San Francisco, 1939), 4, 7, 9, 10, 11.

85. *Alta*, August 13, 1862.

86. *Herald*, October 27, December 29, 1851, February 18, March 22,

July 23, November 1, 1853, December 18, 1855, March 16, May 7, 1856, January 28, 1857, April 20, 1858; *Alta*, June 29, October 19, 1852, July 19, 1854, September 10, 13, 1855, May 22, July 11, 1857, February 19, 1858, February 20, March 1, 5, 1862, August 3, 6, September 18, 1866, July 15, 1869; San Francisco *Occidental and Vanguard*, July 5, 1867.

87. Conwell, *Why and How*, 221.

88. Griffin, *Clippers and Consuls*, 99.

89. *United States Statutes at Large, December 5, 1859, to March 3, 1863*, 340–41; Tien-lu Li, *Congressional Policy of Chinese Immigration, or Legislation Relating to Chinese Immigration to the United States* (Nashville, 1916), 11. For attempts by American officials in China to control the coolie trade see Griffin, *Clippers and Consuls*, 199.

90. *Alta*, June 12, 1852.

91. *Herald*, July 4, 1854; *Alta*, August 1, 1854, February 26, 1856, July 4, 1857, May 21, 1860.

92. Fred Blackburn Rogers, ed. *A Navy Surgeon in California, 1846–1847; The Journal of Marius Duvall* (San Francisco, 1957), 11.

93. Loomis to Lowrie, March 1, 1860, Correspondence of the Presbyterian Board of Foreign Missions; *Alta*, April 27, July 24, August 20, 22, 1851, February 26, March 14, 28, June 12, September 25, 1852, April 20, October 14, 1854, May 6, 1857, August 3, 1860, October 17, 1861; *Herald*, May 17, June 26, August 20, 1851, April 11, 12, June 27, 1852, March 2, November 1, 1853, July 2, 6, 1857; *Daily Evening News*, February 16, 1854; Huie, *Reminiscences*, 24.

CHAPTER IV. Chinese California

1. Naosaku Uchida, *The Overseas Chinese: A Bibliographical Essay Based on the Resources of the Hoover Institution* (Stanford, 1959), 8.

2. J[an]. J[acob]. M[aria]. de Groote, *Het Kongsiwesen van Borneo. Eene Verhandeling over den Grondslag en den Aard der Chineesche Politieke Vereenigingen in de Kolonien, met eene Chineesche Geschiedenis van de Kongsi Lanfong* ('s Gravenhage, 1885), 34–38.

3. Purcell, *Chinese in Malaya*, 78–79. The character *hui* is frequently transcribed as *hoey, hooey, hoe, hué, huey, hwi, ooi, ooy, ui, whay*, or *wui*, according to the dialect or the romanization.

4. William Speer set the general tenor for sympathetic historical accounts of the Chinese associations in California with a series of articles in the *Oriental, or Tung-Ngai San-Luk*, in February and March 1855. They were reprinted under the title "The Chinese Companies" by Benjamin S. Brooks, *Appendix to the Opening Statement and Brief of B. S. Brooks, on the Chinese Question, Referred to the Joint Committee of the Senate and House of Representatives, Consisting of Documentary Evidence and Statistics Bearing on the Question Involved* (San Francisco, 1877), 141–157. The information provided the body of the

chapter, "The Six Companies in California," in Speer, *Oldest and Newest Empire*, 554–571. James Hanley, Chinese Interpreter at Chinese Camp, Tuolumne County, pirated Speer's original articles for his "Statistics of the Chinese Population" in the Sonora *Union Democrat*, reprinted in the *Alta*, December 10, 1856. The opposite approach crystallized in B[enjamin]. E. Lloyd, "The Six Chinese Companies," *Lights and Shades in San Francisco* (San Francisco, 1876), 276–279, and [G. B. Densmore], "The Chinese Six Companies," *The Chinese in California; Description of Chinese Life in San Francisco. Their Habits, Morals and Manners* (San Francisco, 1880), 15–19.

5. Frank Marryat, *Mountains and Molehills; or Recollections of a Burnt Journal* (New York, 1855), 172, 299–300.

6. *Alta*, December 10, 1849, May 12, 1851, May 5, 1852; Mary Floyd Williams, ed. *Papers of the San Francisco Committee of Vigilance of 1851. III. Minutes and Miscellaneous Papers, Financial Accounts and Vouchers* (Berkeley, 1919), 163–172, 319; "Appendix E, Prisoners Arrested by the Committee of Vigilance," Williams, *Papers of S. F. Com. of Vigilance*, 825. For biographical details on Selim E. Woodworth see *Alta*, December 18, 1868, March 21, 1871; Bancroft Scraps, Educated Men of California, Biographies (Bancroft Library, University of California), XXX, 291; Soulé, *Annals*, 794–798; W[illiam]. F. Swasey, *The Early Days and Men of California* (Oakland, 1891), 212–219.

7. San Francisco *City Directory*, 1850, 8.

8. *Alta*, August 11, 13, 14, 26, 27, 28, 29, 30, September 1, October 27, 31, 1850; O'Meara, "Chinese in Early Days," *Overland Monthly*, 3:478–479 (2nd s., May 1884).

9. *Alta*, September 1, October 31, 1850, February 3, 1851, July 7, 1852.

10. *Alta*, August 11, 1851, June 16, October 1, 3, 1852, January 14, 16, 21, 1853; *Herald*, July 28, October 9, 1851, June 9, 1852, January 13, 1853; San Francisco *City Directory*, 1854, 228.

11. *Alta*, July 1, November 8, 9, 15, December 14, 15, 16, 24, 1851.

12. *Herald*, March 7, 8, December 12, 14, 16, 24, 1851, January 7, 21, 24, February 22, 1852; *Alta*, March 6, 8, May 1, 16, 1851, February 20, July 2, August 13, 15, 29, 1852, February 12, 1853; San Francisco *Examiner*, January 23, 1881; Georgia Willis Read and Ruth Gaines, eds., *Gold Rush; The Journals, Drawings, and other Papers of J. Goldsborough Bruff, Captain, Washington City and California Mining Association, April 2, 1849–July 20, 1851*, 2 vols. (New York, 1944), II, 1129; Lula May Garrett, "San Francisco in 1851 As Described by Eyewitnesses," *California Historical Society Quarterly*, 22:270 (September 1943); Alexandre Holinski, *La Californie et les Routes Interocéaniques* (Bruxelles, 1853), 119; Clarkson Crane (trans.), *Last Adventure; San Francisco in 1851, Translated from the Original Journal of Albert Bernard de Russailh* (San Francisco, 1931), 89; Soulé, *Annals*, 384; Williams, ed., *Papers of the San Francisco Vigilance Committee of 1851*, 319.

13. Alexander McLeod, *Pigtails and Gold Dust; A Panorama of Chinese Life in Early California* (Caldwell, Idaho, 1947), 36–38, 175–177, furnishes a recent example.

14. Marryat, *Mountains and Molehills*, 172.

15. *Herald*, September 24, 1854.

16. William Hoy, *The Chinese Six Companies. A Short, General Historical Resumé of its Origin, Function, and Importance in the Life of the California Chinese* (San Francisco [1942]), [ix], thinks it "probable that they were organized concurrently."

17. *Alta*, December 10, 1849, May 10, 1852.

18. Liang Ch'i-ch'ao, *Hsin-ta-lu yu-chi chieh-lu*, 111.

19. Tai Chuang Meng, "A Preliminary Study of the Basic Social Organization of the Chinese in America," unpub. diss., Stanford University, 1932, 34. At Berkeley, the following recent studies came to my attention: Kian Moon Kwan, "Assimilation of the Chinese in the United States: an exploratory study in California," unpub. diss., University of California, 1958; Stanford Morris Lyman, "Structure of Chinese Society in Nineteenth-Century America," unpub. diss., University of California, 1961; and Ellen Rawson Wood, "Californians and Chinese: the first decade," unpub. diss., University of California, 1961.

20. Hoy, *Chinese Six Companies*, 2.

21. The following history of the district companies' rise is based on these sources: Tong K. Achick, a prominent San Francisco merchant and agent of the Yeong Wo Company, translated in 1853 the testimony of the leading merchants of the Four Houses, Gee Atai, Lee Chuen (Sze Yap), Wong Sing, Lee Yuk-nam (Yan Wo), Tam Sam, Chun Aching (Sam Yap), and Lum Teen-kwei (Yeong Wo), before the Committee on Mines and Mining. It was published by the California State Legislature, *Assembly Journal*, 4 Sess., 1853, Appendix, 7–12. On August 12, 1854, in a letter to the Shasta *Courier*, Ha-Sing, Ge-Ti, and Ah-Ching described the operation of the district companies on the California scene. The *Herald*, September 4, 1854, printed extracts from another survey of the five companies by Tong K. Achick, originally published in the *Courier*. William Speer claimed to have translated the account of another Chinese merchant, Lai Chun Chuen, *Remarks of the Chinese Merchants of San Francisco, upon Governor* [John] *Bigler's Message and Some Common Objections; with Some Explanations of the Character of the Chinese Companies, and the Laboring Class in California* (San Francisco, 1855). These remarks appeared also in the *Oriental* in the same year and have been reprinted in Brooks, *Appendix to the Opening Statement*, 136–141. Additional evidence recording the beginnings of the companies came from trials connected with [James] Speer *v. See Yup Company*, 13 Cal. 73, and *Alta*, May 27, 29, 31, July 15, 16, August 26, 1853, February 27, 1854, November 21, 1858, May 18, 1861; *Herald*, June 6, August 27, 1853, November 19, 1855, December 10, 1856, October 27, 1858; *California Police Gazette*, March 20, November

25, 1859; Liang Ch'i-ch'ao, *Hsin-ta-lu yu-chi chieh-lu*, 111–117; Hoy, *Chinese Six Companies*, 2–9, 10, 13–14.

22. The *California Assembly Journal*, 4 Sess., 1853, Appendix, 9, printed the figures of the Four Houses. The compilation of Tong K. Achick appeared in the *Herald*, September 4, 1854.

23. San Francisco *City Directory*, 1856, 125; *City Directory*, 1858, 379; *City Directory*, 1862, 559.

24. *Alta*, April 5, 1856. See also *Alta*, July 8, 1851, April 5, 1856, June 19, 1859, January 24, August 16, 1860, August 17, 1867; *Herald*, January 10, 1857.

25. *Alta*, July 10, 15, 16, 1853, April 5, 1856, May 11, June 19, 1859, January 24, August 16, 1860, January 28, 1861, August 23, 1864, July 27, 1865, August 17, 1867; *Herald*, December 20, 21, 22, 1853, January 10, 1857, October 27, 1858; William Chandless, *A Visit to Salt Lake City; Being a Journey Across the Plains and a Residence in the Mormon Settlements of Utah* (London, 1857), 332; Rev. J. C. Holbrook, "Chinadom in California. In Two Papers — Paper the First," *Hutchings' Illustrated California Magazine* (San Francisco), 4:131–132 (September 1859); Holbrook, "Chinadom in California. In Two Papers — Paper the Second," *Hutchings' Magazine*, 4:173 (October 1859); John Todd, *The Sunset Land; Or, the Great Pacific Slope* (Boston, 1870), 275–277; Harvey Rice, *Letters from the Pacific Slope; Or First Impressions* (New York, 1870), 71–72; [Union and Central Pacific Railroads], *A Souvenir of the Trans-Continental Excursion of Railroad Agents, 1870* (Albany, 1871), 59–60; Samuel Williams, "The City of the Golden Gate," *Scribner's Monthly* (New York), 10:285 (July 1875); James F. Rusling, *Across America; or the Great West and the Pacific Coast* (New York, 1875), 312–315; Hermann W. Vogel, *Vom Indischen Ocean bis zum Goldlande. Reisebeobachtungen und Erlebnisse in vier Erdtheilen* (Berlin, 1877), 420–421. Otheto Weston, *Mother Lode Album* (Stanford, [1948]), 121, 149, reproduced photos of the joss houses at Fiddletown, Amador County, and Auburn, Placer County. Wolfram Eberhard, "Economic Activities of a Chinese Temple in California," *Journal of the American Oriental Society* (Baltimore), 82:362–371 (July-September 1962), discussed the operation of a temple at Marysville; Mariann Kaye Wells, "Chinese Temples in California," unpub. diss., University of California, 1962, traced the remnants of joss houses.

26. *Oriental, or Tung-Ngai San-Luk*, April 28, May 26, 1855.

27. *Oriental*, April 28, May 26, 1855. William Speer published in several places information on company rules which he collected. His literal translation of a copy of the Yeong Wo Wui Kun's articles can be found in *Oldest and Newest Empire*, 557–564, and on pages 565–567 of the same study he reprinted the answers to his questions concerning the principles and operations of the several companies.

28. Speer, *Oldest and Newest Empire*, 569–571.

29. *Alta*, May 31, 1853.

30. *Herald*, May 28, 29, 1853; *Alta*, June 7, November 17, 18, 1853.

31. *Alta*, November 18, 1853.

32. San Francisco *Golden Hills' News, or Kim-Shan Jit San-Luk*, June, 1854; Shasta *Courier*, July 22, 29, August 5, 12, 1854; *Alta*, June, 2, 18, July 21, August 1, 1854, November 17, 1856; *Herald*, June 6, July 26, August 1, 12, 1854; Bernhard Marks to Jacob Solis-Cohen, July 30, 1854, J[acob]. Solis-Cohen, Jr., ed. "A California Pioneer; The Letters of Bernhard Marks to Jacob Solis-Cohen (1853–1857)," *Publications of the American Jewish Historical Society* (New York), 44:50 (September 1954).

33. *Alta*, June 2, July 21, August 1, 1854, November 17, 1856; *Courier*, June 3, July 22, 29, August 5, 12, 1854; Herald, August 12, 1854; John Carr, *Pioneer Days in California* (Eureka, 1891), 266–273; Isaac Cox, *The Annals of Trinity County, Containing a History of the Discovery, Settlement and Progress, Together with a Description of the Resources and Present Condition of Trinity County. Also Sketches of Important Events that Have Transpired Therein from its Settlement to the Present Time. Finally, Short Biographical Sketches of its Prominent Citizens. Compiled and Arranged from the Most Authentic Sources* (San Francisco, 1858), 160–164; Pringle Shaw, "War in China," *Ramblings in California; Containing a Description of the Country, Life at the Mines, State of Society, &c. Interspersed with Characteristic Anecdotes, and Sketches from Life, Being the Five Years' Experience of a Gold Digger* (Toronto, [1856?]), 227–231.

34. *Herald*, October 29, November 10, 1856; *Alta*, October 31, 1856 (quoting Columbia *Gazette*).

35. *Herald*, June 3, 5, 6, July 29, 30, September 10, 13, 27, 1856, April 25, 1858; *Alta*, February 4, September 27, 1856, April 19, 1857.

36. *Alta*, March 20, May 29, June 2, 8, 9, 18, July 21, August 28, September 6, 9, 10, 1854, January 3, February 8, 10, 11, 1855, January 21, 28, February 4, 10, April 3, September 27, October 31, November 17, 1856, April 10, October 16, 17, 18, November 12, 1857, April 20, 1858; *Herald*, March 17, 23, 26, April 15, May 29, June 3, 5, 6, July 19, 26, 30, August 1, 12, September 13, 1854, January 3, July 21, December 11, 1855, October 6, 27, November 10, 17, 1856, April 29, October 16, 17, 18, 1857, April 25, 1858.

37. For a series of minor affairs see *Alta*, May 18, 1861, September 7, 17, 18, 26, October 5, 22, 1862, January 16, 18, September 8, 1863, March 7, May 30, 31, June 1, 2, 4, 6, 8, August 1, 17, 18, 19, 30, 1864, October 17, 1867, September 23, 1869; *Herald*, January 8, 1860.

38. *Alta*, September 17, 18, 26, October 5, 22, 1862, September 8, 1863, March 7, 1864.

39. *Alta*, May 28, 29, 1862; S. Garfielde and F. A. Snyder, (comps.), *Compiled Laws of the State of California* (Benicia, 1853), 274–275. For

the attempt of the Hip Kat Company to file articles of corporation see *Alta*, April 17, 1868.

40. *Alta*, January 10, July 11, 1864.

41. *Alta*, May 31, June 15, 1853, November 21, 1858; *Herald*, November 19, 1853. Mary Coolidge, *Chinese Immigration*, 57, 514, insistently used Six Companies and even inserted "Six" into the title of a pamphlet on the five companies that appeared in 1855.

42. Meng, Preliminary Study of the Basic Social Organization of the Chinese in America, 37, 38–39; Hoy, *Chinese Six Companies*, 10, 13–14.

43. Hoy, 11. William Hoy maintains that "scholarly men" from various districts served as heads of the district companies and — automatically — ruled the Six Companies. Faced with the obvious absence of Chinese literati in California during these decades, he suggests that the companies imported these scholars from their native districts. Only at the close of the century, Hoy argues, was this custom gradually abandoned in favor of merchant control. In the light of the traditional attitude of Confucian scholars toward emigration, Hoy's argument lacks persuasive power.

44. A[ugustus]. W[ard]. Loomis, "The Chinese Six Companies," *Overland Monthly*, 1:222 (September 1868). For other evidence of merchant leadership see *Alta*, May 8, August 13, 1852, June 1, 7, 15, 23, July 16, November 17, 18, 1853, August 25, 1857, October 18, 21, 1859, October 4, 8, 11, November 26, 1861, August 22, 1862, January 15, July 2, 1863, February 5, April 24, 25, August 30, September 20, December 25, 1864, April 5, August 18, 1865, January 7, June 2, September 18, December 28, 1866, April 11, September 1, 1868; *Herald*, April 12, July 9, 23, September 28, October 29, 1852, May 28, 29, August 5, September 30, November 19, December 20, 21, 22, 1853, February 8, 1857, October 27, 1858; *Daily Evening News*, January 28, 1854; *California Police Gazette*, February 9, 1867.

45. *California Assembly Journal*, 4 Sess., 1853, appendix, 9.

46. *Herald*, January 21, 1861 (quoting San Francisco *Le Mineur*).

47. *Alta*, December 28, 1866.

48. *Alta*, August 18, 1865.

49. *Alta*, January 7, 1866.

50. *Alta*, August 22, 1862. For obituaries of other prominent merchants see *Alta*, August 25, 1862, July 2, 1863, April 24, 25, August 30, 1864, September 1, 1868, February 28, 1869.

51. The Grand Jury of San Francisco County reported on May 30, 1853, that the Four Great Houses prevented their "countrymen from purchasing tickets from any but themselves." *Alta*, May 31, 1853. Reverend Otis Gibson, *The Chinese in America* (Cincinnati, 1877), 339–345, who established a mission of the Episcopal Methodist Church to the Chinese in San Francisco, in 1868, described his futile attempts to alter or to break the regulation.

52. Robert Morrison, ed. "Some Account of a Secret Association in China, entitled the Triad Society. By the late Dr. [William] Milne, Principal of the Anglo-Chinese College [at Malacca]," *Transactions of the Royal Asiatic Society of Great Britain and Ireland* (London), 1:240–250 (part I, 1824); Lieutenant [T. J.] Newbold and Major-General [F. W.] Wilson, "The Chinese Secret Triad Society of the Tien-ti-huih," *Journal of the Royal Asiatic Society of Great Britain and Ireland* (London), 6:120–158 (1841); Gustave Schlegel, *Thian Ti Hwui. The Hung-League or Heaven-Earth-League. A Secret Society with the Chinese in China and India* (Batavia, 1866); W[illiam]. A. Pickering, "Chinese Secret Societies and Their Origin," *Journal of the Straits Branch of the Royal Asiatic Society* (Singapore), 1:63–84 (July 1878); Pickering, "Chinese Secret Societies," *Journal of the Straits Branch of the Royal Asiatic Society*, 2:1–18 (July 1879); William Stanton, *The Triad Society, or Heaven and Earth Association* (Shanghai, 1900); L[ennox]. A[lgernon]. Mills, "The Chinese in British Malaya," in "British Malaya, 1824–1867," *Journal of the Malayan Branch of the Royal Asiatic Society* (Singapore), 3:199–213 (part II, November 1925); J[ohn]. S[ebastian]. M[arlow]. Ward and W[illiam]. G[eorge]. Stirling, *The Hung Society, or, The Society of Heaven and Earth*, 3 vols. (London, 1925); Purcell, "Chinese Secret Societies in Malaya," *Chinese in Malaya*, 155–173; Comber, *Chinese Secret Societies in Malaya*.

53. A. H. Hill (trans.), "The Hikayat Abdullah," *Journal of the Malayan Branch of the Royal Asiatic Society* (Singapore), 28:180–192 (part 3, June 1955).

54. The *Herald*'s romanization, "Hung-Shun-Tong Association" and "E Hing Society," surpassed less inspired Western attempts to fathom Cantonese. *Herald*, February 5, 6, 7, 11, 1855.

55. Thomas F. Turner, "Chinese and Japanese Labor in the Mountain and Pacific States," in "Reports of the Industrial Commission on Immigration, Including Testimony, with Review and Digest, and Special Reports. And on Education, Including Testimony, with Review and Digest," *House Ex. Doc. 184*, 57 Cong., 1 Sess., 19 vols., XV, 745–802. See specifically, "Highbinders and Highbinderism," *House Ex. Doc. 184*, 762–794. The statement of Lieutenant of Police William Price to Hart H. North, a regional commissioner of immigration, about tong activities in San Francisco, *House Ex. Doc. 184*, Exhibit D, 775–782, was reprinted in part, Hart H. North, "Chinese Highbinder Societies in California," *California Historical Society Quarterly*, 27:19–31 (March 1948).

56. John J. Manion, Chinese Tongs (typewritten manuscripts, in the possession of the family until 1962, and since then in the Bancroft Library, University of California). Richard H. Dillon, *The Hatchet Men; The Story of the Tong Wars in San Francisco's Chinatown* (New York, [1962]), 363–365, gives a sketch of Inspector Manion's work.

57. Amy Elizabeth Nims, "Chinese Life in San Antonio," unpub. diss. Southwest Texas State Teachers College, 1941, p. 64, furnished one of many examples for the usage. The attempts to compare, or to equate, the Triad Society with Freemasonry goes back to Milne's paper which remarked on the resemblances between the societies. Morrison, ed. "Some Account of . . . the Triad Society. By . . . Dr. Milne . . . ," *Transactions of the Royal Asiatic Society of Great Britain and Ireland,* 1:249–250 (Part I, 1824). The term "high-binder" appeared first in a news report, "Riot," in the *Weekly Inspector* (New York), 1:184 (December 27, 1806).

58. Schlegel, *Thian Ti Hwui,* 18.

59. Rose Hum Lee, *The Chinese in the United States of America* (Hong Kong, 1960), 440, warned against the use of the character *t'ang* and favored *tang,* evidently on the ground that the second character's literal translation (a clique, a faction, a gang, a party, an association in opposition to the government) approximated closer the true nature of tongs. Historically inaccurate, her substitution failed to fathom the dimensions of tongs.

60. Schlegel, *Thian Ti Hwui,* 4.

61. Stewart Culin, "The I Hing or 'Patriotic Rising,' A Secret Society Among the Chinese in America," *Report of the Proceedings of the Numismatic and Antiquarian Society of Philadelphia 1887–89* (Philadelphia, 1889), 1–7; Culin, "Chinese Secret Societies in the U. S.," *Journal of American Folklore* (Boston), 3:39–43 (January–March 1890).

62. Schlegel, *Thian Ti Hwui,* 135–144.

63. *Alta,* January 4, 5, 1854; *Herald,* January 4, 5, 1854; *Daily Evening News,* January 4, 5, 1854; Schlegel, *Thian Ti Hwui,* 33–34, 135–144.

64. *Alta,* March 10, 16, 1854; *Herald,* March 10, 1854; Schlegel, *Thian Ti Hwui,* 36–38.

65. *Alta,* February 27, March 3, 10, 12, 17, 25, 26, April 1, 11, 16, July 27, September 2, October 7, December 9, 1854, February 8, 1855; *Herald,* January 7, February 14, 15, March 10, 12, 21, 26, April 2, 20, 21, 23, 27, June 28, July 27, 30, August 27, October 7, 8, November 4, 17, December 10, 1854, February 5, 6, 7, 8, 10, 11, April 21, May 21, November 19, 1855; Huggins, (comp.), *Continuation of the Annals of San Francisco,* 16, 40. For obituaries of Charles T. Carvalho turn to *Alta,* January 31, February 1, 2, 1870, and San Francisco *Call,* January 30, February 1, 3, 1870.

66. Liang Ch'i-ch'ao, *Hsin-ta-lu yu-chi chieh-lu,* 118.

67. *Herald,* May 21, 1855.

CHAPTER V. Work Camp and Chinatown

1. A few accounts, such as Arnold Genthe and Will Irwin, *Pictures of* [San Francisco's] *Old Chinatown* (New York, 1908), and Edgar M.

Kahn, "Chinatown and the Cable Cars," *Cable Car Days in San Francisco* (Stanford, [1940]), 77–84, in passing touch on this function of Chinatown.

2. [Alfred Trumble], *The 'Heathen Chinee' at Home and Abroad. Who He Is; What He Looks Like; How He Works and Lives; His Virtues, Vices and Crimes. A Complete Panorama of the Chinese in America. By an Old Californian* (New York, [1882]), and Walter J. Raymond, *Horrors of the Mongolian Settlement, San Francisco, Cal. An Enslaved and Degraded Race of Paupers, Opium Eaters and Leepers* (Boston, [1886?]), combine several aspects.

3. William Purviance Fenn, *Ah Sin and His Brethren in American Literature* (Peking, [1933]), and John Burt Foster, "China and the Chinese in American Literature, 1850–1950," unpub. diss. University of Illinois, 1952, looked into the literary merits of the writings on Chinatown. Chester B. Fernald, *The Cat and the Cherub and Other Stories* (New York, 1896), and William Norr, *Stories of Chinatown. Sketches from Life in the Chinese Colony of Mott, Pell and Doyers Streets* (New York, [1892]), proved to be helpful.

4. *Alta*, November 21, 1853, October 15, 1857, February 8 (quoting Oroville *Record*), 18, 1858, February 17, 1859; *Herald*, April 12, July 10, 1852, January 17, June 23, 1853; William H. Goetzmann, *Army Exploration in the American West, 1803–1863* (New Haven, 1959), 401. Foster, China and the Chinese in American Literature, 1850–1950, p. 141, dates the application of the name Chinatown "only after 1860."

5. William J. Hoy, "Chinatown Devises Its Own Street Names," *California Folklore Quarterly* (Berkeley), 2:72 (April 1943); Hoy, (trans.), "Gold Mountain, Big City, Chinese Map," *California Historical Society Quarterly*, 27:256–258 (September 1948).

6. "San Francisco As It Is. Chinese Population," *Herald*, April 12, 1852; *Herald*, December 8, 1853, August 22, 1854, June 12, 1857; *Alta*, October 30, 1851, April 25, November 15, 1853, February 15, September 2, 3, 4, 1854, October 15, 1857, May 7, 23, 1858. Willard B. Farwell, *The Chinese at Home and Abroad* (San Francisco, 1885), also has the map, originally part of the Appendix of the San Francisco *Municipal Reports for 1884–85*.

7. Loomis to Lowrie, December 10, 1860, April 17, 1862, CPBFM.

8. J. D[ouglas]. Borthwick, *Three Years in California* (Edinburgh, 1857), 266–267, describes briefly the interior of a store.

9. *Herald*, August 8, 1853, quoting the Mokelumne *Calaveras Chronicle*, about Chinese gambling and women at Mokelumne Hill.

10. Fern Coble Trull, "The History of the Chinese in Idaho from 1864 to 1910," unpub. diss., University of Oregon, 1946, p. 30.

11. Demas Barnes, *From the Atlantic to the Pacific, Overland. A Series of Letters, Describing a Trip from New York, via Chicago, Atchison, the Great Plains, Denver, the Rocky Mountains, Central City, Colorado, Dakota, Pike's Peak, Laramie Park, Bridger's Pass, Salt Lake*

City, Utah, Nevada, Austin, Washoe, Virginia City, the Sierras and California to San Francisco, Thence Home, by Acapulco, and the Isthmus of Panama (New York, 1866), 93–95; Hoffmann, *Californien, Nevada und Mexico*, 282–283.

12. For examples see Harry T. Peters, *California on Stone* (Garden City, New York, 1935), plates 44, 108.

13. In 1860 Chinese California numbered 34,919 inhabitants. They concentrated in the following counties: El Dorado (4,762), Calaveras (3,657), San Francisco (2,719), Amador (2,568), Placer (2,392), Sierra (2,208), Butte (2,177), Nevada (2,147). "The Indians and Chinese in California," *Alta*, January 13, 1863; Sandmeyer, *Anti-Chinese Movement in California*, 19; Rose Hum Lee, "The Decline of Chinatowns in the United States," *American Journal of Sociology* (Chicago), 54:424 (March 1949).

14. Erwin Gudde (comp.), *California Place Names; The Origin and Etymology of Current Geographical Names* (2nd rev. ed., Berkeley, 1960), 59.

15. Loomis to Lowrie, March 5, 1864, CPBFM; *Alta*, September 20, October 1, 1849, May 11, 1850, March 31, 1851, March 1, August 28, October 1, 18, 1852, March 24, 28, April 25, May 20, September 28, 1853, February 2, March 25, 1854, August 26, September 16, 1856, October 15, 1857, May 30, July 17, 23, August 13, 1858, June 16, October 29, November 2, 3, December 13, 1859, February 9, 26, May 24, July 7, October 20, 1860, January 14, 28, March 1, 5, 16, 17, 19, April 16, August 22, 1861, March 12, May 7, October 17, November 14, 1862, May 5, July 28, December 9, 1864, March 2, June 6, 1865, January 14, April 1, 5, July 26, September 16, 1866, May 12, June 9, September 29, 1867, May 9, 1868; *Herald*, April 12, August 29, 1852, May 16, 23, 1853, January 11, 1854, October 27, 1855, July 2, 18, 24, August 13, 1858, June 6, 1859, May 12, June 16, 1860; [Augustus W. Loomis], "How Our Chinamen Are Employed," *Overland Monthly*, 2:231–240 (March 1869). For data on Orientals in specific industries turn to Ping Chiu, *Chinese Labor in California, 1850–1880; An Economic Study* (Madison, 1963).

16. "Report of the Joint Select Committee Relative to the Chinese Population of the State of California," Appendix B, Brooks, *Appendix to the Opening Statement*, 73.

17. John S. Hittell, *The Resources of California, Comprising the Society, Climate, Salubrity, Scenery, Commerce and Industry of the State* (6th rev. ed., San Francisco, 1874), 40–41; Rodman W. Paul, *California Gold, The Beginning of Mining in the Far West* (Cambridge, 1947), 320.

18. Speer to Lowrie, December 18, 1852, Loomis to Lowrie, March 1, 9, June 25, September 19, 1860, April 17, 1862, June 29, 1863, CPBFM; *Alta*, May 2, 18, July 29, 1851, February 26, March 28, May 2, 5, June

8, 1852, May 14, October 14, 1854, May 6, 1857, June 8, August 3, 1860, October 17, 1861; *Herald*, May 17, August 20, December 29, 1851, April 11, 1852, March 2, 1853, July 2, 6, 1857, May 10, 1859; *Daily Evening News*, February 16, 1854; Robert Glass Cleland, ed., *Apron Full of Gold; Letters of Mary Jane Megquier from San Francisco, 1849–1856* (San Marino, 1949), 58.

19. Speer, *Humble Plea*, 18; *Alta*, June 15, 1853, June 16, 1855 (quoting Georgetown *News*), May 24, July 31 (Stockton *Argus*), 1857, February 18, September 23, 1860; *Herald*, April 21, 1852 (Sacramento *Union*), October 28, November 24, 1854; John Russell Bartlett, *Personal Narrative of Explorations and Incidents in Texas, New Mexico, California, Sonora, and Chihuahua; Connected with the United States and Mexican Boundary Commission, During the Years 1850, '51, '52, and '53*, 2 vols. (New York, 1854), II, 12; "Mining Life in California," *Harper's Weekly*, 1:632 (October 3, 1857).

20. *Herald*, June 5, 1858 (quoting Stockton *Republican*). For a brief description of the Sacramento agency see Speer to Lowrie, December 18, 1852; for Placerville, Marks to Solis-Cohen, January 13, 1854, Solis-Cohen, "A California Pioneer; The Letters of Bernhard Marks to Jacob Solis-Cohen (1853–1857)." *Publications of the American Jewish Historical Society*, 44:22–23 (September 1954).

21. Edward Eberstadt, ed. *Way Sketches; Containing Incidents of Travel Across the Plains, From St. Joseph to California in 1850, With Letters Describing Life and Conditions in the Gold Region By Lorenzo Sawyer, Later Chief Justice of the Supreme Court of California* (New York, 1926), 124.

22. Charles Loring Brace, *The New West: Or, California in 1867–1868* (New York, 1869), 227.

23. *Herald*, November 28, 1857.

24. *Alta*, August 24, 1858 (quoting Mariposa *Gazette*), describes such a Chinese village in the vicinity of Coulterville, Mariposa County. Additional details appear in "Chinese Coulterville Burned Down," *Alta*, July 22, 1859 (Mariposa *Star*), which reports the complete destruction of the village by fire. Rebuilt, fire destroyed Chinese Coulterville again on August 8, 1862; *Alta*, August 22, 1862. Borthwick, *Three Years in California*, 143; Marryat, *Mountains*, 295–296.

25. "Chinamen in Rich Diggings," *Alta*, October 9, 1858 (quoting Sacramento *Union*), depicts the operation of a successful Chinese company on the junction of the North and Middle forks of the American River.

26. Rossiter W. Raymond, *Statistics of the Mines and Mining in the States and Territories West of the Rocky Mountains* (Washington, 1872), 4. This report was also published as *House Ex. Doc. 10*, 42 Cong., 1 Sess.

27. For pictures of Chinese miners and camps see "A Series of In-

teresting Sketches and Scenes in California," *Gleason's Pictorial Drawing Room Companion* (Boston), 3:277 (October 30, 1852); Borthwick, *Three Years in California*, facing 264; "The Cradle and the Manner of Using It," in "Mining for Gold in California," *Hutchings' Magazine*, 2:5 (July 1857); J. Ross Browne, "Washoe Revisited [Third Paper]," *Harper's Monthly* (New York), 31:160 (July 1865); [Charles Peters], *The Autobiography of Charles Peters, In 1915 the Oldest Pioneer Living in California Who Mined in 'The Days of Old, The Days of Gold, The Days of '49'. Also Historical Happenings, Interesting Incidents and Illustrations of The Old Mining Towns in The Good Luck Era, The Placer Mining Days of the '50s* (Sacramento, [1915]), 142; Carl I. Wheat, ed. " 'California's Bantam Cock,' The Journals of Charles E. DeLong, 1854–1863," *California Historical Society Quarterly*, 9: facing 348 (December 1930); Peters, *California on Stone*, plates 22, 28; Newell D. Chamberlain, *The Call of Gold; True Tales on the Gold Road to Yosemite* ([Mariposa, 1936]), facing 26; Mae Hélêne Bacon Boggs, (comp.), *My Playhouse Was A Concord Coach; An Anthology of Newspaper Clippings and Documents Relating to Those Who Made California History During the Years 1822–1888* ([Oakland, 1942]), 119.

28. Agnes and Helen Stephenson, (trans.), *Pekin, Jeddo, and San Francisco. The Conclusion of a Voyage Round the World. By the Marquis* [Ludovic] *de Beauvoir* (London, 1872), 252.

29. *Autobiography of Charles Peters*, 141–142; James W. Bartlett, "Annotations to Cox's Annals of Trinity County," Isaac Cox, *The Annals of Trinity County* (Eugene, Oregon, 1940), 210; Robert F. G. Spier, "Tool Acculturation Among 19th-Century California Chinese," *Ethnohistory* (Bloomington), 5:111 (Spring 1958).

30. Borthwick, *Three Years in California*, 263.

31. *Autobiography of Charles Peters*, 143–145. "A Chinaman in Luck," *Herald*, March 24, 1856, records the discovery of a hidden purse in an abandoned cabin by a Chinese miner. See also C. B. Glancock, *A Golden Highway; Scenes of History's Greatest Gold Rush Yesterday and Today* (Indianapolis, [1934]), 122.

32. *Herald*, June 6, 1853.

33. Eduard Vischer, "A Trip to the Mining Regions in the Spring of 1859. 'Californischer Staats-Kalender' in the Leap Year A. D. 1860," *California Historical Society Quarterly*, 11:230 (September 1932); Brace, *New West*, 218.

34. The general picture of Chinese miners is chiefly based on: *Alta*, May 2, 18, July 29, 1851, May 2, 5, 14, 15, June 26, 1852, February 16, June 15, October 12, 13, December 29, 1853, March 4 (quoting Jackson *Sentinel*), 14 (Nevada *Journal*), 29 (Mokelumne *Calaveras Chronicle*), July 6, August 23 (Marysville *Express*), September 11 (Grass Valley *Telegraph*), 1854, May 21 (Mokelumne *Calaveras Chronicle*), June 11 (Sacramento *Union*), June 16, October 26 (Nevada *Democrat*), 1855,

October 13, 1856 (Shasta *Republican*), May 19 (Auburn *Press*), July 13 (Auburn *Placer Herald*), 21 (Mariposa *Gazette*), 23 (Mariposa *Democrat*), August 8, October 8, December 2 (Marysville *Express*), 1857, February 1, 13 (Hornitas *Democrat*), 15, March 1 (Sacramento *Bee*), 14 (Placerville *Index*), August 5, 24, October 9, November 11 (Shasta *Courier*), December 5, 6, 1858, January 19 (Auburn *Placer Herald*), 31 (Sonora *Democrat*), February 16 (Coloma *Times*), May 21, October 9 (Sacramento *Standard*), 1859, September 23, December 8 (Mariposa *Gazette*), 1860, April 3 (Sacramento *Union*), August 10 (Stockton *Independent*), October 8 (Mariposa *Gazette*), 1861, March 12, 1862, January 13, May 3 (North San Juan *Hydraulic Press*), 1863, July 26, August 6, 1866, November 10, 1867, June 17, 1869; *Herald*, October 27 (Mokelumne *Calaveras Chronicle*), December 29, 1851, March 6, April 25, May 9 (Sacramento *Union*), 10 (Mokelumne *Calaveras Chronicle*), 12 (Marysville *Express*), June 9 (Sacramento *State Journal*), November 26, 1852, March 18, May 24, June 6, 8, 9, July 4, November 9, 26, December 8, 1853, March 27, 1854, July 31 (Butte *Record*), August 6 (Mokelumne *Calaveras Chronicle*), November 12, 1855, March 24 (Auburn *Press*), April 21 (Mariposa *Gazette*, Jackson *Ledger*), May 4, 11, 1856, March 15, 23 (Mariposa *Gazette*), June 12, November 10 (Shasta *Courier*), 1858, March 16, April 2, 1861; Carr, *Pioneer Days*, 69–70; William Shaw, *Golden Dreams and Waking Realities; Being the Adventures of a Gold-Seeker in California and the Pacific Islands* (London, 1851), 50, 56, 64, 65–66, 81–82, 86, 94–95, 122; Franklin Langworthy, *Scenery of the Plains, Mountains and Mines: A Diary Kept upon the Overland Route to California, By Way of the Great Salt Lake: Travels in the Cities, Mines, and Agricultural Districts — Embracing the Return by the Pacific Ocean and Central America, In the Years 1850, '51, '52 and '53* (Ogdensburg, New York, 1855), 184; Marryat, *Mountains*, 295–297; Speer, *Humble Plea*, 19–26; "Mining for Gold in California," *Hutchings' Magazine*, 2:5 (July 1857); "Mining Life in California," *Harper's Weekly*, 1:632–633 (October 3, 1857); Borthwick, *Three Years in California*, 51, 55, 143–145, 262–267, 319; Holbrook, "Chinadom in California. In Two Papers. — Paper the Second," *Hutchings' Magazine*, 4:173 (October 1859); Horace Greeley, *An Overland Journey, from New York to San Francisco, in the Summer of 1859* (New York, 1860), 288–289; Francis P. Farquhar, ed. *Up and Down California in 1860–1864. The Journal of William H. Brewer, Professor of Agriculture in the Sheffield Scientific School from 1864 to 1903* (Berkeley, 1949), 330, 481; Browne, "Washoe Revisited," *Harper's Monthly*, 31:159–161 (July 1865); Bowles, *Our New West*, 400; Conwell, *Why and How*, 126–127; de Beauvoir, *San Francisco*, 250–253.

35. Albert D. Richardson, *Beyond the Mississippi: From the Great River to the Great Ocean. Life and Adventure on the Prairies, Mountains, and Pacific Coast, 1857–1867* (Hartford, 1867), 462.

36. *Senate Rept. 689*, 44 Cong., 2 Sess., 667, 723; "How Our China-men Are Employed," *Overland*, II (March, 1869), 232.

37. "Monthly Record of Current Events," *Hutchings' Magazine*, 4:238 (November 1859).

38. Eliot Lord, *Comstock Mining and Miners. A Reprint of the 1883 Edition* (Berkeley, 1959), 253, 355.

39. *Senate Rept. 689*, 44 Cong., 2 Sess., 724.

40. *Alta*, June 24, 1869, contains a statement by a foreman of the Central Pacific about the contract of Chinese laborers.

41. "Chinese Arrivals at San Francisco Custom House," Coolidge, *Chinese Immigration*, 498; Richardson, *Beyond the Mississippi*, 462.

42. [F. S. Hickman, publisher], *The Pacific Rail Road, Congressional Proceedings in the Thirty-seventh, Thirty-eighth, and Forty-first Congresses* (West Chester, Pennsylvania, 1875); *Senate Ex. Doc. 51*, 50 Cong., 1 Sess.

43. Robert Hancocks, Assistant Editor, Bureau of News, Southern Pacific Company, to G. Barth, September 2, 1959; Irene Authier Keeffe, Director, Union Pacific Historical Museum, to G. Barth, September 17, 1959.

44. Hoffmann, *Californien, Nevada und Mexico*, 210–225. See also Effie Mona Mack, *Nevada, A History of the State from the Earliest Times through the Civil War* (Glendale, California, 1936), 374–375; Wesley S. Griswold, *A Work of Giants; Building the First Transcontinental Railroad* (New York, [1962]), 108–125; and Robert West Howard, *The Great Iron Trail; The Story of the First Trans-Continental Railroad* (New York, [1962]), 224–236.

45. *Alta*, April 25, 30, May 1, 8, 12, 1869; J. N. Bowman, "Driving the Last Spike at Promontory, 1869," *California Historical Society Quarterly*, 36:265–266 (September 1957).

46. Densmore, *Chinese in California*, 64–66, lists the main festivals of the Chinese in San Francisco.

47. Raymond, *Statistics of Mines and Mining*, 4.

48. *Alta*, October 30, 1853, February 17, 1855, February 16, May 7, 1858, January 23, 1860, February 18, 1863; *Herald*, April 4, 1852.

49. *Alta*, February 3, 1851, February 8, 1853.

50. *Alta*, February 14, 1858.

51. *Alta*, February 8, 1853, January 29, 30, 1854, February 8, 17, 1855, January 25, 26, 1857, February 14, 16, 1858, February 2, 4, 1859, January 21, 22, 23, 31, 1862, February 18, 19, 1863 January 14, February 6, 9, 1864, January 2, 26, 27, 28, 1865, January 1, February 12, 14, 15, 1866, February 3, 1867, February 9, 10, 1869; *Herald*, February 15, 20, 1855, February 5, 6, 1856, January 25, 26, 1857, February 13, 14, 1858, February 3, 5, 1859, January 23, 1860, February 11, 12, 1861, January 29, 31, 1862; Huggins, (comp.), *Continuation of the Annals of San Francisco*, 36. For additional descriptions of the New Year's festivi-

ties see Farquhar, ed. *Journal of William H. Brewer*, 243, 360–370; Hoffmann, *Californien, Nevada und Mexico*, 316; Rusling, *Across America*, 311–312; J. W. Ames, "Day in Chinatown," *Lippincott's Magazine* (Philadelphia) 16:496–497 (October 1875); Mary Cone, *Two Years in California* (Chicago, 1876), 188–190.

52. "Chinese Temple at Lone Mountain," *Alta*, January 10, 1864. See also *Alta*, November 25, 1863.

53. *Herald*, April 3, 4, 5, 12, 1852, October 11, 1853, April 3, 4, 21, 1856, April 19, 1858 (quoting Butte *Record*), April 5, 1860 ("The Chinese Festival Tsing Ming," from Sacramento *Standard*), April 5, October 12, 1861; *Alta*, April 4, 5, September 30, October 22, 1852, April 11, October 11, 1853, February 25, 1854, October 20, 1855, April 27, 1856, March 28, 1861, April 6, 1862, August 23, 1866, April 4, 1868; Caroline C. Leighton, "Chinese Feast of the Dead," *Life at Puget Sound with Sketches of Travel in Washington Territory, British Columbia, Oregon and California, 1865–1881* (Boston, 1884), 215–217.

54. [Augustus W. Loomis], "The Old East in the New West," *Overland Monthly*, 1:363 (October 1868).

55. *Alta*, July 27, August 21, 1851, March 28, 1852, February 25, 1854, November 14, 1855, December 10, 1856, October 10, 1857, February 18, 19, 21, April 23, June 9, 1858, May 9, June 19, July 9, August 24, 1859, January 9, June 7, August 5, 16, December 2, 17, 1860, March 28, 1861, June 22, October 6, 24, 1862, February 19, June 3, October 28, 1863, February 28, November 2, 1864, September 14, 1866, April 5, 8, 27, May 26, November 4, 1867; *Herald*, April 8, November 15, 16, 1855, December 20, 22, 1857, February 20, June 26, 1858, April 25, 1859, March 28, 1861; Huggins, (comp.), *Continuation of the Annals of San Francisco*, 80.

56. *Alta*, July 10, 15, 16, 1853, April 5, 1856, May 11, June 19, 1859, January 24, August 16, 1860, January 28, 1861, August 23, 1864, January 27, 1865, August 17, 1867; Eldridge *v.* See Yup Company, 17 Cal. 45; Williams, "City of the Golden Gate," *Scribner's Monthly*, 10:285 (July 1875); Lloyd, *Lights and Shades in San Francisco*, 272–275.

57. Loomis to Lowrie, November 18, 1859, CPBFM.

58. *Alta*, July 10, 15, 16, 1853; Harold Kirker, "Eldorado Gothic, Gold Rush Architects and Architecture," *California Historical Society Quarterly*, 38:33–34 (March 1959). Lewis R. Townsend is listed in the San Francisco *City Directory*, 1854, 134, as architect and in the *Directory*, 1858, 271, as architect and civil engineer; he is briefly mentioned in Harold Kirker, *California's Architectural Frontier; Style and Tradition in the Nineteenth Century* (San Marino, 1960), 76, 215.

59. "The Chinese Quarter," *Herald*, July 25, 1853; "Chinese Houses on Jackson Street," *Herald*, January 7, 1858; Benjamin, *Three Years in America*, I, 281; Hoy, "Chinatown Devises Its Own Street Names," *California Folklore Quarterly*, 2:71–75 (April 1943).

60. *Alta*, April 5, 1856, July 24, 1860, August 23, 1864, January 27, 1865; *Herald*, April 21, 1856; Holbrook, "Chinadom in California. In Two Papers — Paper the First," *Hutchings' Magazine*, IV (September, 1859), 131–132; Todd, *Sunset Land*, 275–277; Robert von Schlagintweit, *Californien, Land und Leute* (Köln, 1871), 332–334; Cone, *Two Years in California*, 191–195; Densmore, *Chinese in California*, 61–62; Theodor Kirchhoff, *Californische Kulturbilder* (Kassel, 1886), 99–100.

61. *Alta*, October 4, 25, 1849, January 11, September 18, 1850, May 15, 1862; *Herald*, September 30, 1858, May 2, 1860; E[lisha]. S[mith]. Capron, *History of California, From Its Discovery to the Present Time; Comprising Also a Full Description of Its Climate, Surface, Soil, Rivers, Towns, Beasts, Birds, Fishes, State of Its Society, Agriculture, Commerce, Mines, Mining, etc. With a Journal of the Voyage from New York to San Francisco, and Back, via Panama* (Boston, 1854), 154–156; C. J. W. R., "A Dinner with the Chinese," *Hutchings' Magazine*, 1:512–513 (May, 1857); Ames, "Day in Chinatown," *Lippincott's Magazine*, 16:497–500 (October 1875); "A Chinese Reception," *Harper's Weekly*, 21:466 (June 9, 1877); F. Taylor, *Between the Gates* (Chicago, 1878), 107–110; Densmore, *Chinese in California*, 47–48; William Henry Bishop, *Old Mexico and Her Lost Provinces; A Journey in Mexico, Southern California, and Arizona by Way of Cuba* (New York, 1883), 338; Daniel Knower, *The Adventures of a Forty-Niner. An Historic Description of California, with Events and Ideas of San Francisco and its People in those Early Days* (Albany, 1894), 49, 81; Genthe and Irwin, *Pictures of Old Chinatown*, 26–32.

62. *Alta*, October 6, 7, 18, 20, December 20, 25, 1852, April 1, September 2, December 19, 1853, December 14, 1856, May 11, August 12, 15, 1857, February 23, 1859, January 6, May 10, 11, 12, 14, 15, 16, 17, 1860, February 17, 1865, November 21, 1867, January 28, June 18, September 20, 1868; *Herald*, August 16, October 6, 8, 10, 17, 18, 19, 20, 21, 22, 23, 24, December 22, 1852, March 10, 27, 31, April 1, November 27, 1853, April 26, 1858, May 11, August 11, 1860; "The Royal Theatre, A Popular Performance," in "Character Sketches in San Francisco: An Evening in the Chinese Quarter," *Frank Leslie's Illustrated Newspaper* (New York), 46:422 (August 24, 1878); Densmore, "Chinese Theatres," *Chinese in California*, 54–58; George Augustus Sala, "The Drama in China Town," *America Revisited: From the Bay of New York to the Gulf of Mexico, and From Lake Michigan to the Pacific*, 2 volumes (3rd ed., London, 1883), II, 238–252; MacMinn, "Celestial Entertainments," *Theater of the Golden Era in California*, 493–508; Lois Rodecape, "Celestial Drama in the Golden Hills; The Chinese Theatre in California, 1849–1869," *California Historical Society Quarterly*, 23:97–116 (June 1944), Alice Henson Ernst, "The Chinese Theatre," *Trouping in Oregon Country; A History of Frontier Theatre* (Portland, [1961]), 96–102.

63. Loomis to Lowrie, November 18, 1859, CPBFM; *Herald*, December 22, 1852, July 15, 1853, September 22, December 29, 1854, April 14, July 28, August 17, 1855, March 22, 26, 27, October 31, November 1, 1857, January 16, November 28, 1858; *Alta*, September 18, 1853, September 22, 1854, August 28, 1863, January 11, 1864, February 15, 1866; Bowles, *Our New West*, 406; Williams, "City of the Golden Gate," *Scribner's Monthly*, 10:283–284 (July 1875); Ames, "Day in Chinatown," *Lippincott's Magazine*, 16:500 (October 1875); Vogel, *Vom Indischen Ocean bis zum Goldlande*, 421; "Elysium of the Opium Smoker, in "Character Sketches in San Francisco: An Evening in the Chinese Quarter," *Leslie's Illustrated*, 46:422 (August 24, 1878); Taylor, *Between the Gates*, 115–116; Densmore, *Chinese in California*, 99–101; Iza Duffus Hardy, "In China Town," *Belgravia* (London), 43:218–219 (December 1880).

64. Stewart Culin, "Popular Literature of the Chinese Laborers in the United States," *Oriental Studies, A Selection of Papers Read Before the Oriental Club of Philadelphia, 1888–1894* (Boston, 1894), 54–55.

65. Speer to Lowrie, December 18, 1852, CPBFM; *Alta*, November 12, 1852, May 18, 1855, March 2, September 2, 4, 5, 11, 12, 1857, November 13, 17, December 17, 18, 22, 1858, October 2, 1860; *Herald*, October 29, 1852, March 21, July 23, 25, 1853, February 11, 22, June 30, 1854, March 30, 1856, September 6, 12, December 12, 1857, December 3, 16, 17, 1858, February 25, March 13, November 2, 1859, September 29, October 2, 1860; California State Senate, *Chinese Immigration 1876*, 44, 47, 60, 89, 100, 110, 116, 124, 152; *Senate Rept. 689*, 44 Cong., 2 Sess., 10, 151, 191, 192, 196, 222, 224, 240, 309, 829; California State Senate, *Chinese Immigration 1878*, 109, 112, 125, 165, 175, 187, 189, 217; Capron, *History of California*, 150–151; Soulé, *Annals*, 382–383; Balduin Möllhausen, *Wanderungen durch die Prairien und Wüsten des westlichen Nordamerika vom Mississippi nach den Küsten der Südsee im Gefolge der von der Regierung der Vereinigten Staaten unter Lieutenant* [Amiel Weeks] *Whipple ausgesandten Expedition* (2nd ed., Leipzig, 1860), 461–462; Todd, *Sunset Land*, 277–280; Charles Nordhoff, *California* (New York, 1872), 87–89; Albert S. Evans, *À la California. Sketches of Life in the Golden State* (San Francisco, 1873), 287–290; Rusling, *Across America*, 310–311; Densmore, *Chinese in California*, 97–98; Chamberlain, *Call of Gold*, 145. For scenes in Chinese gambling houses see Peters, *California on Stone*, 57, 62, 69, 121, plates 22, 61; Soulé, *Annals*, 383 (also reproduced in Henry Evans, *Curious Lore of San Francisco's Chinatown* (San Francisco, 1955), 7); Sala, *America Revisited*, II, 272; Bishop, *Old Mexico and Her Lost Provinces*, 339; Wheat, ed. "Journals of Charles E. DeLong," *California Historical Society Quarterly*, 9:facing 348 (December 1930); Boggs, (comp.), *Anthology of Newspaper Clippings and Documents*, 119.

66. For a description of the games among the Chinese in the United States see Stewart Culin, *The Gambling Games of the Chinese in America. Fán t'án: the Game of Repeatedly Spreading Out. And Pák kòp piú or, the Game of White Pigeon Ticket* (Philadelphia, 1891), and "Chinese Games [in America] with Dice and Dominoes," *Report of the U.S. National Museum, under the Direction of the Smithsonian Institution, For the Year Ending June 30, 1893* (Washington, 1895), 491–537, based on a preliminary study, *Chinese Games with Dice — Read Before the Oriental Club of Philadelphia, March 14, 1889* (Philadelphia, 1889).

CHAPTER VI. Strife

1. Gibson, *Chinese in America*, 224; Coolidge, *Chinese Immigration*, 30; Eaves, *History of California Labor Legislation*, 105–106; Fenn, *Ah Sin*, 2.

2. Charles Howard Shinn, *Mining Camps: A Study in American Frontier Government* (New York, 1885), 212–218; Bancroft, *History of California*, VI, 211–212.

3. Josiah Royce, *California, From the Conquest in 1846 to the Second Vigilance Committee in San Francisco: A Study of American Character* (Boston, 1886), 271–376.

4. Coolidge, *Chinese Immigration*, 55.

5. Sandmeyer, *Anti-Chinese Movement in California*, 25.

6. Rodman W. Paul, "The Origin of the Chinese Issue in California," *Mississippi Valley Historical Review* (Cedar Rapids, Iowa), 25:182 (September 1938).

7. Leonard Pitt, "The Beginnings of Nativism in California," *Pacific Historical Review*, 30:23, 38 (February 1961).

8. Doris Marion Wright, "The Making of Cosmopolitan California: An Analysis of Immigration, 1848–1870," *California Historical Society Quarterly*, 19:324–329 (December 1940).

9. New York *Herald*, April 3, 1849; Taylor, *Eldorado*, I, 84–87; José Francisco Velasco, *Noticias estadísticas del estado de Sonora* (Mexico City, 1850), 288–291; Richard H. Dillon, "Kanaka Colonies in California," *Pacific Historical Review*, 24:17–18 (February 1955).

10. *Herald*, October 27, 1851 (quoting Mokelumne *Calaveras Chronicle*).

11. Allen B. Sherman, ed. "Sherman Was There: The Recollections of Major Edwin A. Sherman," *California Historical Society Quarterly*, 23:351–352 (December 1944).

12. J. Ross Browne, *Report of the Debates in the Convention of California, on the Formation of the State Constitution, in September and October, 1849* (Washington, 1850), 43–50, 137–152, 331–340; "Free Negroes," *Herald*, January 7, 1851; Paul S. Taylor, "Should California

Enter the Union Slave or Free?" in "Foundations of California Rural Society," *California Historical Society Quarterly*, 24:194–202 (September 1945).

13. *California Assembly Journal*, 1 Sess., 1850, 805–811.

14. Paul, *California Gold*, 48–49.

15. William Shaw, *Golden Dreams and Waking Realities; Being the Adventures of a Gold-Seeker in California and the Pacific Islands* (London, 1851), iv, 27, 86–87.

16. *Alta*, July 26, 1849. See also Sacramento *Placer Times*, July 9, 25, 1849.

17. *Alta*, May 4, 1850.

18. *California Senate Journal*, 1 Sess., 1850, 232–233, 250–258, 493, 496–497, 1110, 1147. For a brief history of the Foreign Miners' Tax in California between 1849 and 1866 see Carl I. Wheat, "Notes on the Journal of Charles E. DeLong for 1855," *California Historical Society Quarterly*, 8:353–355 (n. 4) (December 1929).

19. Browne, *Report of the Debates in the Convention of California*, 144.

20. *Alta*, May 24, October 7, 12 (quoting Sacramento *Placer Times*), 1850.

21. Friedrich Gerstaecker, *Californische Skizzen* (Leipzig, 1856), 159–195.

22. *Californian*, November 4, 1848.

23. *California Senate Journal*, 3 Sess., 1852, 15.

24. Browne, *Report of the Debates in the Convention of California*, 339.

25. *Alta*, July 23, August 21, 23, 25, 1851; H. Brett Melendy, "Who Was John McDougal?" *Pacific Historical Review*, 29:239–240 (August 1960).

26. *Alta*, March 8, 1852.

27. *Alta*, "The Chinese," February 1, 21, 23, March 24, April 10, 11, "Chinese Tax," October 27, "Exodus of the Chinese," November 2, 1855, "Chinese Question," January 26, 1856, "The Chinese Problem," July 6, "The Chinese," July 11, 28, "Our Chinese Population," December 7, 1857, "The Abuse of the Chinese," January 23, April 10, 20, "The Chinese Exodus," June 28, 1858, January 13, "More Chinese Legislation," February 7, "Chinaman and Taxation," February 11, "The Chinese Question," February 19, 1859, "Lo the Poor Chinaman," May 13, 1860, January 29, "The Chinese Question," February 20, March 1, "The Chinese Question in its Constitutional Aspects," March 3, 5, 1862, "The Crusade Against the Chinese," April 16, "Chinese Labor," July 26, August 14, 15, 16, 17, 18, 1866, "The Labor Question," January 16, "Chinese Labor," March 8, "The Civil Rights Bill and Chinese Testimony," November 19, 1867, "The Tax on Chinese Miners," January 18, 1868, "The Civil Rights and the Chinese Testimony," January

15, "The Chinese Necessary to the Prosperity of Our Mining Industry," June 17, "The Chinese on the Pacific Coast," June 24, "Novel View of the Chinese Question," July 8, "Citizen John Chinaman," July 24, "Is the Coolie Trade Practicable," August 2, 1869; *Herald*, November 7, December 18, 27, 30, 1855, "The Chinese Question," February 11, 13, 14, 18, 21, March 1, "A Plea for the Chinese," April 4, "Chinese Question," April 10, 1856, "Thoughts about the Chinese," July 13, "The Chinese," December 29, 1857, "Immigration of the Inferior Races," March 28, April 9, "The Chinese Question," April 11, 1858, "The Chinese — An Imperium in Imperio," March 21, November 6, 1859, "The Chinese Question," March 15, August 27, 29, 1860; *California Police Gazette*, "Chinese Defiance of Law," November 25, 1865; *Occidental*, "The Radicals and Chinese Suffrage," May 17, 1867; "Report of Joint Select Committee Relative to the Chinese Population of the State of California," *Appendix to California Legislative Journals*, 13 Sess., 1862, No. 23; George F. Seward, "Objections which Have Been Advanced Against Chinese Immigrants," *Chinese Immigration, In Its Social and Economical Aspects* (New York, 1881), 136–291; Wen Hwan Ma, "The Objections to Chinese Immigration," *American Policy Toward China As Revealed in the Debates of Congress* (Shanghai, [1934?]), 123–173.

28. "The Chinese in California," *Herald*, October 9, 1859 (quoting Sacramento *Democratic Standard*).

29. Coolidge, *Chinese Immigration*, took the side of the defenders of the Chinese; Sandmeyer, *Anti-Chinese Movement in California*, favored the opponents of Chinese.

30. *Alta*, March 10, 21, 1852; *California Assembly Journal*, 3 Sess., 1852, 353; *California Senate Journal*, 3 Sess., 1852, 303, 305–307.

31. *Alta*, March 8, 10, 21, 1852; "Celestials Faithless," *Herald*, March 25, 1852.

32. *Daily Evening Picayune*, March 10, 1852; Sacramento *Union*, March 20, 1852.

33. *Herald*, March 12, 1852 (quoting Stockton *Republican*); Stockton *Times*, March 5, 8, 12, 15, 20, 22, 1851; *Alta*, March 15, 21, 1851; *California Assembly Journal*, 2 Sess., 1851, 1334–1335; *California Senate Journal*, 2 Sess., 1851, 318, 391, 396.

34. Browne, *Report of Debates in the Convention of California*, 144, 333.

35. [Philip A. Roach], "Minority Report of the Select Committee on Senate Bill, No. 63, 'an act to enforce contracts and obligations to perform work and labor'," *California Senate Journal*, 3 Sess., 1852, Appendix 669–674.

36. Diary of Isaac McCullough, July 19, 1852 (MS, Houghton Library); *Alta*, April 21 (quoting Sacramento *Union*), May 1, 12, 14, 15, 16, 21, 22, 26, 29 (Shasta *Courier*), June 9 (Sacramento *Democratic State Jour-*

nal), 26 (Stockton *Republican*), July 13, September 25, 30 (Sonora *Herald*), October 9 (Mokelumne *Calaveras Chronicle*), 1852, January 26, 28, February 16, 1853; *Herald*, May 6, 9 (Sacramento *Union*), May 10 (Mokelumne *Calaveras Chronicle*), 11, 12 (Marysville *Express*), 14 (Marysville *Express*), 15, 20, 21, 22, June 2 (Nevada *Transcript*), 4 (Sacramento *Union*), July 24, October 11, 1852, March 1, 1853.

37. "Report of the Committee on Mines and Mining Interests (April 16, 1852)," *California Assembly Journal*, 3 Sess., 1852, Appendix, 831.

38. *Herald*, March 18, 1853; *Alta*, January 13, 24, 1859; "Majority and Minority Reports of the Committee on Mining and Mining Interests, No. 28 [March 9, 1853]," *California Assembly Journal*, 4 Sess., 1853, 5–6; "Minority Report of Select Committee on Resolutions of the Miners' Convention of Shasta County, No. 16 [March 17, 1855]," *California Senate Journal*, 6 Sess., 1855, Appendix; [Wilson Flint], "Report from the Select Committee to Whom was Referred the Resolutions of the Miners' Convention at Shasta County [March 28, 1855]," *California Senate Journal*, 6 Sess., 1855, Appendix; *California Legislative Journals*, 6 Sess., 1855, 704, 722–723, 755, 779, 786; People v. Downer, 7 Cal. 170.

39. *Alta*, November 2, 3, 6, December 9, 10, 1859, January 30, September 23, October 31, November 3, 5, 1860, January 14, 16, 22, March 5, 6, 17, 1861, August 5, 1863, July 28, 1864, February 13, 14, 15, 18, 20, 21, 22, 23, 24, 26, 27, March 1, 5, 7, 8, 10, May 14, June 2, 1867, June 24, 25, July 18, 21, September 12, November 26, 1869; *Herald*, November 18, December 11, 1859, October 3, 1861; San Francisco *Bulletin*, July 12, 1862; San Francisco *California Police Gazette*, February 23, March 2, 9, May 4, 1867, December 25, 1868; San Francisco *Occidental*, March 13, May 17, July 5, 12, August 30, 1867; [Anti-Chinese Union of San Francisco], *Constitution and By-Laws of the Anti-Chinese Union of San Francisco* ([San Francisco], 1876). See also Ira B. Cross, *A History of the Labor Movement in California* (Berkeley, 1935), 31–32, 34, 73–87.

40. Based on reports in California newspapers. For specific dates see Barth, unpubl. diss., pp. 250–252, or turn to excerpts from the files of the San Francisco *Evening Bulletin* from December 3, 1855, to September 27, 1876, which Brooks printed as "Appendix 'A': Outrages on Chinese," *Appendix to the Opening Statement*, 1–72.

41. The murder of Martin Van Buren Griswold on November 7, 1857, at Jackson, Amador County, and the capture and prosecution of his four Chinese assassins may serve to illustrate the point. A wealth of documentation sustains the viewpoint; it would go far beyond the scope of this argument to reproduce it here in detail. *Alta*, November 10, 18, 19 (Stockton *Republican*), 24 (Jackson *Ledger*), 1857. Charles Carvalho, the Chinese interpreter of the San Francisco Police Court, translated during the trial at Jackson. *Alta*, February 22, 1858. *Herald*, November 11 (Jackson *Ledger*), 17, 19 (Stockton *Republican*), 23, 24, 1857, April

6 (Jackson *Ledger*), 17 (Sacramento *Union*), 20 (Jackson *Ledger*), 1858. On May 7, 1858, after the execution of the murderers, the *Herald* published and praised the poems which the condemned men had written in the death cell. See also [Springer & Co.], *Murder of M. V. B. Griswold*.

42. For the trials, tribulations, and rewards in the life of collectors of the Foreign Miners' Tax turn to Wheat, ed. "Journals of Charles E. DeLong," *California Historical Society Quarterly*, 8:338–349 (December 1929); Sherman, ed. "Recollections of Major Edwin A. Sherman," *California Historical Society Quarterly*, 24:177–179 (June 1945); "Hard Times Among the Chinese Miners," *Herald*, April 21, 1856; *Alta*, July 31, 1867.

43. *Alta*, February 19, May 23, 24, 1851, October 26, 1871; *Herald*, May 23, 26, 1851; Los Angeles *Star*, October 25, 26, 1871; Los Angeles *News*, October 26, 1871; "Chinese Massacre," W. W. Robinson, ed. *Reproduction of Thompson and West's History of Los Angeles County, California* (Berkeley, 1959, original edition, 1880), 84–85; C[hester]. P. Dorland, "Chinese Massacre at Los Angeles in 1871," *Annual Publications of the Historical Society of Southern California* (Los Angeles), 3:22–26 (part II, 1894); P. S. Dorney, "A Prophecy Partly Verified," *Overland Monthly*, 7:230–234 (2nd s., March 1886); Paul M. De Falla, "Lantern in the Western Sky," *Southern California Quarterly* (Los Angeles), 42:57–88 (March 1960), 42:161–185 (June 1960).

44. *Alta*, October 18, 1860.

45. [Francis P. Farquhar, ed.], *Joaquin Murieta, The Brigand Chief of California: A complete history of his life from the age of sixteen to the time of his capture and death in 1853* (San Francisco, reprinted, 1932), 22–23, 28–29, 59, 72.

46. Joseph Henry Jackson, "Introduction," *The Life and Adventures of Joaquin Murieta, The Celebrated California Bandit, By Yellow Bird [John Rollin Ridge]* (Norman, 1955), xii. Franklin Walker, *San Francisco's Literary Frontier*, 45–54, suggests that Ridge, in his penny dreadful of 1854, taking the side of the Mexican down-and-outer, "was supporting the minority cause of his fellow Indians."

47. *Alta*, March 25, 1866; San Francisco *Elevator*, August 27, October 22, November 19, 26 (quoting Charleston *Missionary Record*), December 3, 17, 1869.

48. *Alta*, March 24, May 2, 1851, June 14, September 2, 3, October 31, 1853, January 24, February 14, April 7, September 1, 2, October 6, 27, 1854, January 25, October 25, 27, 31, November 22, December 7, 1857, February 26, March 12, July 22, October 26, 1858, January 6, October 24, November 17, 1860, February 13, August 4, 1861, December 16, 1867; *Herald*, August 8, 1853, January 20, October 22, 1858; *Daily Evening News*, February 14, 1854; *California Police Gazette*, October 7, 1865, June 16, 1866; "Mining Life in California," *Harper's Weekly*,

1:633 (October 3, 1857); Sherman, ed. "Recollections of Major Edwin A. Sherman," *California Historical Society Quarterly*, 24:177–179 (June 1945); Farquhar, ed. *Journal of William H. Brewer*, 250–251.

49. *Alta*, April 25, 26, 27, 30, May 10, 1852; *Herald*, April 30, 1852; "The Chinese in California. Letter of the Chinamen to His Excellency, Gov. Bigler," *Littell's Living Age* (Boston), 34:32–34 (July 3, 1852); *California Senate Journal*, 3 Sess., 1852, 373–378.

50. *Herald*, May 1, 4, 8, 10, 20, June 12, 1852. The pioneer study on the Chinese in the United States, Coolidge, *Chinese Immigration*, 55–56, 67, selects John Bigler as villain, evidently under the influence of John S. Hittell, *A History of the City of San Francisco and Incidentally of the State of California* (S. F., 1878), 280–281; Royce, *California*, 277, 494; Bancroft, *History of California*, VI, 659; Theodore H. Hittell, *History of California*, 4 vols. (San Francisco, 1898), IV, 180.

51. *Herald*, February 20, March 26, April 10, May 4, "Hegira of the Chinese," 18, 21, June 8, 10, 15, 17, "The Chinese Hegira," 30, July 4, 22, August 2, "The Chinese Everywhere," 16, 18, September 2, 1852; *Alta*, March 26, 29, April 10, 23, 28, "Chinese Emigration," May 10, June 3, 4, 7, 9, 10, 11, 12, 15, 18, July 23.

52. *California Senate Journal*, 3 Sess., 1852, 373; *Alta*, May 4, 1852.

53. Herald, July 10, "The Chinese Question at the East," August 15 (quoting *China Mail* and *Overland Register*), September 26, 28, 1852; *Alta*, August 12 (London *Times*), 23 (New York *Evening Mirror*), 29 (London *Times*), October 5 (New York *National Police Gazette*), 28 (Hong Kong *Friend of China*), 1852; London *Times*, June 18, 1852; Thomas Greaves Cary's manuscript, The Chinese in California, (Houghton Library) is primarily a copy of the first Chinese answer to Governor Bigler and of an editorial in the New York *Times*, commenting favorably on the Chinese letter.

54. A later editorial of the *Alta*, published on August 23, 1852, mentions Norman Assing instead of Hab Wa as second signer of the remonstrance.

55. *Herald*, June 6, 1852.

56. "Curious Features of California Life," *Herald*, June 7, 1852.

57. *Herald*, June 6, 7, 22, July 9, 23, December 10, 1852.

58. *Alta*, June 6, 1852; *Herald*, June 12, 1852, February 6, 1855, [San Francisco *Herald*], *An Analysis of the Chinese Question. Consisting of a Special Message of the Governor, and, in Reply Thereto, Two Letters of the Chinamen, and a Memorial of the Citizens of San Francisco* (San Francisco, 1852); Speer, trans. *Remarks of the Chinese Merchants*; Speer, *Oldest and Newest Empire*, 588–603; [Presidents of the Six Companies and President of Chinese Young Men's Christian Association], "A Memorial to His Excellency U. S. Grant, President of the United States, From Representative Chinamen in America," Layres, *Facts Upon the Other Side of the Chinese Question*, 20–24.

59. *California Senate Journal*, 3 Sess., 1852, 373–376.

60. People *v.* George W. Hall, 4 Cal. 399. See also the precedent established by Justice Solomon Heydenfeldt in 1852 who turned down the testimony of Malay sailors on the ground that they were Indians and could not testify against white men. In 1854 he concurred in Chief Justice Hugh C. Murray's opinion. "Chinese Oaths," *Herald*, December 20, 1852.

61. *California Assembly Journal*, 4 Sess., 1853, Doc. 28, 10–12, *Herald*, March 18, 1853; *Alta*, March 25, 1853.

62. "Circular Addressed by the California Chinamen to their Countrymen," *Herald*, May 16, 1852.

63. *Alta*, September 26, 1852 (quoting Hong Kong *China Mail*).

64. "Decrease of the Chinese Population in California," *Alta*, July 31, 1867.

65. *Alta*, March 8, May 8, 11, 1850, February 3, "The Chinese Quarter," October 5, November 21, 1853; *Herald*, April 4, 12, July 10, 1852, July 25, 1853.

66. *Alta*, August 30, 1851, January 6, May 13, 1852, February 5, 22, 1854; *Herald*, July 10, 1852, January 17, December 8, 26, 1853; January 26, 1854.

67. *Alta*, March 20, 1850, February 14, 1851, March 1, 8, April 17, November 1, 1852, March 28, October 30, 1853, August 30, September 2, 1854; *Herald*, October 25, 27, 1851, March 13, October 21, 23, December 20, 1852; Huggins (comp.), *Continuation of the Annals of San Francisco*, 16.

68. Albert M. Friedenberg, ed. "Letters of a California Pioneer [Alexander Mayer to his uncle Lazarus Mayer]," *Publications of the American Jewish Historical Society*, 31:135–171 (1928).

69. "Report of the Special Committee of the Board of Supervisors of San Francisco, on the Condition of the Chinese Quarter of that City," Farwell, *Chinese At Home and Abroad*, part II, 5.

70. *Herald*, February 22, August 22, 24, 25, September 4, 1854; *Alta*, August 21, 22, 30, September 3, 4, October 7, 8, 1854.

71. Speer, *Humble Plea*, 20, estimated that Chinese paid the following monthly rates to property owners prior to 1856: San Francisco, $13,200; Sacramento, $3,000; Auburn, $1,200; Marysville, $1,000; Jackson, $600; Stockton, $320.

72. *Herald*, August 15 (quoting Marysville *Herald*), 23 (Sacramento *Union*), November 6 (Sonora *Democrat*), 1854; *Alta*, August 22, 23 (Sacramento *Union*), 1854.

73. *Alta*, July 12, 1859; San Francisco *Municipal Reports*, 1859–1860, 62–63; 1865–1866, 124–126; Gibson, "Missionary Work Among Chinese Women in California," *Chinese in America*, 200–222; Condit, *Chinaman As We See Him*, 136–155; Carol Green Wilson, *Chinatown Quest; The Life Adventures of Donaldina Cameron* (Stanford, 1931). The "Official

Map of Chinatown in San Francisco," a part of the *Municipal Reports for 1884–85* and also published in Farwell, *Chinese at Home and Abroad*, gives the location of the houses of prostitution.

CHAPTER VII. Acculturation

1. *Alta*, March 29, 1852, June 10, 1853, "Gold at Canton," July 23, 1854 (quoting *China Mail*); *Herald*, July 23, 1853.

2. *Alta*, May 18, 1851.

3. "Missionary Effort Among the Chinese in America," Gibson, *Chinese in America*, 138–199; "Origin of Chinese Missions in America," Condit, *Chinaman as We See Him*, 90–100; Robert Seager II, "Some Denominational Reactions to the Chinese Immigration to California, 1856–1892," *Pacific Historical Review*, 28:49–66 (February 1959); Lionel U. Ridout, "The Church, The Chinese, and The Negroes in California, 1849–1893," *Historical Magazine of the Protestant Episcopal Church* (New Brunswick), 28:115–138 (June 1959).

4. Speer to Lowrie, November 15, 1852, Lowrie to Speer, January 20, 1854, Trustees of Chinese Mission to Lowrie, November 4, 1858, CPBFM.

5. Speer to Lowrie, November 15, 1852, September 15, 1853; H. Channing Beals to Lowrie, June 30, 1855, CPBFM.

6. Thomas C. Hambly to Speer, November 8, 1853, CPBFM; *Alta*, September 9, 1853; Albert Williams, *A Pioneer Pastorate and Times, Embodying Contemporary Local Transactions and Events* (San Francisco, 1879), 122–123.

7. *Alta*, August 11, 13, 14, 26, 27, 28, 29, 1850; Soulé, *Annals*, 287–288; Williams, *Pioneer Pastorate*, 121–122.

8. *Alta*, August 30, 1850, February 24, June 22, August 8, 11, 1852, July 15, 1854, February 24, 1859, April 20, 1865; *Herald*, February 21, 24, July 5, 7, August 4, 5, 7, 11, 1852, September 29, 1858; Sacramento *Union*, September 30, 1858; Helen Throop Pratt, "Crescent City on the Tuolumne; A Prophecy that Failed," *California Historical Society Quarterly*, 11:361 (December 1932); Helen Throop Pratt, ed. "The California Letters of Edward Hotchkiss," *California Historical Society Quarterly*, 12:100, 102–103 (June 1933); Soulé, *Annals*, 287–288, 294; Wheat, ed. "Journals of Charles E. DeLong," *California Historical Society Quarterly*, 9:360 (December 1930), 360; George Hamlin Fitch, "How California Came Into the Union," *Century Illustrated Monthly Magazine* (New York), 40:791 (September 1890); Helen Throop Purdy, "Portsmouth Square," *California Historical Society Quarterly*, 3:40–41 (April 1924).

9. William Taylor, *California Life Illustrated* (New York, 1861), 310–319; James Woods, *Recollections of Pioneer Work in California* (San Francisco, 1878), 99–102; Williams, *Pioneer Pastorate*, 122–123;

C. V. Anthony, *Fifty Years of Methodism; A History of the Methodist Episcopal Church Within the Bounds of the California Annual Conference from 1847 to 1897* (San Francisco, 1901), 295.

10. Beals to Lowrie, June 30, 1855; Trustees of Chinese Mission to Lowrie, November 14, 1858; Loomis to Lowrie, November 18, 1859, January 18, 1861, CPBFM; *Alta*, April 2, 1857, "Christianize the Chinese by Importing Them," June 20, 1869 (quoting New York *Journal of Commerce*); Speer, *China and California*, 26–27.

11. *Herald*, February 11, 1853; *Alta*, February 12, 1853; Condit, *Chinaman as We See Him*, 90, contains a photograph of the chapel.

12. *Herald*, June 5, 6, 1854; *Alta*, June 5, 6, October 25, 1854; *Daily Evening News*, June 5, 1854.

13. Loomis to Lowrie, September 17, 25, 1859, CPBFM; *Herald*, November 11, 1853; *Daily Evening News*, October 20, 27, 1854; Jeter, ed., *Memoir of Mrs. Henrietta Shuck*, 6; Speer, *Oldest and Newest Empire*, 661; K[enneth]. S[cott]. L[atourette]., "Shuck, Jehu Lewis," *DAB*, XVII, 137.

14. *Alta*, July 17, 1854; [Edward W. Syle], "Chinese in California," *Spirit of Missions* (New York), 20:38 (February 1855); William I. Kip, "California," *Spirit of Missions*, 20:141 (April 1855); Speer, *Oldest and Newest Empire*, 661.

15. *Herald*, June 27, 28, July 4, 1853, November 24, December 2, 3, 4, 5, 8, 1855; Loomis to Lowrie, November 18, 1859, CPBFM.

16. Msgr. Walter J. Tappe to G. Barth, August 11, 1959; Gibson, *Chinese in America*, 241–403; [Augustus W. Loomis], "Annual Report of the Chinese School, In charge of the Presbyterian Chinese Mission, Submitted by Rev. A. W. Loomis, D. D., Feb. 6, 1877, On the Occasion of its 24th Anniversary," [Chinese Presbyterian Mission School], *The Twenty-Fourth Anniversary of the Chinese Presbyterian Mission School, or, A Practical Answer to the Question, "Are the Chinese capable and desirous of assimilating with us, and learning our language and habits?"* [(San Francisco, 1877)], 6–7; " 'The Chinese Must Go: Father Bouchard Says So,' " John Bernard McGloin, *Eloquent Indian, The Life of James Bouchard, California Jesuit* (Stanford, [1949]), 172–187; Robert Seager II, "Some Denominational Reactions to the Chinese Immigration to California, 1856–1892," *Pacific Historical Review*, 28:54–59 (February 1959).

17. *Kim-Shan Jit San-Luk*, July 8, 1854; William I. Kip, "Chinese in California," *Spirit of Missions*, 20:89 (March 1855); Lloyd, *Lights and Shades in San Francisco*, 284, in 1876, referred in passing to "Father Thomas" who "came to San Francisco from Siam . . . as long ago as 1853." Henry L. Walsh, *Hallowed Were the Gold Dust Trails: The Story of the Pioneer Priests of Northern California* ([Santa Clara], 1946), 476, n. 31.

18 *Herald*, August 3, 1854 (quoting Sacramento *Union*); San Francisco *City Directory*, 1856, 35, 124; *Directory*, 1858, 90, 376; *Directory*, 1859,

86, 385; *Directory*, 1860, 93, 437; *Directory*, 1862, 553–554; Rev. John B. McGloin, S.J., Archivist, University of San Francisco, to G. Barth, July 14, 1961; Walsh, *Hallowed Were the Gold Dust Trails*, 476, n. 31.

19. Lloyd, *Lights and Shades in San Francisco*, 284; John P. Young, *San Francisco: A History of the Pacific Coast Metropolis*, 2 vols. (San Francisco, [1912]), I, 239–240; John B. McGloin, ed., "A California Gold Rush Padre: New Light on the 'Padre of Paradise Flat,'" *California Historical Society Quarterly*, 40:64 (March 1961).

20. Speer to Lowrie, September 15, 1853, Lowrie to Speer, May 18, Beals to Lowrie, June 30, Lowrie to David S. Turner, August 5, 1855, Lowrie to Speer, September 20, Trustees of the Chinese Mission to Lowrie, November 4, 1858, CPBFM; *Alta*, July 23, August 1, September 9, November 13, 1853, June 12, 1855; *Herald*, June 18, September 5, 7, 1853; Sacramento *City Directory*, 1856, 27; Holbrook, "Chinadom in California. In Two Papers — Paper the Second," *Hutchings' Magazine* 4:173 (October 1859); [Sacramento Book Collectors Club], *Sacramento Illustrated; A Reprint of the Original Edition Issued by Barber & Baker in 1855* (Sacramento 1950), 101–102.

21. *Alta*, November 25, 1855, February 22, 1856; Kip, "Chinese in California," *Spirit of Missions*, 20:85–90 (March 1855); Wm. Ingraham Kip, *The Early Days of My Episcopate* (New York, 1892); D[wight]. O. Kelley, *History of the Diocese of California, From 1849 to 1914* (San Francisco, [1915?]), 32–33, 34, 85, 360; Ridout, "The Church, The Chinese, and The Negroes in California, 1849–1893," *Historical Magazine of the Protestant Episcopal Church*, 28:119–126 (June 1959).

22. Loomis to Lowrie, September 17, 23, December 15, 19, 1859, December 10, 1860, CPBFM; *Alta*, December 12, 1856, March 28, August 1, 1857; *Herald*, January 16, 1855, March 28, 1857; *DAB*, XVII, 137.

23. Lowrie to Speer, January 14, W. C. Anderson to Lowrie, February 19, Rev. J. K. Davis, of Stockton to Lowrie, March 3, Anderson to Lowrie, March 5, Turner to Lowrie, April 4, 1857, A. A. Scott to Lowrie, November 4, 1858, Lowrie to Trustees of Chinese Mission, February 22, Lowrie to Scott, February 25, 1859, CPBFM.

24. Loomis to Speer, January 14, Anderson to Lowrie, February 19, 1857, CPBFM; *Herald*, September 22, 1860; *California Police Gazette*, December 2, 1865.

25. For examples see the table, "Total Number of Chinese Christians Baptized in America," Gibson, *Chinese in America*, 198, and Bryan J. Clinche, "The Chinese in America," *American Catholic Quarterly Review* (Philadelphia), 9:69 (January 1884).

26. See in particular Loomis to Lowrie, March 1, 9, June 25, 1860, June 29, 1863.

27. McGloin, ed., "A California Gold Rush Padre: New Light on the 'Padre of Paradise Flat,'" *California Historical Society Quarterly*, 40:58 (March 1961).

28. *Herald*, April 8, 1855, contains the first recorded civil marriage

between "Mr. Ah He and Miss Say Sung" before "Orrin Bailey, Esq., Justice of the Second Township." See also Huggins (comp.), *Continuation of the Annals of San Francisco*, 41.

29. Kip, "Chinese in California," *Spirit of Missions*, 20:89 (March 1855) provides an early example of the argument.

30. [John Archbald], *On the Contact of Races: Considered Especially with Relation to the Chinese Question* (San Francisco, 1860) elaborates the view.

31. A remonstrance to the California Legislature crowned Speer's labor. It appeared as a pamphlet under the title, *An Humble Plea.* *Herald*, February 29, 1856, noticed the publication. It was followed by *An Answer to the Common Objections to Chinese Testimony; and an Earnest Appeal to the Legislature of California for Their Protection by Our Law* (San Francisco, 1857). The *Alta* recorded its appearance on April 2, 1857.

32. Loomis to Lowrie, January 3, 30, 1860, January 19, February 21, 1861, CPBFM.

33. Speer to Lowrie, November 15, 1852, September 15, 1853, Loomis to Lowrie, November 18, 1859, December 10, 1860, CPBFM; *Alta*, November 13, 1853; *Herald*, September 5, 1853, September 22, 1860.

34. Loomis to Lowrie, September 17, 25, December 15, 1859, March 1, 8, 9, December 10, 1860, January 19, 1861, CPBFM; *Herald*, September 20, 1860.

35. Yung, *My Life in China and America*, 39.

36. Speer to Lowrie, September 15, 1853, Beals to Lowrie, June 30, 1855, Loomis to Lowrie, September 17, 25, December 2, 15, 1859, March 1, 8, 9, June 25, September 19, December 10, 1860, January 19, 1861, April 17, August 2, 27, 1862, June 29, 1863, CPBFM. Speer, *Oldest and Newest Empire*, 659.

37. Loomis to Lowrie, December 10, 1860, CPBFM.

38. *Herald*, March 17, 1853; *Alta*, April 24 1855; "Our Social Chair," *Hutchings' Magazine*, 4:186–187 (October 1859); *California Police Gazette*, May 24, 1866.

39. Loomis to Lowrie, November 18, 1859, January 19, 1861, CPBFM; *Alta*, January 3, 1853, January 15, 1866.

40. *Alta*, August 4, 1861 (quoting Placerville *El Dorado County Daily Union*).

41. [Edward C. Moore and James L. Barton], *General Report of the Deputation Sent by the American Board to the Chinese in 1907* (Boston, 1907), 37.

42. Foreign Mission School: Including some letters relating to the education of Heathen Youth before the establishment of the School. Received before Sept. 1, 1824, Letters from Agencies, General Series, II, ABCFM Papers. The printed annual reports of the Board from 1817 to 1824 deal with affairs of the school. For a brief history of the work at Cornwall turn to Edward C. Starr, "The Foreign Mission School," *A*

History of Cornwall, Connecticut; A Typical New England Town
([New Haven?], 1926), 138–157. S. Wells Williams to Rufus D. Anderson, March 20, 1848, September 24, 1853, III, ABCFM Papers.

43. *Alta*, March 1, 4, 1851.

44. Loomis to Lowrie, September 15, 25, 1859, January 3, 1860, November 12, 1861, CPBFM; *Alta*, November 7, 1855, January 1, 3, 1860, May 23, 1861, November 12, 1862, February 5, August 21, 1867; *California Police Gazette*, March 2, 1867.

45. *Gazette*, December 14, 1860. In the early 1860's the San Francisco *City Directory* lists "Lanctot, B., teacher Chinese School." *Directory*, 1860, 192, 1861, 207, 1862, 234, 1863, 219. *Directory*, 1864, 241 registers Lanctot's advancement to the position of principal.

46. *Alta*, April 18, 1861; August 27, 1864.

47. Speer, *Oldest and Newest Empire*, 661; Gibson, *Chinese in America*, 166, 173–199; Condit, *Chinaman as We See Him*, 101–102; William Chauncey Pond, *Gospel Pioneering: Reminiscences of Early Congregationalism in California, 1833–1920* ([Oberlin], 1921), 128–145. Pond opened the Congregational Mission in San Francisco in 1870. He came to California in 1853. Pond, *Gospel Pioneering*, 21; Clifford M. Drury, *San Francisco YMCA; 100 Years by the Golden Gate, 1853–1953* (Glendale, 1963), 65–67. For a sketch of the missionary work among the Chinese in the United States in its later phases turn to Marjorie M. Carter, ed., *The Chinese in the United States and the Chinese Christian Churches. A Statement Condensed For The National Conference on the Chinese Christian Churches. From a Study by Horace R. Cayton and Anne O. Lively; Incorporating Field Work and Consultation by Dr. Peter Y. F. Shih* ([New York], 1955).

48. *Alta*, August 27, 1867, February 12, July 12, 26, September 27, December 20, 1869.

49. *Alta*, December 23, 1850, August 2, 1852, March 25, June 10, 28, July 10, 11, 13, 18, August 22, September 1, 26, 29, October 7, 31, November 10, 23, 1853, July 19, 1854, July 1, August 24, 1857, June 23, September 6, November 10, December 22, 1858, June 15, November 10, 1859, February 27, 1860, June 30, 1861, January 27, 1862, June 14, 1864, May 11, September 20, 1866, February 20, May 30, June 2, 1867, November 10, 18, 23, December 21, 1869; *Herald*, May 19, June 20, July 15, August 8, September 14, November 17, 1852, August 6, 7, 8, 11, 21, 22, 24, September 17, 27, December 11, 1853, April 16, August 17, 1854, February 22, 1855, January 26, 28, June 20, 1857, May 21, 1858, February 7, May 19, 1860.

50. Speer to Lowrie, November 15, December 18, 1852, September 15, 1853, Beals to Lowrie, June 30, 1855, CPBFM; *Alta*, February 5, June 28, 29, July 20, 21, 23, August 11, 12, 1853, January 8, 11, 12, February 8, March 7, April 11, 1854, August 4, 1855, October 9 1869; *Herald*, November 14, 1852, January 1, March 26, June 14, 21, 23, 24, 25, 26, 27, 28, 29, July 4, 13, 14, 15, 16, 19, 20, 21, 22, 23, August 11, 12, Novem-

ber 18, 1853, January 7, 10, 11, 12, 13, 17, 19, 21, February 9, March 8, 9, 1854; *Daily Evening News*, January 19, 1854.

51. *Alta*, December 9, 1860 (quoting Columbia *Gazette*).

52. *Alta*, May 13, June 8, 1852, January 10, July 30, September 22, 1853, February 13, 1854, November 7, 1855, October 13, 1858, February 7, 1859, July 6, September 9, 1864, April 5, 1868; *Herald*, April 29, 1854, December 29, 1857, January 22, 1861; Quelp (pseud., trans.), "Chinese Letters," *Pioneer* (San Francisco), III (March 1855), 161–166.

53. *Herald*, April 29, 1854. For Mrs. Partington see B. P. Shillaber, ed. *Life and Sayings of Mrs. Partington* (New York, 1854).

54. *Herald*, July 28, October 27, 1851; *Alta*, February 5, June 27, 1853, November 4, 1854, August 22, 1857; Speer to Lowrie, May 10, 1859, CPBFM; Stanislas Hernisz (comp.), *A Guide to Conversation in the English and Chinese Languages for the Use of Americans and Chinese in California and Elsewhere* (Boston, 1854); A[ugustus]. W[ard]. Loomis, *English and Chinese Lessons* (New York, 1872).

55. *Alta*, April 29, 1854; *Herald*, April 29, 1854; *Daily Evening News*, April 29, 1854. For other lithographic work done by F. Kuhl see Peters, *California on Stone*, 151–152, who restricts Kuhl's activity in San Francisco to the years 1856–57.

56. *Alta*, July 10, 1854.

57. *Golden Hills' News*, July 9, 1854. *Alta*, July 14, 1854, reprinted the editorial.

58. Edward C. Kemble, "History of California Newspapers," Sacramento *Union*, December 25, 1858. For a reprint turn to Helen Harding Bretnor, ed., *A History of California Newspapers, 1846–1858, by Edward C. Kemble* (Los Gatos, 1962).

59. *Herald*, January 30, August 19, 1857; *Alta*, August 3, 1859 (quoting Sacramento *Bee*). Katherine Chandler (comp.), *List of California Periodicals Issued Previous to the Completion of the Transcontinental Telegraph (August 15, 1846–October 24, 1861)* (San Francisco, 1905), 10, gives "Dec., 1856–58" as dates of publication.

60. *Oriental*, January 4, 1855; *Herald*, July 23, 1853; Speer, *China and California*, 23. *Alta*, and *Daily Evening News* announced the forthcoming publication on December 18, 1854.

61. *Herald*, July 23, 1853, May 8, 1855.

62. *Oriental*, January 4, 1855.

63. Condit, *Chinaman as We See Him*, 93.

64. Solis-Cohen, Jr., ed. "A California Pioneer. The Letters of Bernhard Marks to Jacob Solis-Cohen (1853–1857)," *Publications of the American Jewish Historical Society*, 54:41 (September 1954); Henry Miller Madden, ed. "California for Hungarian Readers; Letters from Janos Xantus, 1857 and 1859," *California Historical Society Quarterly*, 28:128 (June 1949).

65. Exceptions were the Sacramento *Chinese Daily News*, discussed above, and the San Francisco *California China Mail and Flying Dragon*,

issued first on January 1, 1867, by Frederick Marriott, with the beginning of direct steam communication between San Francisco and Hong Kong. The latter aimed, as a prospectus announced, primarily at furnishing information about California to Oriental merchants. *Alta*, November 24, 1866; *California Police Gazette*, December 1, 1866; Henry R. Wagner, "Edward Bosqui, Printer and Man of Affairs," *California Historical Society Quarterly*, 21:22–24 (December 1942).

66. *Herald*, June 25, 1852, January 4, 5, 1854, October 29, November 20, December 10, 1856, January 4, February 26, 1857, June 19, 1858; *Daily Evening News*, November 2, 1853; *Alta*, December 9, 1855, December 24, 1860, August 28, 1864.

67. W. Hazlitt (trans.), *Travels in Tartary, Thibet, and China, During the Years 1844–5–6. By [Evariste Regis] Huc.* 2 vols. (London, [1852]); *Alta*, July 26, 1855. The paper had reviewed the book on June 17, 1853.

68. *Herald*, January 24, 1852; *Alta*, May 5, 1852.

69. "Chinese Citizenship," *Alta*, May 21, 1853.

70. *Alta*, December 3, 9, 29, 1854, June 5, 1860, April 16, 1866, April 14, 1867, June 15, 1868, July 24, 1869; *Herald*, December 31, 1854; Huggins (comp.), *Continuation of the Annals of San Francisco*, 29, Brace, *New West*, 218.

71. *Herald*, November 6, 1852, August 5, 1853, January 29, 1854, May 1, 1860; *Alta*, August 18, 1857, June 22, 1863, July 20, 1864, February 6, May 21, 1869; "Appendix 'H'," Brooks, *Opening Statement and Brief*, 135.

72. *Alta*, May 16, 19, 20, June 11, August 13, 1850, April 13, 1851, April 14, 1852, February 3, 5, 27, 1853, January 10, 1855; *Herald*, May 17, 1853, January 10, 1855; Pratt, "Crescent City on the Tuolumne; A Prophecy that Failed," *California Historical Society Quarterly*, 11:360 (December 1932).

73. *Alta*, September 15, 1866.

74. Loomis to Lowrie, March 9, 1860, CPBFM; *Alta*, November 7, 1858, March 13, 1860, March 2, 14, June 6, 1865, May 17, 1867. For the names of Chinese physicians turn to the San Francisco *City Directory*.

75. Stuart W. Hyde, "The Chinese Stereotype in American Melodrama," *California Historical Society Quarterly*, 34:357–367 (December 1955), collected examples from one area of public life.

76. [F. Bret Harte], "Plain Language from Truthful James," *Overland Monthly*, 5:287–288 (September 1870); "John Chinaman, Esquire," [Beadle and Adams], *Girls, Don't Fool With Cupid, Songster* (New York, 1871), 39.

CHAPTER VIII. Aftermath: From Sojourners to Immigrants

1. John Meares, *Voyages Made in the Years 1788 and 1789, From China to the North West Coast of America. To which are prefixed an*

Introductory Narrative of a Voyage performed in 1786, from Bengal, in the Ship Nootka; Observations on the probable Existence of A North West Passage and Some Account of the Trade Between the North West Coast of America and China; and the Latter Country and Great Britain (London, 1790), 3, 32–33, 88, 115–116, 220–221, 243.

2. F[rederick]. W[illiam]. Howay, ed., *The Journal of Captain James Colnett Aboard the Argonaut From April 26, 1789, to Nov. 3, 1791* (Toronto, 1940), 15, 40, 41, 42, 125, 142–143. Joseph Antonio de Villa-Señor y Sánchez, *Theatro Americano, Descripcion General de los Reynos, y Provincias de la Nueva-Espana, y sus Jurisdicciones,* 2 vols. (Mexico City, 1746–1748), I, 186–190; Bancroft, *History of California,* VII, 335; William Lytle Schurz, *The Manila Galleon* (New York, 1939), 63–98. See also George I. Quimby, "Culture Contact on the Northwest Coast, 1785–1795," *American Anthropologist* (Menasha, Wisconsin), 50:247–255 (April–June 1948).

3. Portland *Weekly Oregonian,* October 31, 1857; Viola Noon Currier, "The Chinese Web in Oregon History," unpub. diss., University of Oregon, 1928, 24.

4. San Francisco *Globe,* May 16, 1858; E[thelbert]. O[laf]. S[tuart]. Scholefield and F[rederick]. W[illiam]. Howay, *British Columbia, From the Earliest Times to the Present,* 4 vols. (Vancouver, B. C., 1914), II, 567.

5. "Chinese Address to the Governor," Victoria *British Colonist,* April 5, 1864.

6. Nevada *Journal,* September 28, 1855; [William Wright], Dan de Quille (William Wright), *History of the Big Bonanza: An Authentic Account of the Discovery, History, and Working of the World Renowned Comstock Silver Lode of Nevada* (Hartford, 1877), 26.

7. *Alta,* May 21, 1866; Lord, *Comstock Mining and Miners,* 119, 204, 253; Mack, *Nevada,* 160.

8. *Alta,* October 5, 1866; *Occidental,* August 30, 1867; Trull, Chinese in Idaho, 8–9; Robert G. Bailey, *River of No Return (The Great Salmon River of Idaho). A Century of Central Idaho and Eastern Washington History and Development, Together with the Wars, Customs, Myths, and Legends of the Nez Perce Indians* (Lewiston, 1935), 378–380.

9. Boulder *County News,* November 2, 1870; Patricia K. Ourada, "The Chinese in Colorado," *Colorado Magazine* (Denver), 29:275 (October 1952). For some aspects of the movement of the Chinese into the Rocky Mountains turn also to William J. Trimble, *The Mining Advance Into the Inland Empire: A Comparative Study of the Beginnings of the Mining Industry in Idaho and Montana, Eastern Washington and Oregon, and the Southern Interior of British Columbia; and of Institutions and Laws Based Upon That Industry* (Madison, 1914), 144–146; William S. Greever, *The Bonanza West:*

The Story of the Western Mining Rushes, 1848–1900 (Norman, [1963]), 88, 94–95, 151, 203, 220, 235, 254–255, 259–260, 272, 321; Rodman Wilson Paul, *Mining Frontiers of the Far West, 1848–1880* (New York, [1963]), 143–144, 149, 182.

10. *Alta*, May 12, 1869; Opelousas *Courier*, August 21, 1869; New Orleans *Commercial Bulletin*, September 1, 1870; A. P. Merrill, "Southern Labor," *De Bow's Review* (New Orleans), 7:587–588 (n.s., July 1869). For the preceding years note the documentation in Oscar Zeichner, "The Transition from Slave to Free Agricultural Labor in the Southern States," *Agricultural History* (Baltimore), 13:25–26 (January 1939).

11. Joe Creason, "William Kelly of Kentucky — Maker of Steel," Louisville *Courier-Journal*, February 27, 1949; Creason, "Kelly Did It First — A Kentuckian's Idea Caused Revolution in Steel-Making," *Courier-Journal*, September 9, 1955; Creason, "Kelly's Furnace vs. Barkley Dam — Another Relic of Kentucky Is About To Be Eradicated," *Courier-Journal*, August 8, 1956; John Newton Boucher, *William Kelly: A True History of the So-Called Bessemer Process* (Greensburg, Pa., 1924), 24–26; James Grant Wilson and John Fisk, eds. *Appleton's Cyclopaedia of American Biography*, 7 vols. (New York, 1887–1901), III, 508–509. The Frankfort newspapers for 1854 did not refer to the Chinese. The 1860 Federal Census of Lyon County, Kentucky, listed Jim Fo on page 697 of the manuscript. Frances Coleman, Librarian, Kentucky Historical Society, to G. Barth, September 22, 1959. See also Thomas La Fargue, "Some Early Chinese Visitors to the United States," *T'ien Hsia*, 11:138 (October–November 1940).

12. Thomas S. Staples, *Reconstruction in Arkansas, 1862–1874* (New York, 1923), 341–342; E. Merton Coulter, *The Civil War and Readjustment in Kentucky* (Chapel Hill, 1926), 345–346; David Y. Thomas, *Arkansas in War and Reconstruction, 1861–1874* (Little Rock, 1926), 423–424; W[illiam]. B[est]. Hesseltine, "Tennessee's Invitation to Carpet-Baggers," *East Tennessee's Historical Society's Publications* (Knoxville), 4:114–115 (January 1932); Bert James Loewenberg, "Efforts of the South to Encourage Immigration, 1865–1900," *South Atlantic Quarterly* (Durham), 33:363 (October 1934); E. Merton Coulter, *The South During Reconstruction, 1865–1877* ([Baton Rouge], 1947), 105–106; Rowland T. Berthoff, "Southern Attitudes Toward Immigration, 1865–1914," *Journal of Southern History* (Lexington), 17:328 (August 1951).

13. New Orleans *Commercial Bulletin*, January 16, 1867 (quoting Franklin St. Mary's *Planters' Banner*); Lexington *Observer and Reporter*, July 12, October 30, 1869; Edward King, "The Great South: The South Carolina Problem. The Epoch of Transition," *Scribner's Monthly*, 8:137,142 (June 1874): Anne Kendrick Walker, *Backtracking in Barbour County: A Narrative of the Last Alabama Frontier* (Richmond, 1941), 228; Robert D. Reid, "The Negro in Alabama During the

Civil War," *Journal of Negro History* (Washington), 35:278–279 (July 1950).

14. Frances Butler Leigh, *Ten Years on a Georgia Plantation Since the War* (London, 1883), 145–147.

15. *Alta*, August 29, 1869 (quoting Charleston *News*).

16. New Orleans *Daily Picayune*, "The Chinamen," June 5, "Chinese Immigration," July 7, "The Chinamen and the Negroes," July 13, "Letter from California," February 7, May 18, July 11, 1869.

17. Memphis *Appeal*, June 27, July 18, 1869; Little Rock *Arkansas Gazette*, June 30, 1869; "Chinamen in the South; Organization of a Company in Arkansas to Promote the Immigration of Chinese Laborers," *Alta*, July 11, 1869. For a biographical sketch of George W. Gift (1833–1879) see his obituary in the Napa *County Reporter*, February 14, 1879, and J. Thomas Scharf, *History of the Confederate States Navy: From Its Organization to the Surrender of Its Last Vessel* (Albany, 1894), 618–619.

18. *Picayune*, July 14, 15, 1869. For a biography of Isham G. Harris turn to F[rank]. L[awrence]. O[wsley]., "Harris, Isham Green," *DAB*, VIII, 310–311.

19. The reports in the Nashville *Daily Press and Times*, the Memphis *Appeal*, and the New Orleans *Picayune*, July 14, 15, 1869, reflect the convention's mood. The sober second thoughts appeared two months later, "The Chinese Again," *Hunt's Merchants' Magazine*, 61:214 (September 1869). A detailed review of the importation scheme and a dispassionate discussion of its implications in the Louisville *Journal* has been reprinted in the *California Police Gazette*, July 17, 1869. Other views, expressed in newspapers and periodicals, are evaluated by William M. Burwell, "Science and the Mechanic Arts Against Coolies," *De Bow's Review*, 7:557–571 (n.s., July 1869); and "The Cooley-ite Controversy," *De Bow's Review*, 7:709–724 (n.s., August 1869). [Edward Jenkins], *The Coolie, His Rights and Wrongs, By The Author of Ginx's Baby* (New York, 1871), 114–116, refers to the South American venture of Tye Kim Orr.

20. "Waiting for Koopmanschap," *Alta*, July 15, 1869.

21. Gemeentelijke-Archiefdienst van Amsterdam to G. Barth, February 11, June 25, 1963; Rijksarchieven in de Provincie Noordholland, Haarlem, to G. Barth, July 3, 1963; Liber Matrimoniorum, M I, 1855–1876 (Notre Dame des Victoires, San Francisco), 297; C. C. Andrews, United States Consul General at Rio de Janeiro, to Department of State, September 19, 1882 (Consular Despatches, National Archives); *Alta*, July 15, 1869, September 21, 1882; *California Police Gazette*, November 30, 1867; San Francisco *Abendpost*, September 21, 1882; San Francisco *Bulletin*, September 21, 30, 1882; San Francisco *Call*, September 21, 1882; San Francisco *Chronicle*, September 21, 26, 1882; San Francisco *City Directory*, 1854, 81, 1858, 176, 1860, 190, 1861, 204, 1862, 231, 1863, 216, 1864, 147, 237, 584, 1865, 263, 636, 1867, 64, 289,

568, 1868, 328, 651, 1869, 362, 724, 1870, 263, 1871, 381, 765, 1872, 379, 770, 1873, 357, 733, 1874, 383, 798, 1875, 432, 1877, 472, 1878, 502, 1879, 492, 963, 1880, 502, 990, 1881, 519, 1023, 1882, 546, 1094, 1883, 572, 1107; [San Francisco Union Club], *By-Laws, Officers and Members of the Union Club, of San Francisco* (San Francisco, 1867), 25, *Constitution and By-Laws of the Union Club, of San Francisco. 1874* (San Francisco, 1874), 38, *Constitution and By-Laws of the Union Club of San Francisco. 1875* (San Francisco, 1875), 41; *Senate Rept. 689*, 44 Cong., 2 Sess., 1116. For Koopmanschap's view on Chinese laborers see "Koopmanschap Interviewed," New York *World*, July 21, 1869; "Chinese in the South," *Alta*, October 6, 1869.

22. *Picayune*, July 15, 27, 1869.

23. *Alta*, March 12, 1869.

24. Sacramento *Reporter*, July 14, 1869; *Alta*, July 16, 21, 30, December 11, 1869.

25. New York *Tribune*, June 23, 1870.

26. Nashville *Daily Press and Times*, September 1, 1869; *Acts of Tennessee*, 36 Gen. Assembly, 1 Sess., 188; *Picayune*, July 14, 1869; Burwell, "Science and the Mechanic Arts Against Coolies," *De Bow's Review*, 7:570 (n.s., July 1869). Richard Harvey Cain, the editor of the Charleston *Missionary Record*, came out in favor of Chinese laborers in the South. For repercussions of the debate among Negroes turn to the columns of the *Elevator*, August 27, September 17, October 29, November 19, 26, December 3, 17, 31, 1869, June 17, 1870. See also Hesseltine, "Tennessee's Invitation to Carpet-Baggers," *East Tennessee's Historical Society's Publications*, 4:115 (January 1932) and C. G. Belissary, "Tennessee and Immigration, 1865–1880," *Tennessee Historical Quarterly* (Nashville), 7:235 (September 1948).

27. New York *Herald*, July 23, 1869; *Picayune*, January 5, 6, 1870; Leigh, *Ten Years on a Georgia Plantation*, 146.

28. *Call*, May 30, 1872; Robert Somers, *The Southern States Since the War, 1870–71* (London, 1871), 163–164; A. B. Moore, "Railroad Building in Alabama During the Reconstruction Period," *Journal of Southern History* (Lexington), 1:428 (November 1935).

29 *Call, Chronicle*, September 21, 1882.

30. *Picayune*, January 8, 9, 1870.

31. *Courier*, October 23, 1869; *Commercial Bulletin*, November 9, 1870; J. Carlyle Sitterson, *Sugar Country: The Cane Sugar Industry in the South, 1753–1950* (Lexington, [1953]), 237–238; Somers, *Southern States*, 225; Leigh, *Ten Years on a Georgia Plantation*, 146; [James Wentworth Leigh], "Rice-Cultivation," appendix 4, Leigh, *Ten Years*, 269; *Senate Rept. 689*, 44 Cong., 2 Sess., 1116; Work Projects Administration, *Arkansas, A Guide to the State* (New York, 1941), 346; William Hyde and Howard L. Conard, eds., *Encyclopedia of the History of St. Louis*, 4 vols. (New York, 1899), I, 357–358.

32. For the visit of merchants from the Chicago Board of Trade to

San Francisco, investigating the possibility of "introducing Chinese labor into the Northwest," see *Alta*, July 23, August 18, 28, 1869.

33. North Adams *Transcript*, March 24, June 14, 1870; Newark *Daily Advertiser*, June 15, 1870; "Chinese in Massachusetts," *Leslie's Illustrated*, 30:261 (July 9, 1870); James L. Bowen, "The Celestials in Sunday-School," *Scribner's Monthly*, 1:556 (March 1871); William F. G. Shanks, "Chinese Skilled Labor," *Scribner's Monthly*, 2:496 (September 1871); Hamilton Child, *Gazetteer of Berkshire County, Massachusetts, 1725–1885* (Syracuse, N. Y., 1885), 248; "Editor's Easy Chair," *Harper's Monthly*, 42:137 (December 1870); Washington Gladden, *Recollections* (Boston, 1909), 172; Coolidge, *Chinese Immigration*, 498, 501. For details of Calvin T. Sampson's struggle with the Crispins see Frederick Rudolph, "Chinamen in Yankeedom: Anti-Unionism in Massachusetts in 1870," *American Historical Review* (New York), 53:1–29 (October 1947). Excerpts from news report were reprinted in John R. Commons *et al.*, eds. *A Documentary History of American Industrial Society*, 12 vols. (rev. ed., New York, 1958), IX, 84–88.

34. S. Proctor Thayer, "Adams and North Adams," [Thomas Cushing and J. E. A. Smith, eds.], *History of Berkshire County, Massachusetts; With Biographical Sketches of its Prominent Men*, 2 vols. (New York, 1885), I, 501.

35. "North Adams — An Industrial Battle," Daniel Pidgeon, *Old-World Questions and New-World Answers* (London, 1884), 146.

36. Springfield *Republican*, June 17, 1870; *Daily Advertiser*, June 22, 1870; Gladden, *Recollections*, 171–172.

37. New York *Nation*, July 14, 1870; Boston *Commonwealth*, June 25, 1870.

38. *Alta*, July 18, 1869; *Nation*, June 23, August 11, 1870.

39. *Nation*, June 30, 1870; Gladden, *Recollections*, 173. For the encounter between the Chinese laborers at North Adams and Niishima Jo, a Japanese student from the Theological Seminary at Andover, in August, 1871, turn to Arthur Sherburne Hardy, ed., *Life and Letters of Joseph Hardy Neesima* (Boston, 1891), 107–109.

40. New York *Independent*, February 27, 1873.

41. *Nation*, June 23, 1870; *Commonwealth*, June 25, 1870.

42. *Advertiser*, September 22, "The Situation at Belleville," September 28, 1870 (quoting New York *Star*). For incidental information on the Passaic Steam Laundry turn to Theodore Sandford, "Belleville Township," William H. Shaw, (comp.), *History of Essex and Hudson Counties, New Jersey*, 2 vols. (Philadelphia, 1884), II, 879–890k; H. Holmes, *Brief History of Belleville* (n.p., n.d., after 1890), 92.

43. Edward Sothern Hipp, "Newarker 'Father' of Chinese Laundry; George T. Casebolt, 93, Reveals That He Brought First Chinamen East to Break Strike, But They Started Their Own Business," Newark *Call*, October 9, 1932.

44. *Advertiser,* September 22, 28, 1870.

45. *Advertiser,* September 23, 28, 29, 1870; February 2, April 6, July 14, 15, 1871; August 13, 1872.

46. *Advertiser,* September 29, October 4, 8, 10, 21, November 22, 29, 30, December 19, 1870, February 2, 17, November 13, 1871, May 15, 1872.

47. *Advertiser,* May 4, 13, 15, 16, September 28, 1871, June 7, August 30, September 2, December 23, 27, 1872.

48. *Advertiser,* December 19, 1870, September 23, November 29, December 5, 1872, January 20, 21, 1873; *Call,* October 9, 1932.

49. Beaver County's Chinatown, Read By Charles Reeves May At Meeting Of Beaver County Historical Society, May 15, 1925, a manuscript in the Carnegie Free Library, Beaver Falls, Pennsylvania, and placed at the disposal of the writer by the Librarian, Miss Fern Medley, provided the major portion of the evidence. See also Albert Rhodes, "The Chinese at Beaver Falls," *Lippincott's Magazine,* 19:708–712 (June 1877); Joseph H. Bausman, *History of Beaver County, Pennsylvania, and Its Centennial Celebration,* 2 vols. (New York, 1905), II, 670; Huie, *Reminiscences,* 41.

50. New York *Times,* June 20, 1859; "Chinese Marriages in New York," *Harper's Weekly,* 1:630 (October 3, 1857); [James H. Lanman], "The Chinese Museum in Boston," *Hunt's Merchants' Magazine,* 14:347–349 (April 1846); [Nathan Dunn], *"Ten Thousand Chinese Things." A Descriptive Catalogue of the Chinese Collection in Philadelphia. With Miscellaneous Remarks upon the Manners, Customs, Trade, and Government of the Celestial Empire* (Philadelphia, 1839); E[noch]. C[obb]. Wines, *A Peep at China, in Mr. Dunn's Chinese Collection; With Miscellaneous Notices Relating to the Institutions and Customs of the Chinese, and Our Commercial Intercourse with Them* (Philadelphia, 1839); John R. Peters, Jr. *Guide to, or Descriptive Catalogue of the Chinese Museum, in the Marlboro' Chapel, Boston, with Miscellaneous Remarks upon the Government, History, Religion, Literature, Agriculture, Arts, Trades, Manners and Customs of the Chinese. To be had only at the Museum* (Boston, 1845); R. L. Brunhouse, "Lascars in Pennsylvania: A Side-light on the China Trade," *Pennsylvania History* (Philadelphia), 7:20–30 (January 1940); LaFargue, "Some Early Chinese Visitors to the United States," *T'ien Hsia,* 11:128–139 (October–November 1940); [Maryland Historical Society], " 'The China Trade in Baltimore', An Exhibition Illustrating 165 Years of Commerce with the Orient, at the Maryland Historical Society, June 15 to October 15, 1950," *Maryland History Notes* (Baltimore), 7:[1–4] (August 1950); George C. D. Odell, *Annals of the New York Stage,* 15 vols. (New York, 1927–1949), II, 305, IV, 42, 43, 106, 177, 186, V, 398, 399, 500, 501, 505, 577, 579, 580, VI, 169, 202, 242, 270, 275, 286.

INDEX